Praise for *The Wrong Stuff*

"The funniest book to come out of the locker room since Jim Bouton's *Ball Four*!"

—Jonathan Yardley, *Washington Post Book World*

"*The Wrong Stuff* will keep you in stitches. The Spaceman pitcher for the Boston Red Sox and Montreal Expos gets a laugh on every page."

—Larry King, *USA Today*

"Full of funny and sometimes telling anecdotes about wild and crazy guys playing a kid's game under adult pressures."

—Gene Lyons, *Newsweek*

"As crazy and delightful as Bill Lee."

—Dick Schaap

"An accurate picture of what it's like to be in the major leagues."

—Terry Pluto, *Cleveland Plain Dealer*

Other Books by the Authors

BY BILL LEE AND RICHARD LALLY
The Wrong Stuff

BY BILL LEE
The Little Red (Sox) Book

BY RICHARD LALLY
Bombers
Baseball for Dummies (with Joe Morgan)
Long Balls, No Strikes (with Joe Morgan)

HAVE GLOVE,
WILL TRAVEL

Adventures of a Baseball Vagabond

BILL "SPACEMAN" LEE

AND RICHARD LALLY

Crown Publishers • New York

Copyright © 2005 by Bill Lee and Richard Lally

Published by Crown Publishers, New York, New York.
Member of the Crown Publishing Group, a division of Random House, Inc.
www.crownpublishing.com

CROWN is a trademark and the Crown colophon is a registered trademark of
Random House, Inc.

Printed in the United States of America

Design by Cynthia Dunne

Library of Congress Cataloging-in-Publication Data
Lee, Bill, 1946–
    Have glove, will travel : adventures of a baseball vagabond /
Bill "Spaceman" Lee and Richard Lally.—1st ed.
    Includes index.
    1. Lee, Bill, 1946– 2. Pitchers (Baseball)—United States—Biography.
I. Lally, Dick. II. Title.
    GV865.L36A34 2005
    796.357'092—dc22   2004004077

ISBN 1-4000-5407-9

10 9 8 7 6 5 4 3 2 1

First Edition

To Diana Lee Donovan
—*Bill Lee*

In memory of my parents, Richard, the Marine,
and Anne, the Brooklyn Dodgers fan
—*Richard Lally*

ACKNOWLEDGMENTS

I want to thank my father, William Lee Jr., my mom, Paula Hunt Lee, my brother, Paul, and my aunt Annabelle for their enduring love and encouragement. My daughters, Caitlin and Anna, my sons, Mike and Andy, and their wives, Shelley and Leslie, are a continual source of joy and inspiration as are my three grandchildren, Logan, Kazden, and Hunter. I also want to thank all of my Vermont neighbors, particularly Mr. and Mrs. David Reed and Doctor and Mrs. Lorraine Starr and their families for their friendship and support. Richard Lally continues to be a friend as well as a partner, the best Sacco any Vanzetti could ask for. I would be remiss if I did not thank all those highway patrolmen in Canada and New England who have often chosen to look the other way. And special thanks to every player I competed with or against over the last forty years and then some. Each one of you is a teammate.

—*Bill Lee*

I must first thank our brilliant editor, Annik La Farge, for believing in this project and guiding us to its completion. During the months when this book was all I thought about, my agent, Mark Reiter, once again proved to be a loyal ally and friend. He always makes my job easy.

Whenever I needed a fact checked or some unmanageable copy smoothed or just craved encouragement, I turned to my Gang of Usual Suspects: Billy Altman, Rob Neyer, Jordan Sprechman, Bill Daughtry, Jim Gerard, John Collett, Eve Lederman, Bill Shannon, and Vincent Parker. Pete Fornatale rates a special mention for encouraging us to write this book back when it was barely more than an idea. Annik La Farge's assistant editor, Mario Rojas, helped to keep us on schedule, and sharp-eyed copy editor Sue Warga made sure we were always properly punctuated.

I also want to thank those friends and relatives who have given me the emotional sustenance every writer needs. My heart is crowded with love for all of them: my brothers Joseph and Sean; cousins Michael and Bernard; Aunt Kathy and Uncle Tom; my violet-eyed, raven-tressed partner-in-crime Maria DiSimone; the late Brother Leo Richard and his Clan of the Cave, including Dr. Patrick Murphy, Father Ed Doran, Brother James Norton, Brother Regis, Chris Dougherty, Ray DeStephens, Brother Dan O'Riordan, and two absent friends: Brother Ronald Marcellin and Dr. Robert Englud; that superb English teacher Joseph Smith for teaching me to revere the written word; my blood brother Al "Sonny" Lombardo who has amazingly survived the streets of Brooklyn, Iraq, and Afghanistan as well as our teens, and his wife, Cathy; Karl Durr, the Burgermeister of Forest Hills Gardens and his gorgeous wife, Margrid; Richard Erlanger, Fenway's own Duke of Earl and his duchess, Jessie, with the laughing eyes; Joyce and Emma Altman; The Budny Family: Alecks and Michaela, Paulina the budding artist, Mathilda, who never lets us forget she's in charge, and my very best pal Rasmus, also known as the incredible "Mr. Mookie"; the gang at the gym, including Stan Enden and Andrew Alexander, two men I can count on; Alan Flusser, my SGI godfather; President Daisaku Ikeda and all the members of my Soka Gakkai International family, especially David Edwards and Arthur Fitting; and Vesna, Jean, Joey G., Gil and Roz, Chris and Hazel, Andy, the golden-throated Cy Curnin, and the rest of my rollicking crew of madcaps at Q Thai Bistro in Forest Hills, still the best damned restaurant on the planet.

—*Richard Lally*

CONTENTS

Authors' Note:

This book describes Mr. Lee's experiences while playing baseball throughout the world from 1982 to 2003. The authors have recorded these events as Mr. Lee remembers them. They have changed the names and identifying details of some of the individuals presented in these pages in order to protect the guilty.

Mr. Lee does not know any innocents.

HAVE GLOVE,
WILL TRAVEL

PROLOGUE

Frozen Out in Port Hawkesbury

I t is a November night in 1984. My name is Bill Lee, and I used to play professional baseball with the Boston Red Sox and Montreal Expos. I just unpacked my bags in a chilly, narrow locker room. Now I stare at a spot. Well, bigger than a spot actually, it is a stain, a dark inverted triangle of damp seeping through the ceiling directly above me and trailing midway down the wall of my locker. If you call this a locker: a concrete cubicle, stark and bare with metal hooks to hang my clothes on. We do not have a clubhouse boy to pick up after us.

I rest my feet on a worn rubber mat, coal black in parts but faded to dusky gray at the edges. Dull wooden slats lead out the door to a colorless hallway. This room smells of stale sweat and camphor. I sit on a wobbly red bench whose legs some large razor-clawed beast must have recently used for a scratching post.

My uniform clings to my body even though we have yet to play. Perspiration has soaked through these double knits. Our team has appeared in thirteen towns in the last fourteen days; we live out of a bus and must cram our clothes into duffel bags immediately after each game and the fabrics never get an opportunity to completely dry. As I walked from the shower a few days ago, a teammate pointed out a growth on my left calf. It resembled a small chanterelle. A closer look revealed that I had contracted a body fungus, the price for continually playing in a mildewed uniform. A doctor prescribed Lamisil tablets for this condition. The fungus uses them for after dinner mints.

Breath hovers above me in a wreath of fog. It felt so cold when I walked through the door, I expected to find a side of beef hanging from one of the clothes hooks. Except it could never fit in here. Unlike the spacious big-league clubhouses that allow players to spread out, this room is cramped. My teammates and I sit huddled in front of our lockers, facing each other as if we were attending a consciousness-raising group. All we need to complete the setting is for Tony Robbins to appear clapping those big ham hands of his and exhorting us to go for it. With the mood I'm in, though, the only thing I would go for is his throat.

Actually, the close confines count as a plus, since the body heat we generate staves off frostbite. Some of the older players sitting near me claim we are lucky. They recall how as teenagers they sat around smudge pots to keep warm when they played in outdoor venues farther north of here. That comes as a surprise. I didn't think you could get any farther north of here without being south.

Clearly, this is not the major leagues.

We are visiting the town of Port Hawkesbury on Cape Breton, an island separated by the Strait of Canso from the Nova Scotia mainland. The locker room sits in the back of an old minor-league hockey arena the community built during the 1950s. It resembles an oversized Quonset hut constructed from concrete rather than aluminum.

A Canadian promoter arranged this event for the Tour de Hockey Legends Team. No, I have not adopted a second sport. You might say I act as the team's halftime show or mascot. It was the promoter's idea to stick me on the bill, his way of increasing ticket sales. I have never played hockey and have no connection with the game in the public mind. That does not matter. This promoter would have booked acrobats to soar above the rink while a SWAT team took potshots at them if he thought people would pay money to watch.

In an hour or so, the team will trot me out between periods of tonight's charity hockey match between the Legends and a club composed of players from the 1978 Junior League champions of Nova Scotia. I might skate a bit at first. Not a particular skill of mine. Maintaining my feet on the ice while standing or moving at moderate speed hardly presents a challenge, but once I accelerate, stopping poses a problem. The only sure way I can halt is to slam into a wall.

Shortly after the collision, I will remove my skates and wobble up a long red carpet to a portable plywood mound at the center of the rink to demonstrate "trick" pitches—curveballs, sliders, palm balls, screwballs, knuckle curves, perhaps a spitter if my saliva has not frosted over to ice—for an arena filled with ravening hockey carnivores who consider baseball to be as macho an athletic endeavor as knitting.

It should all be quite classy, like a minstrel show at a KKK rally. I will perform the same function as some carny geek who bites off the heads of live chickens for the deranged amusement of the paying customers, most of whom will be wearing plaid.

You are wondering how I got here. Funny, I just asked myself that question.

We could blame any number of people for my predicament—Jim Fanning and John McHale immediately come to mind—but let's face it, I screwed up, albeit with the best intentions. It all started more than two years ago on the night when the Montreal Expos' front office released Rodney Scott.

Rodney had started at second base for Montreal since 1979. Cool Breeze impressed me as a wide-ranging fielder who routinely saved our groundball-throwing pitching staff with his jaw-dropping, rally-killing plays. Rodney rarely hit much more than .235, but he walked frequently enough to contribute on offense and ranked among the best percentage base stealers in the major leagues. Our manager, Dick Williams, named him our MVP three years running even though such

Hall of Fame-quality players as Gary Carter, Tim Raines, and Andre Dawson also appeared on our roster.

The Expos' front office did not share Williams's high opinion of Scott. As soon as Dick left the organization in the middle of the 1981 season, his successor, Jim Fanning, began searching for an alternative at second base. The quest bordered on an obsession for Jim. After the 1981 season ended, Fanning and I occasionally ran into each other in the Olympic Stadium Nautilus room. He knew I considered Rodney my best friend on the team and I guess he wanted to send a message. No matter where our conversations started, they invariably ended in the middle of the Expos diamond. I might say, "Jim, did you see where the price of gold dropped again?" and Fanning would reply, "Yes, but can we afford to keep Rodney at second base next season?"

My answer was always the same emphatic yes. Rodney had established himself as the Expos' most reliable infielder, an important consideration for a team that played its home games in Olympic Stadium, a park that suppresses run scoring. We also depended on our second baseman to jump-start our offense. Whenever Rodney worked his way on base, the threat his base-stealing skills represented so distracted pitchers, they often forgot to concentrate on the hitter. As Ken Griffey Sr. once said to a sportswriter, "No one in baseball can drive a pitcher crazy like the Breeze." I also pointed to the team's record over the last few years. Montreal did not emerge as a bona fide contender until Rodney entered our lineup as a regular.

Fanning usually nodded and tried to look thoughtful, as if my arguments just might sway him. Then he would change the subject. Apparently nothing I nor any other player said in support of Rodney exerted any impact. The Expos started the 1982 season with rookie Wallace Johnson playing second base.

Wallace had flashed some skills the few times I saw him play. A line drive hitter. Good power to the gaps. Excellent speed. The flip side: Johnson possessed little aptitude for defense. He reacted slowly to balls off the bat and lacked the delicate rhythm and footwork a second baseman needs to consistently turn the double play. Once Wallace stopped hitting, his weak glove forced Fanning to remove him from the lineup. In Johnson's place, he used every infielder on our roster. Everyone except Rodney. I think even Margaret Trudeau took a turn at second. Rodney stayed the good soldier. He did not complain or demand more playing time, just came to the park every night ready to help us win.

Scott's professionalism did not persuade Fanning to return him to the regular lineup. On the evening of May 8 I entered our clubhouse after a pregame workout to find Rodney at his locker packing his bags. His movements appeared slow and disoriented. He looked around the room through car-crash-victim eyes. He did not say a word. He was not Rodney. Someone asked what he was doing.

"Leaving. Fanning just released me."

All right, you don't want Rodney starting for the team, fine. But he still could have made significant contributions to the Expos as the perfect utility player: a switch-hitter who could get on base and a versatile fielder equally adept at second, short, or third. Rodney even had enough talent to play the outfield in an emergency, and no manager could ever find a better pinch runner. Releasing him for no good reason struck me as pure vendetta, a move so mean-spirited and idiotic, I had to protest. When the trainer brought over my game uniform for that night, I ripped it down the middle and draped it over Fanning's desk. I scribbled a note, informing the manager that one of his pitchers had just gone AWOL. "I cannot put up with this bullshit," I wrote. "Going over to the bar at Brasserie 77. If you want to, come and get me."

Read those words as a deliberate challenge. That very morning Fanning had made a clubhouse speech before the entire team. We had lost to the Dodgers the night before in a sloppily played game, and he thought we needed a kick in the rump. Fanning did not pull a Knute Rockne, imploring us to win one for the Gipper. Instead, he adopted a tough-love approach. He told us we did not deserve to be on the field with Los Angeles. We were not as classy as the Dodgers. We did not execute plays as well as they did. Even their uniforms looked better than ours. We were an embarrassment to the organization. A disgrace to the city.

Fanning had finished his tirade by going weirdly John Wayne on us. He recalled how his father had once given him a pair of white boxing gloves for Christmas, and he told us he knew how to lace them on again should anyone care to challenge his authority. Why he needed to wave his macho before a roomful of powerful young athletes—any one of whom could have stuffed him in the nearest wastepaper basket—I will leave for the armchair psychiatrists among you to analyze. Remembering his words pushed enough of my own silly buttons to inspire the addition of this P.S. to my note: "Bring along those lily-white gloves your dad gave you."

Fanning never appeared. I watched the Expos' game on the

bar's TV while drinking beers with the political cartoonist Terry Mosher and playing pool with a quiet gentleman whose cerebral palsy made his hands shake violently except when he held a cue stick. Then his fingers turned so rock-steady, he ran the table on us. By the sixth inning the Dodgers were once again shellacking us, and I realized our team was about to run out of pitchers. The walkout immediately ended. I wanted to stick it to Fanning and the front office, not my teammates. My friends hustled me back to Olympic Stadium.

I reached the ballpark just before the bottom of the seventh inning. Fanning refused to put me in the game, and we tangled in his office afterward. He accused me of deserting the team; I accused him of lying to Rodney. He sputtered. He fumed. His face swelled red. But his boxing gloves stayed locked away. He pointed me back into the clubhouse and said, "[Montreal general manager] John McHale wants to see you in his office tomorrow. Bright and early. This is between you and him now."

"What's wrong with right now?"

"John does not want to see you in the state you're in. The morning will be fine."

I had walked off a ball club once before to protest management's mistreatment of a teammate. In 1978, the Boston Red Sox traded Bernie Carbo—for my money, the most dangerous left-handed hitter on our roster—to the Cleveland Indians simply because they did not appreciate Carbo's colorful late-night lifestyle. I left the team for twenty-four hours right after the front office announced the deal. Boston fined me one day's salary over that incident. I expected a similar punishment from McHale.

What else could he do? The edge belonged to me. McHale would never jettison his best left-handed reliever. During the previous season I had topped the Expos in earned run average while finishing second on the team in games pitched and holds. I even hit .348. And I still ranked among the most popular players on the team. People chanted my name the moment I appeared on the field not just in Montreal but in ballparks around the league. I led the club in speaking engagements. My fans were so passionate, they lowered bottles of tequila to me in the bullpen before the start of every game. At one point I collected sixty-seven bottles in less than two months, an all-time record in the annals of sport that will undoubtedly remain unbroken for years to come. Most teams considered my sort of player invaluable.

Irreplaceable.

Untouchable.

Wouldn't you think?

"We just released you from your contract," McHale announced not ten minutes into our meeting. Just seven words, but they instantly altered my identity. I could no longer call myself a professional ballplayer. I had become a line of agate type on the AP transactions wire. A black hole on the rosters of rotisserie league managers across North America. A blurb on tonight's evening news that began, "And now a sad note from the world of baseball . . ."

In calculating my worth to the Expos, I had let ego throw off the math. Not exactly a first for me. In essence, the Expos had decided they would rather pay me $225,000 not to play than keep me on the team. It rankled to discover how expendable they considered me. The Lee Irish temper flared. I shook my fist at McHale and shouted, "You want to cut me, fine. There are plenty of clubs in this league desperate for left-handed pitching. One of them will sign me. You just watch."

McHale's cold eyes brightened. A smug look crossed his face as he leaned over his desk to whisper, "Don't bet on it."

A blackball had just thudded onto the floor, but the sound took its time reaching my ears. The next day, my wife and I sent letters offering my services to the other eleven National League clubs. We did not contact anyone in the American League. I liked hitting too much, and the designated hitter rule would prevent me from taking my cuts at the plate.

We expected teams to overwhelm us with offers. My contract stipulated that the Expos had to pay the rest of my salary. Any club could have signed me for the major-league minimum. If I did not perform well, the team could release me without losing any more money than they might have paid to the greenest rookie. What a bargain! So how many replies did we receive? How about one, and that from Hank Peters, the general manager of the Pittsburgh Pirates, who took the time to write, "Our club has enough problems without adding you to the list."

Not everyone considered me a headache. The Montreal chapter of the YMCA circulated a petition demanding that the Expos immediately reinstate me. Over ten thousand people signed, including Charles Bronfman, the team owner. Pure window dressing, that—a billionaire playing to the masses, spreading a bit of the old Magoo. In the organizational hierarchy, Fanning was the manager. He managed the team in the clubhouse and on the field. McHale was the general manager. He managed the team's business affairs. Bronfman was the owner. He owned everything—Fanning, McHale, the players, the uniforms, the balls, the bats, me until the day of my release. Had Bronfman told McHale to kiss my ass in the middle of Olympic Stadium, I would still be wiping lipstick from my cheeks, so don't believe Charlie wanted me back on the club.

Anyway, McHale had no intention of letting any petitions alter his stance. Word went around he preferred giving Lefty Grove the opportunity to pitch before handing me the ball. Mr. Grove was a Hall of Famer, but he had died seven years earlier. Even after Woodie Fryman, Montreal's only other reliable southpaw reliever, injured his arm, McHale and Fanning still refused to call me.

In early July, my friend Bill Brownstein asked if he could contact the American League teams. Desperation made me agree. Each club replied with a verbal form letter: "Thank you for thinking of us. We have our roster set. Yes, it is true we are in last place; yes, it's true we are twenty games out and it's only June; and yes, our starting rotation is so tattered we can barely flesh out a complete pitching staff. We do not need Mr. Lee at this time." At this time. Another way of saying at any time. Ever.

We did not give up. Richard Lally, my coauthor for this book as well as my first autobiography, *The Wrong Stuff,* called Atlanta Braves assistant general manager Pat Nugent in early August. Atlanta had opened the 1982 season with thirteen consecutive wins and entered the All-Star break with a hefty lead in the National League West. In late July, however, the Braves fell into a protracted slump when most of the club's starting pitchers lost their effectiveness. The losing streak allowed the Los Angeles Dodgers, San Francisco Giants, and San Diego Padres to pull nearly even in the division title race.

Richard buried Nugent under a landslide of statistics that revealed how well I had pitched in Atlanta's home park. My friend also pointed out that I had compiled a career ERA of 2.54 against the Dodgers, Giants, and Padres, the very three teams that were threatening to overtake the Braves. Even I didn't know that.

Nugent expressed surprise over the numbers and promised to give us an answer within a few days. A week passed. No call. So Richard phoned Braves vice president John Mullen and repeated his pitch. Read the tail end of their conversation:

Mullen: "Those stats are excellent, but I'm not sure we have a spot for Bill. We already have our twenty-five-man roster set."

Lally: "Yes, John, I understand that, but at the moment they are sinking faster than the *Andrea Doria,* so let's talk business. You do not have a single proven left-handed pitcher on your staff. You do not have any left-handers in the minors ready to come up. Bill can start for your team or pitch out of the bullpen as a setup man or long reliever. You can even use him as a left-handed specialist. He is willing to fly to Atlanta or anywhere else you choose at his own expense to show what he can do. The tryout has no obligations attached to it. Bill would even sign a minor-league deal if you like what you see but can't find a place for him yet. And if he fails in the tryout, you've lost nothing but time."

Mullen's response offered us some hope. He asked several questions about my contract with Montreal and wondered how quickly I could get into playing shape. Richard assured him that I had been pitching regularly with a semipro team since my release. I could pitch that night if the Braves needed me. "All right," Mullen said, "I'll discuss Bill's situation with [Braves manager] Joe Torre and get back to you soon as I have a decision." They must be slow talkers—twenty years have passed. We are still waiting for Mullen's call.

Shortly after that conversation, I asked Marvin Miller, the president of the Players' Association, whether he thought we could sue all twenty-six major-league teams for colluding to exclude me from baseball. Marvin showed great sympathy. He did not offer any encouragement. "If you really want to do that," he said, "the union will help you as much as possible. But I have to tell you, you won't win. Collusion is the most difficult thing to prove in a court of law. What evidence do you have to support your claim?"

Evidence? McHale's ominous parting words. My own gut feeling. The lack of offers. Not good enough. I did know the Expos had spread damaging stories about me and Rodney Scott around the league. One player said he had overheard Montreal scout Eddie Lopat telling some reporters that my arm was shot and I could not pitch anymore. Absurd. I had allowed only one run in my last six innings of work. When I appeared on David Letterman's show, Yankees pitcher Tommy John told me his general manager had mentioned a rumor regarding Rodney's alleged homosexuality. Even if the story had foundation, it should not have made any difference. What does sexual preference have to do with ability anyway? But I knew Rodney was straight. He had hit on my wife on at least ten occasions.

After I realized no club would hire me on any terms, it took several weeks to recover from the pain of all that rejection. My mood turned defiant. *All right,* I thought, *screw them. Who needs major-league baseball?* It had become nothing but a business, corrupted by greed and run by agents who persuaded the players they represented to sell their skills to the highest bidder. Team loyalty had become arcane. Comradeship no longer mattered. And I had tired of the false glitz and glamour marketers used to sell the game.

The owners had done me a favor chucking me out of their sport; now I could travel the world, searching for the game in its purest form. I made up my mind to play wherever I could find a diamond for any team that needed my talents. Hardball, softball, stickball, Wiffle ball, cricket, pay me in cash, pay me in pelts, pay me not at all—it did not matter. Performing in front of large crowds no longer appealed to me. After spending thirteen years in the major league limelight, I desired anonymity. If you owned a club of Nerfball-playing kangaroos with a home park situated somewhere just beyond the dark side of the moon and you needed someone to fill that last spot on your roster, I would catch the next space shuttle. My left hand, you see, felt incomplete without a baseball gripped between its fingers. I just wanted to stand on a mound again, even one made of plywood in the middle of an ice rink, doing what I do best.

And that is how I came to be starring in a sideshow for the Hockey Legends in the town of Port Hawkesbury on Cape Breton, an island separated by the Strait of Canso from the Nova Scotia mainland on this arctic November night.

1

A SEASON UNDER
THE INFLUENCE

That chessboard would not stop shape-shifting. I leaned over the bar in the Cul de Sac, a Montreal hangout on lower Crescent Street, trying to place a pawn on a black square that kept slithering out of reach. The white boxes melted over the lines and swirled into the blacks. Next the board expanded and flopped over the sides of the bar. A tablecloth. But only for a moment. It rapidly shrank again until it appeared no larger than a postage stamp. And then back one more time to normal size, only now the squares re-formed as cubes, elevated off the board in descending heights. An M. C. Escher etching.

Sounds like some nefarious drug held me in its clutches. No, I'd just run a minimarathon through the heart of Montreal. My blood sugar had dropped to my ankles, and dehydration had sucked up all my bodily fluids. My lungs felt scarred after inhaling ten kilometers' worth of car exhaust. This weakened state left me prone to hallucinations as all the toxins stored in my body after a week-long debauchery recycled to deliver a haymaker to my senses.

My chess opponent had introduced himself moments earlier as Milos, a fat, brooding man with a scraggly beard and thick Slavic accent. Never seen him before. I'd come in for a beer, and he challenged me to a game. It took him only a few minutes to notice my disorientation.

"You look all in," he said.

"Rough week. Not enough sleep. Ran too fast too far today. Didn't eat enough. A cold brew will put me right."

"Try this."

Milos handed over a stunted joint wrapped in black rolling paper. I assumed it contained either pot or hash and merrily struck a match. I know. Accepting drugs from a stranger is a stupid thing to do. Nancy Reagan would never approve of me; I rarely say no to anyone offering a good time. I never thought her antidrug slogan got it right anyway. Really want to drive a drug dealer crazy? Don't say no. Say maybe. Dealers hate to wait around while you make up your mind.

I toked twice, paused, and again considered how to outflank my opponent. The board had stopped playing tricks. But as I raised the pawn to shoulder height, the head of the piece grew bulbous and top-heavy. It pulled me backward.

I teetered on the edge of my stool for a moment and swooned. I surrendered to buoyancy. Buoyancy failed me. I could not float. Down, down, down my body fell, off a bar stool the height of a skyscraper. My brain went as well, rolling, tumbling ass over cerebellum down a velvet staircase studded with spikes.

Customers and staff ran over to help. I heard them babbling somewhere far off, cushioned snub-nosed sounds from under a bubble, imploring me to get up. Betty Boop shimmied naked on the pale, hairless chest of Koko the Clown. He passed an opium pipe to Cab Calloway, who was spinning on his heels, fronting an orchestra of skeletons. Hot jive. Hot jive. Cold fingers played hot jive. Bone bebopped against cold metal until . . . jazz slid into dirge . . . and then . . . craba-locker fishwife . . . sheep . . . barking . . . like . . . frogs . . . semolina pilchard . . . rat-faced gremlins . . . flagellating . . . Toulouse-Lautrec . . . yellow matter custard dripping . . . ban-shees devouring . . . flamenco dancers . . . dead dog's eye . . . a chanting castrato chorus . . . the egg man . . . Gertrude Stein buggering . . . Dr. Billy Graham . . . mouth . . . opens . . . goo goo goo joob . . . Davy . . . Davy Crockett . . . could . . . not . . . com . . . plete . . . a . . . senten . . .

Four hours later I awoke in a beer cooler, splayed on top of six cases of Labatt's. *Oh, fuck. Not even my brand.* Josh, the bartender, grabbed the front of my sweatshirt and gently hefted me to my feet.

"What the hell did you stick me on ice for? Did I look overheated?"

"No, Bill. You looked dead. We figured this was the best place to preserve the body."

My tongue tasted of glue mixed with sand. I gulped two tankards of water and joined Milos at the bar. "What was that shit," I asked, "opium? Angel dust?"

"Just some pot."

"Really?"

"Yeah. Laced with a little powdered heroin."

"Heroin! Jesus, why didn't you warn me? You could have damaged me!"

He waved me off. "Not with just two tokes. Besides, you fall pretty good."

"I've had lots of practice."

I first experimented with pot, hash, mescaline, peyote, and other hallucinogens during the sixties and continued to indulge throughout my major-league career. Guess that means the experimental phase is over. Drugs erased my shyness, made me more sociable. They wiped the mind clear of extraneous thoughts, so I could listen intently to what other people said without judgment or expectation.

A philosophy teacher once told me that all conversation represents a form of persuasion. On pot, I never tried persuading anyone of anything. My weed-wacky friends and I stopped confusing discussions with competitions. I became convinced that if everyone took drugs, we could put aside our egos and differences to improve the planet. There would be no quarrels, no borders, no governments. Instinct and telepathy would render language superfluous. Love would guide our actions, armed conflicts would become passé, the loaves would inherit the fishes, and the lambs would sleep with the dinosaurs.

Don't ask me what those last few sentences mean. I smoked several joints just before writing this.

I might not have gotten stoned so regularly had someone made me pay for the privilege. But when you win even the smallest fame as a pro ballplayer, fans give you drugs gratis just for the chance to hang with you. In Boston, a jock-sniffing doctor regularly supplied me and several Red Sox—I'm not naming any names, but there were a half dozen of us—with pharmaceutical-grade cocaine. One hit of that powder and my body instantly fell into suspended animation. I would sit on a stool for hours in some Inman Square bar unable to move anything except the top joint of my pinky while my mind floated to Rio de Janeiro and rumbaed at Carnival.

We often participated in coke relay races during the wee hours. Fans would pour two white parallel lines down the length of the bar. Two teams of three Red Sox each would line up on either side of those powdery trails and stand about three feet apart. The first player would snort as much coke as his nose could hold in one inhalation before passing the straw to his partner. Whichever team finished the line first won the prize: its members got to sit down.

In Montreal, fans rained hashish on me in the Expos bull-pen and pressed joints in my hand as I left the ballpark. Go to the Cul de Sac, the 1234 Club, or Grumpy's and you could always tell when the coke had arrived; the line outside the men's room stretched longer than the one outside the ladies' room. Several Expos and I snorted blow off twenty-dollar bills in the bathroom stalls free of charge. Most fans insisted that we keep the twenties. Or they presented us with a bullet shooter, a Vicks VapoRub tube packed with coke guaranteed to clear your sinuses by drilling a hole through them. We also

frequented a club called the Longest Yard, a name that described the amount of coke the average patron snorted there
in a night.

I rented my basement to a drug dealer, a mysterious gentleman who called himself Alex. His last name changed from
week to week. I strictly enforced one rule during his stay: he
could not deal inside the house. So he set up shop on our
stoop. Alex would sprinkle several lines of coke on a dish the
first of every month and send it up to my bedroom via the
dumbwaiter. His rent. It was the closest I ever came to paying
for drugs, but the arrangement suited me. I've always supported the barter system.

During the regular baseball season, I tried staying straight
on game days and generally succeeded. Once the Expos let me
go, though, I had plenty of time to fall into trouble. A typical
day started with a joint. Then a friend might drop in and lay
some hash on me. We'd smoke; he'd throw me four joints for
later. I would trade two of them for four tabs of mescaline.
That evening I would exchange two hits of mesc for a gram of
cocaine and head to a local restaurant where the head chef and
I smoked his hookah—a Middle Eastern water pipe filled with
hash. After that, I started partying.

My friends and I snorted coke to stay up, smoked pot to
come down, or drank several six-packs or a bottle of wine to
soften the edge. We repeated the process twenty-four hours
later. We spent our nights searching for level ground, trying to
strike a balance, to harmonize our yin and yang.

I know what you're thinking. Poor son of a bitch loses his
career and he just completely falls apart; next he'll be telling us
how he slept among garbage cans under blankets of newspa-

pers. Getting thrown out of baseball had nothing to do with this. I was not trying to escape. I just enjoyed feeling dopey. And I hadn't drifted all that far from the game.

Six weeks after McHale released me, the doorbell rang as I sat in the bathroom admiring my picture on the cover of *High Times* magazine. I ignored the nagging buzzer. The questioning reporters, the commiserating fans—I had no desire to greet any of them. Just wanted some down time, a chance to reflect on my next move. But that damned bell rang again and again and still again and continued ringing until I finally yanked open the door. He introduced himself as Gino Lemitti, a mailman whose route covered a neighboring district. Should have known. Leave it to a postman to ring more than twice.

Gino stood with his friend Claude in my doorway under the moonlight. A bright star hovering in the sky behind the pair made them resemble two of the wise men from a Nativity scene. "Jesus ain't here," I cracked. "You have any presents for him, just leave them on the stoop." As it turned out, they had arrived bearing gifts.

"How would you like to be pitching again, Bill?"

"Why, you boys just buy the Expos?"

Gino was quick to explain that he did not have an affiliation with any major league club. However, he did manage the Longueuil Senators, a team in the Quebec Senior League. Soon as the news of my release reached him, Gino drove to the Ministry of Sports in Ottawa and persuaded its members to reinstate my amateur athletic status. Now he wanted me to join his pitching staff.

It sounded ideal. The Senators played their home games in a Montreal suburb just across the river from the Expos' Olympic Stadium and only ten miles from my home. I could stay sharp pitching in regular competition against the best over-twenty semipro baseball players in Canada while showcasing my talents for any scouts who visited the area to watch the Expos. Before agreeing, I needed to know only two things.

"How soon can I start, and will you let me bat cleanup?"

"You can hit anywhere in the lineup you want," Gino promised, "and would tomorrow night be soon enough? We need pitching badly."

Culture shock jolted my receptors when I strolled into the Longueuil clubhouse on the evening of June 23. The ample room appeared spic-and-span clean but frill-free. I did not find any lockers or even stalls to dress in. When I asked where to put my clothes, an attendant pointed to a row of small hooks on the wall. Instead of the cavernous shower rooms I had grown accustomed to in the major leagues, he showed me to a midsized bathroom with two shower stalls and a single toilet. The lack of amenities did not discourage me. I felt grateful to be pitching again so soon, and the players greeted me warmly, many with bone-crunching embraces. Longueuil had played six games of a forty-game schedule and had already established itself as one of the strongest offensive clubs in the circuit. With a major leaguer pitching one-third of their games—the Senators played just three times a week—my new teammates believed they had a chance to win a championship.

We walked onto the home field a half hour before game time, and I immediately fell in love. It was an old-time major-league stadium in miniature, a one-tier ballpark with wooden stands topped by a row of modern klieg lights and a chain-link fence lining the outfield. The grounds crew had rolled a portable aluminum bleachers behind that fence to supply additional seating for the overflow crowd. Over fifteen hundred fans had come out that night to watch my return to the mound against the Joliette Beavers.

As I warmed up on the pitching rubber, I checked the players on both sides for gray hair. None of them had any. I was the oldest man on that diamond. Didn't hamper me, though. I pitched a five-hit shutout to beat the Beavers, 4–0. My teammates carried my carcass from the mound to a standing ovation. That performance clearly excited them, but for me it was just another ball game, though I considered the shutout my first step back to the major leagues.

We traveled to our road games in a minibus or drove our own cars, the hops were so short. The Senators competed against teams from nine nearby cities: Verdun, Sorrel, Mascouche, Victoriaville, Thetford Mines, Joliette, Sherbrooke, Quebec City, and Trois-Rivières. Some of the players in these towns demonstrated professional skills, but most of them could not have made even a low-level minor-league team. I noticed early on that many Canadians hit off their front feet. That meant they set up in the batter's box with their weight evenly distributed down the center of their bodies. As the ball arrived at home plate, they would shift their entire mass forward, so they ended up hitting with just their hands and shoulders. Their lower torsos—where most of a hitter's power resides—hardly came into play.

A pitcher could challenge these batters without worrying about surrendering a long ball. Even someone who threw as softly as I did encountered little trouble getting them out while pitching inside. Instead of swinging for home runs, hitters in the Quebec Senior League contented themselves with looping singles and doubles to the opposite field. I believe that had something to do with all the ice sports Canadians play. Ice skating and skiing require you to push and glide. It takes a different exertion, more a plant and push, to smack a baseball for distance. To generate torque, most sluggers must spin off their back legs, a motion skaters and skiers seldom employ.

Many QSL pitchers threw hard, and some could deliver their fastballs in the low nineties, rapid enough to attract the attention of any major-league scout. However, few of these pitchers knew how to change speeds or even location. They could win with nothing more than pure velocity so long as they competed in a circuit where so many players had such slow bats. Major-league hitters would have pulverized them.

Of the forty or so pitchers who played in the QSL, perhaps three owned decent curveballs. That may have represented the biggest difference between this league and the majors. A first-rate professional curve appears to be a fastball when it leaves a pitcher's hand, but it breaks late and hard in a tight spin as it crosses home plate. Unless you identify the pitch early, it's like trying to hit an unraveling ball of yarn. You swing where you think the ball should be, but there is nothing left to connect with except a bit of string. The pitch has already curved under your bat to nestle into the catcher's glove. Good curves also emit a sound—the crackle of static electricity—as the seams of the ball bite into the air.

QSL hurlers threw rinky-dink curves with large orbits, pitches that broke so early, hitters could easily read them.

These pitches swished as they passed over the plate. I hit over .350 that first season; many of my hits came off hanging curves. My own assortment of breaking balls and changeups so baffled the opposing hitters, I won ten games while losing only one, averaged a Randy Johnson–level fifteen strikeouts a game, and finished with an ERA of 1.75. Not a single major-league club noticed, but our team contended all season, and I reclaimed my status as a Montreal sports hero, albeit on a smaller scale.

Meanwhile back at the ranch . . .

My wife divorced me. Mary Lou and I had been married since 1969, but she never completely adapted to being a baseball player's spouse. She wanted me to emulate Mr. Price, our next-door neighbor, who worked nine to five, arrived home every night at six, and sat in front of the fireplace smoking his pipe while the kids told him what they had done in school that day and his wife mixed the martinis and cooked that perfect pot roast. A Douglas Sirk world I could never fit into. I was a midnight rambler, a natural adventurer who relished the night life and meeting new people, the more exotic the better.

I loved my wife; there was much we had in common. Mary Lou and I enjoyed running, hiking, camping, and long drives to nowhere. Our cultural tastes meshed. We read many of the same books and shared concerns over the same social issues. But despite this compatibility, our relationship started deteriorating in 1980. She continually complained that I did not spend enough time with the family—she was right about that—and we bickered over little things. Communication broke down. We grew apart. I pursued other interests that she found unappealing.

After weeks of nearly nonstop fighting, she threw me out of the house, hired an attorney, and eventually filed for divorce. I represented myself in the proceedings, figuring an agile, USC-trained mind could match any lawyer's. When a judge granted our divorce in 1982, Mary Lou came away with custody of our three children, Mike, Andy, and Caitlin, our duplex in Belmont, Massachusetts, the house in Bellingham, Washington, our Jeep, the BMW, all of the furniture and the entire $150,000 in our bank account. Oh, and half my final year's salary from the Expos. But I outfoxed them. I kept the Volkswagen bus and all my rifles.

Precisely the items I would need when the creditors began chasing me.

Amazing how fast money can disappear. In 1979, Montreal signed me to a three-year contract worth $900,000 with 25 percent of it deferred over ten years starting in 1983. So the Expos paid me $225,000 in 1982. Half of that went to my ex-wife. After my divorce, I married Pam Fair, a woman I had met during my separation from Mary Lou. We put $20,000 down on a house in Montreal and invested another $30,000 to fix it up. Estimated taxes swallowed another huge slice of my check. I had expected to receive a refund after factoring in the interest on my mortgage, only to discover the IRS would not allow us to write off any payments we made on a Canadian home.

My savings account showed only $24,000 by September 1, not much when no other money is coming in and your mortgage is $2,400 a month, not to mention the cost of heating. Or the price of food. Or the cost of gasoline. Or clothes. Or toothpaste, soap, floor wax, toilet paper, and all the other incidentals. Now you know why I took drugs. I could not afford cable television.

I freebased cocaine that year. Crack, though no one called it that back then. My first and only time. Not by design, either, but little in my life ever follows a plan. A woman passed me the pipe at a party. She didn't tell me; I didn't ask. Just two puffs and I evaporated. My head curved into a big shiny marble, rolled from my shoulders, and landed on a table. I remember looking back at my torso and thinking, *Here's my chance to find out if people appreciate me for my body or my mind. Let's see which one draws the biggest crowd.* Naturally, my head had no trouble communicating, but my body could not attract anyone's attention unless I talked through my ass.

Something else I've had a lot of practice doing.

I never hid my drug use from anyone. An organization that supported the legalization of marijuana once asked me to speak at a widely publicized conference. I showed up, but none of the group's members appeared. Should have known. Potheads. They had all stayed home to smoke weed.

About now is the time I should express some regret for all the days and nights spent floating in lotus land. No chance. I had a good time gallivanting and enjoyed mind-expanding experiences few people who stay straight their entire lives can fathom. And please don't tell me that athletes—even those as outside the mainstream as I—have an obligation to behave as role models. I have two words for that: *horse* and *shit*.

Writers who cling to the childlike notion that people who play sports for a living qualify as heroes perpetuate the idea that athletes must act as exemplars for society. Team owners endorse that supposition to keep their employees in line, hoping they will conform to whatever standards of behavior serve the owners' interests. Some players and agents continue the charade in the name of good marketing.

When you become a professional athlete you do not sacrifice your right to live your life as you choose, no matter how flawed that existence might be. No one assigns you a smaller quota for making mistakes than the rest of the human race. Nor do you agree to live up to anyone's expectations except your own. Just don't hurt anyone other than yourself while you're doing it.

Let me add one more thought on jock heroism. Many admirable people populate the sports world. How many of them are any braver than the average person? On September 11, 2001, when those planes crashed through the twin towers, two men running from their office noticed a fellow worker in a wheelchair who could not negotiate an escape. They risked their lives taking turns carrying her down more than fifty flights of stairs. I challenge anyone to name one thing an athlete has ever done on the field in any sport to compare to that selfless act. Or come even close.

All right, I'll give you one. Jackie Robinson breaking the color line. That's about it. Attributing heroism to men and women who are simply doing their jobs in return for money and glory cheapens the word. For example, during the 2003 baseball season one prominent sportswriter gushed in his column over the valor the Montreal Expos displayed by remaining in the pennant race despite the handicap of playing one-fourth of their home games in Puerto Rico. He claimed that the Expos "may be the most courageous team of 2003."

Don't know about you, but I wanted to dust off the Purple Hearts after reading that piece. I mean, what feats did the

Expos perform in Puerto Rico that remotely qualified as courageous? Run around the local beaches without wearing sunscreen?

As for role models, check out your mirror tomorrow morning. If you do not find one looking back, all the heroes in the world cannot help you.

◆

Competition in the QSL proved so light, I didn't hesitate to get high during games. My friend Carl Lumerick smuggled ganja resin disguised as coffee into Canada from Jamaica every fall and kept me supplied. No one should mistake Carl as a mere drug dealer. He was an artisan, a Dutch master among purveyors of pot. Carl spent his winters on sun-soaked beaches rolling that brown cannabis gum into ovals. He would painstakingly etch thin lines into each morsel until they resembled coffee beans. After packing his stash in Blue Mountain coffee bags, Carl walked through customs every September without attracting any notice.

Lumerick's compact marijuana beans contained five times the potency of standard pot. One toke and you stared at the TV screen for three hours. Except there was no TV screen. The drug enhanced my visual acuity. I smoked some before a doubleheader in Sorrel and went seven for eight with three home runs. Every pitch thrown to me, no matter how fast, arrived at home plate with the force of a leaf gently tumbling through the air. I could count the seams on the ball, actually watch the horsehide turn from dark to light as it completed each of its revolutions. I only had to catch the ball on the end of my bat and serve it.

I experienced no sense of urgency playing the outfield that

day. One batter smacked a deep fly in my direction, but instead of soaring past me, the ball hovered and spoke. *Take your time, Bill,* it said, *I'll wait until you get under me.* Caught that one behind my back.

In the second game, I took the mound and threw a two-hitter. Every pitch behaved as I instructed it to. I would throw a fastball and follow with a change exactly 9.32456 miles per hour slower, the pot gave me that much precision. My catcher and I decided to eschew conventional pitching strategy in favor of a no-plan plan. Hitters could not think with me because of the simple fact that I had ceased thinking. I threw one batter sixteen straight slow curves. He finally struck out looking for the sinker that never arrived.

With Carl's amazing electric coffee beans keeping me loose but percolating during the pennant stretch, I helped the Senators win enough games to qualify for the QSL playoffs. We met the Verdun team in the first round. The two clubs had little in common. The majority of Longueuil's players were French suburbanites, professional men who worked white collar jobs and did not own a callus. Verdun players were Irish city toughs, longshoremen brick-muscled from years of wrestling heavy cargoes up and down the docks. Longueuil players visited bistros. Verdun players hung out in bars. Longueuil players dressed in Ralph Lauren. Verdun players dressed in Ralph Kramden. Longueuil players ate pâté, escargots, and croissants. Verdun players? They ate players from Longueuil. Their team bested us in three straight to send us home for the winter.

No games left to pitch. I spent much of my time in a seedy Montreal tavern, frequented by drinkers, drug users, and dealers. Some of the men who went to this establishment sported colorful nicknames such as the Joint, the Mustache, the Pelt, the Head, and the Skunk. Interesting characters, but not the sort you would ever find strolling with Big Bird down Sesame Street. For instance, the Pelt served as our mascot until he disappeared into a witness protection program. The Head no longer had one after the Russian Mafia repossessed his car. He was sitting in it at the time, so the mobsters wedged a dozen sticks of dynamite under the chassis to dislodge the vehicle from its parking space.

One of the regulars was a placid sort who hardly ever spoke above a whisper; his wife held the position of family hell-raiser. She once bought a used Chevy that turned out to be a lemon. Instead of taking it back for a refund or exchange, she drove the vehicle onto the dealer's iced-over swimming pool one night and set the machine on fire. It sank through the melted ice just as the dealer pulled into his driveway. He thought someone had crashed into his yard, so he dived into the pool to save the driver. Poor bastard nearly froze to death. When he emerged from the water, she screamed, "You no-good fucking asshole, don't you ever sell us a lemon again or I'll be back." The car dealer was her father-in-law.

The Joint cruised the local waterways every day in a high-powered speedboat equipped with camouflage and twin Gatling guns. He claimed to use the weapons for duck hunting. Given my state, his story sounded plausible.

On Thursday nights, some of the tavern regulars dumped their hashish on the bar so we could comparison-shop. They offered every grade of hash, from the dusty, light Lebanese blond that produced a speedy high to the rich, onyx Turkish blend that acted as a sedative. We closely examined each chunk to separate the pure grades from those dealers had stepped on with darkening agents or fillers such as grape jelly. Finally, we sampled the merchandise using "hot knives," a piece of hash wedged between the blades of two steak knives heated over a flame until we could inhale the vapors. Whoever offered the best quality at the lowest price received our business that week.

The police never bothered us. Many of our friends worked for the force and they smoked with us on weekends. Cops apprehended dealers only when customers complained about being overcharged. You might say the police functioned as a Better Business Bureau for potheads.

That lifestyle could not continue for long. A friend called near the end of 1982 and invited me to a February tryout for a minor-league team in Phoenix. I gratefully accepted. Preparing for spring training would force me to lead a Spartan life, to get my body and brain back into peak condition. If scouts in Arizona discovered I could still get out professional hitters, they might offer me a chance to return to the majors. That was what I wanted. Yes, I know what I wrote about being fed up with the glitz and the greed and the disloyalty and how the right time had arrived for me to leave the Expos. That was me bullshitting me, providing a rationale to soften the pain. Hard on the ego, admitting just how much McHale's punishment had hurt. Felt as though I was conceding a point to him and Fanning, letting them win.

But it did ache. Right down to my marrow. I longed to pitch against the top hitters in the world again, to play in front of large crowds, to bask in all that attention and feel the heat of a big-time pennant race. All right, they got me. I was addicted to major league baseball and needed to satisfy my jones.

I also knew that if I did not take a break from Montreal soon, I would end up the following year bankrupt. Or dead. Or both. Goo goo goo joob.

2

SMALL WORLD

One summer evening during the late sixties, I saw Jim Morrison perform with the Doors at the Fillmore West. I had not experienced drugs yet, but no one in that theater needed them to hallucinate. Just walking through the audience gave us an immediate contact high, like being nonsmokers at a cocktail party. A cannabis haze, wispy as a spiderweb, hung over the crowd, strobe lights raked our eyes, and sparks literally ignited under our shoes—some psychedelic gremlin had sprinkled the floor with phosphorous.

The colorful thrashing amoebas and sinuous collages of the Joshua Light Show played on a screen behind the band. Ray Manzarek on organ, Robbie Krieger on lead guitar, and John Densmore on drums revealed themselves as powerful performers, always on the attack. The music they played rolled over you in a violent, reckless rush, yet every note resonated so cleanly. A stampede you could dance to. But it was Morrison who riveted our attention.

His voice sounded shot. Little more than a rasp, really. It would not have mattered if the son of a bitch failed to hold a note. This was all about presence. From the moment he slinked to center stage, Morrison assumed the robes of the Lizard King holding court. Slouching at the mike, his body a metronome swaying back and forth to rhythms only he could hear, Morrison wielded every dark, poetic lyric like a razor, slicing past the clichéd, the sentimental to uncover some brutal truth about love, hurt, death, and orgasm we dared not confront on our own. Even his pauses sounded eloquent. So filled, so pained.

Morrison intrigued me that night. In the days following the concert I read everything about him I could find. In one interview, he described how the spirit of a long-dead Apache warrior had entered his body during a soul-searching trek through the Gila Wilderness. That was only a warm-up. A few days after the possession, Jim saw God walking through the area's cliff dwellings.

At the time, my religious affiliations were vague. How would you describe me? Lapsed Catholic, definitely. Disorganized Buddhist, perhaps. Seemed everyone in California claimed to be a Buddhist during the sixties, though few people I met could actually tell you anything about the practice beyond the chanting. The Hare Krishnas almost sank their hooks into me, but ultimately I rejected them. Not because of their theology, which sounded fairly hip. Fashion dictated my decision. I liked the saffron togas but hated the haircuts and the wooden clogs.

If you had to assign a label to me, optimistic skeptic might have fit best. That is why I vowed to one day retrace Morrison's steps to find out if the Deity still made personal appearances. Something that tangible could transform me into a true believer. And what if an Indian spirit entered my body during this exploration? Bonus.

I would not visit the Gila Wilderness until February 1983. Pam and I were chugging through New Mexico in the Volkswagen bus on our way to Scottsdale, Arizona, for spring training with the Phoenix Giants, the top farm club in the San Francisco Giants' minor-league system. Phoenix owner Marty Stone had invited me for a tryout. Marty was forty-eight, a multimillionaire in the international publishing industry. We had first met when he pitched batting practice for the Red Sox in Fenway Park during the seventies. This was one tycoon who did not fit any corporate stereotypes. He ate health food, drank organic coffee, read Zen journals, and owned a rustic hunting lodge in upstate New York.

Marty loved to discuss politics and the arts, but he was absolutely nut crazy when it came to baseball. He had nearly bought the Red Sox after Tom Yawkey died and was well aware of my large fan followings in Boston and Montreal. Marty believed signing me would boost ticket sales for his franchise. I accepted, hoping to pitch so well San Francisco would purchase my contract and return me to the major leagues.

To reach Scottsdale, Pam and I had to drive through Mesilla, New Mexico—the former stomping grounds of Billy the Kid—and Hatch, a town along the Rio Grande. Hatch is so small, you might pass through it without ever knowing you'd been there. Except for the roofs. Red roofs topped all the houses in town, and the color was not due to any paint or tiling. Chiles accounted for the crimson tide. Nearly everyone in Hatch raised those hot peppers. They spread the harvest on the roofs of their adobe huts or wooden homes or any other elevated surfaces so they would dry in the sun. We stopped to buy a couple of wreaths for $10 each. Would have paid five or six times that amount in some big city store.

We decided to take a shortcut through the Mimbre Mountains. At the Silver City cutoff, I noticed a large wooden sign that read CLIFF DWELLINGS. *Oh, God,* I wondered, *could it be? Was this the road that would lead us to that sacred spot where Morrison encountered his visions?* We drove for several miles but found no other signs indicating the site's location. I pulled into the driveway of a small cabin near the base of a mountain and got out to ask directions. A knock on the door. No answer. The place looked deserted.

It occurred to us that the cliff dwellings had to lie somewhere up in the nearby rocks so we followed a dirt hiking path that coiled around the mountain face. After twenty minutes of climbing, though, we still had no idea how much further we had to go before reaching our destination. We saw no signs, no landmarks, nobody to guide our journey.

We stopped to get our bearings. Then the singing came. It was a woman's voice but deep, cutting loose with a folk song in some ancient tongue. From around a large boulder leaning over a bend in the path, she appeared on horseback, this female Josey Wales: an oily, copper face; brown dungaree chaps frayed thin at the thighs by hard riding; red speckled bandana knotted around her throat; sun-faded denim shirt; a battered, sweat-stained cowboy hat tilted back on her shoulders. She wore her dark hair in pigtails, thick and coarse as raw wool. A large woman, but on that horse as graceful as any ballerina.

She kept a chaw of tobacco tucked under one cheek. Carried a carbine under her left arm. From a distance, we noticed something slung over the back of her saddle. Only when she pulled alongside us could we identify her cargo—the corpse of a freshly slain mountain lion. Her smile as she passed could not have looked friendlier, but you immediately sensed that no one trifled with this woman. She carried that carbine low and gave the impression she could blow off your balls while spitting a blob of tobacco juice smack in the center of your forehead.

We asked if she knew where we could find the cliff dwellings. She stretched from her saddle to point far up the mountain. "You just keep climbin'," she said, "they'll be on top of you 'fore you know it." She and her horse loped down the trail.

Keep climbing we did, but the higher we stepped, the lower the temperature dropped. It felt like fall at the foot of this mountain; the climate turned wintry as we neared the summit. Frost crunched under our shoes. Snow covered the peaks and boulders. We shivered in our warm-weather clothes and found no comfort when we finally reached the cliff dwellings, only disappointment.

One look told me we had arrived in the wrong place. These dwellings looked half the size of those Morrison had described. God was not Tony Orlando. He or She would never play such a small room. We later found out the caves Morrison had visited were indeed located in the Gila Wilderness, but about three hundred miles south of where we stood. Well, that's me, the Wrong Way Corrigan of modern explorers.

We stopped at the cabin back near the parking lot to sign a guest book resting on a pulpit near the front door. As we walked to our car, I heard a low, breathy whistle behind us.

"Jesus Christ," said a voice ringing with frogs. "Bill Lee was here!"

I spun around to find a disheveled park ranger staring at my autograph. He stood troll-short and feather-thin, with matted, shoulder-length red hair, a flimsy dirty-blond beard, and wild, bloodshot gray eyes peering at us from under the brim of a Smokey the Bear hat. Scabs had crusted in the corners of both nostrils.

Anyone could see that this man's diastolic pressure had soared dangerously high. He lifted his head and revealed the face of a dog tick, red and bloated after sucking too much blood. He could not stop fidgeting. Clearly, here was yet another DNA mishap who had somehow eluded all of God's quality controls before escaping to this haven far beyond the reach of any responsible recall process.

I stuck out my hand. "That's right," I said, "Bill Lee was here. And I'm me." The ranger wrapped his arms around my waist in a bear hug that revealed considerable steel considering his size.

"I'm Bill Calvin, "he hollered, "and I'm your biggest fan in the whole world. The Red Sox are my team. I'm a New Englander, ya know? Come from Maine. Worked on a boat, ya know? I was the captain."

"Well, sir," I said, "you certainly are a long way from port."

As it turned out, my Red Sox teammates and I shared some responsibility for that. Bill had helmed a fishing vessel back in 1975 when he sailed into Boston to watch us take on the Cincinnati Reds in the sixth game of the World Series. As every Red Sox diehard knows, rain delayed that meeting for three straight days. Bill spent most of them getting wasted on boilermakers in a local pub, waiting for Fenway Park to dry. Each day his boat remained anchored in the harbor, the swordfish in his hull ripened a bit more. By the time we finally played, no one would buy that reeking cargo. "I lost my haul, my job, and fifty thousand dollars," he told me, "but it was worth it just to see Fisk hit that game-winning home run. Fuck the fish and the money. I'll have that memory with me forever."

With his captain's bridge yanked from under him, Bill became a full-time wanderer. He drove down to Florida, canoed all the way to Mexico, and hiked across the border into Texas. Bill stopped in Silver City long enough to start an affair with a Native American lap dancer. The two of them did not emerge from her bedroom for three weeks and might have frolicked longer if they had not run out of food, booze, and pot. Bill headed to Fort Worth to restock their provisions only to wake up in a Mobile, Alabama, jail three days later with no idea how he got there. Turned out the police had arrested him on a DWI.

Bill spun this abridged version of his life story in about two minutes flat, jabbering faster than a cattle auctioneer. Fans often corner me to relate how some game I played altered their lives. Bill's tale sounded more interesting than most, so I didn't mind chatting for a bit. Still, we had to go.

"But you can't leave," Bill sputtered, "not without seeing the hot spring. Let me show you where it is."

He walked back in the direction we had just come from, only this time he had us squeeze behind a large rock formation overlooking a plateau. Sure enough, we saw the spring, bubbling low like the water you boil an egg in with a layer of steam rising off the surface.

Once Bill left, Pam and I dropped our clothes and dipped naked into the swirling water. The temperature of the spring had climbed to 102 degrees. Hot tub cozy. All we needed to complete our pleasure was a bottle of champagne chilling on the side and a mirrored ceiling. There was no one around unless you counted the spirits of Geronimo and Cochise. No one, that is, except for the bald eagles circling overhead, sizing up my pecker as if it were an appetizer from a Steak and Brew shrimp bar. It would be nice to write "jumbo shrimp." However, a man cannot sit for long in a hot pool without experiencing shrinkage.

I wanted to put the moves on Pam. Kind of sexy floating naked in the midst of that raw wilderness. But those eagles . . . they kept watching. There is nothing prudish about me, but the bald eagle is our national bird. The thought of making love in front of those two just seemed unpatriotic.

Bill invited us to stay overnight in his trailer, parked only a few yards down a small path hidden behind the visitor's cabin. His refrigerator contained six bottles of vodka, two gallons of gamy bear meat stew, and a large battered tin of marijuana some park ranger from Maui had sent him. You know, the essentials.

We stayed up well past midnight and got hammered while Bill showed slides of him frolicking with the local bears and kayaking around Kodiak Island. I answered his many questions about the Red Sox. Not the greatest entertainment, for sure, but it offered us some taste for the life of the Native Americans who had inhabited these mountains centuries ago. Without *Oprah* or *Seinfeld* reruns to distract them after a day's hunt, they had little to do but sit around the campfire, smoking herb and sharing stories much as we did that evening.

Except those Apaches apparently had greater resilience than we did. They would rise at dawn following a night-long debauch to sow the fields and hunt for food. Afternoon passed before we could rouse ourselves from bed and bid Calvin adieu.

Ten years later, I told this story to a businessman on a golf course. Before I could even mention our host's name, the man said, "Bet it was Bill Calvin the sea captain. That old bastard used to work for me in Sugarbush, Vermont, as a ski instructor until the day he stole my car and drove off to New Mexico. The guy was a con man from day one. On the run ever since he lost that boat."

So Bill had lied about the canoe trip from Florida to Texas, the walking tour across Mexico, and the lap dancer in Silver City. Hell, I appreciated the captain just the same. Outlaws appealed to me. Straight types may be more dependable, but they have zero amusement value. Anyone who can relieve the boredom of existence can always drink from my canteen. Besides, as it turned out, Bill's tall tales were not the last flim-flams laid on me during this trip.

We drove another fifty miles with our Volkswagen coughing and staggering the entire way. The car finally collapsed on the San Carlos reservation. We looked under the hood and discovered a cranky fuel filter had starved our engine. I performed an emergency bypass good enough to get us to Scottsdale.

The car sputtered again as we crossed the city limits and followed a narrow boulevard thick with palm trees and silver garbage pails. We rolled for a few feet before the engine died for good in front of a whitewashed, horseshoe-shaped concrete apartment complex. Turned out the Boston Red Sox used to stay there whenever the team trained in Arizona during the 1930s. I saw that as a good omen. The landlord rented us a one-bedroom right near the heated pool for $325 a month, fully furnished with all the black widow spiders you could kill.

I walked to the Phoenix Giants training facility early the next morning. Crickets sang in a frothy whisper. A heavy dew still coated the lawns, and every few minutes I heard the hushed clatter of milk bottles being gently placed on the stoop of some house whose occupants had yet to stir. I reached the Giants' complex and found an empty parking lot. That troubled me. When you are a veteran trying out for a team, it is never a good idea to be the first to arrive. Makes you look desperate.

While I stacked my gear in a locker, the door swung open. I had hoped to see another player, but instead this tall, deep-chested, middle-aged man with bushels for hands swaggered in as if he owned the place. Tom Haller, a former major-league catcher, was the minor-league director for the San Francisco Giants. His greeting reflected just how much his organization wanted me in camp.

"What the fuck are you doing here?" he shouted.

I explained that Marty Stone had signed me to a personal services contract and that I was trying out for his team and that if I made the roster I would work for Stone, not San Francisco, and that I understood the big-league Giants had no obligation to promote me to their club, and blah, blah, blah. It took nearly five minutes for me to say those few words; Haller kept injecting "Oh, yeah?" between every syllable. When I finished, he stared at me and chewed his lip for a good long while before replying in a voice that scraped my scalp, it sounded so harsh, "Well, we'll just have to see about that."

Ten minutes later a clubhouse boy stopped at my locker to say I could not suit up for practice that day. Instead, Ethan Blackaby, the Phoenix general manager, had already arranged for me to work out with the Arizona State college team. Marty came down before I left and told me to stay in shape throwing batting practice until he straightened everything out with Haller.

I pitched against the collegians in an intrasquad game that very afternoon. Sportswriters ranked Arizona State as a national baseball power, and I could see why; nearly every hitter showed major-league potential. One player stood out, a tall, skinny kid with thick wrists, long muscled arms, and a bat so quick I did not dare throw him a fastball for fear he might hit a laser back up the middle and leave nothing of me behind but a grease smudge and a pair of smoking spikes.

My best bet was a breaking pitch outside. Soon as this hit-

ter fouled it off, he massaged my ears with a few friendly pro-
fanities—nothing out of line for a baseball diamond—and
said, "Is that all you got, old man? Why don't you challenge
someone?" He laughed to let me in on the joke, but the age
reference stung. I dropped down to throw him a hard sidearm
sinker. It ran across home plate and veered inside to jam him
right above the bat handle. He dropped to one knee trying to
swat it and hit a floppy line drive to second base for an out.
"Son of a bitch," the batter yelled. He walked in circles and
shook his hands to get the feeling back into his fingers. Before
leaving the field, the batter smiled and touched the bill of his
cap. A ballplayer's salute.

He seemed surprised I could still run the ball in on him with
so much oomph. That encouraged me. If my sinker could bore
in on a stud with a lightning swing toting an aluminum bat, I
could probably still jam most major-league sluggers. I did not
find out the player's name until after the game. It was Barry.

Bonds.

Yeah, that one.

Three days passed before Haller permitted me to return to
the Giants' camp. Once my arm shaped up, Phoenix manager
Jim Lefebvre put me in a game. The hitters smacked my
pitches as though I had served them up on a batting tee. My
arm felt strong, but I threw too hard, trying to impress Haller
and the Giants' coaching staff. Every sinker lacked tempo and
hovered too long over the heart of home plate.

When you rush your delivery—as I did that afternoon to
increase my velocity—it is difficult to finish your pitches. Your
foot lands too soon. Your arm lags behind the rest of your
pitching motion, and you cannot get your body on top of the

ball to make the sinker sink. You work against yourself. I usually remedied that by lengthening my stride two inches while raising my arm higher over my head, but I could not get synchronized. The top of my body spun at 45 rpm while the bottom rotated at 78. I surrendered three runs in less than an inning.

Despite my poor performance, Lefebvre continued to use me in games. I did not surrender another run over my next nine innings. When Lefebvre called me into his office three weeks into camp, I assumed he wanted to discuss my role with his club. Instead, the manager explained that the front office had decided to fully commit to a youth movement. Phoenix no longer required my services.

Gee, they'd known my age when we arrived in Arizona. No one had said anything then. Had the last three weeks pushed me over the limit? An apologetic Marty Stone met me outside the clubhouse and explained what had happened. He admitted my birthday was not an issue; Giants officials had pressured him into releasing me. They had told Marty major-league baseball would be expanding to Arizona in the near future and that he would be the leading candidate to own the new franchise—unless he pissed them off by keeping me on his team.

Bad news never holds me down for long. I have always believed the adage about a door opening for every one that closes. Lately, though, whenever I walked through a door, the temperature outside was twenty below zero. I needed to find warmer climes.

3

RINGSIDE FOR
THE APOCALYPSE

Four a.m. on New Year's Day, 1984. I strolled down a paved asphalt street just outside Caraballeda, Venezuela. This section of the city resembled a typical U.S. suburb with its picket fences, trim lawns, colorful flower boxes, and modern street lamps. I saw basketball hoops hanging in the backyards of wooden gingerbread houses. Glittering late-model cars and vans filled nearly every driveway.

About a mile into my walk, the pavement thinned before crumbling into dirt and middle-class havens gave way to dismal hovels constructed of plywood and mismatched crating planks. Broken street lamps slouched over the street; a full moon provided the only illumination. Cars loitered alongside some of the homes, rusted vehicles with dead motors. I saw just one toy, the only evidence that children lived in this squalor: a tricycle turned upside down in a ditch. A tricycle without wheels.

A dirt road winding behind this cluster of shanties narrowed into a trail that led up into the mountains. It was important to climb as high as my legs could carry me before the first morning light broke over the countryside. Once the sun appeared, I intended to sit and wait for the explosion. One more hour until dawn. Plenty of time.

Dense woods shrouded the mountain. I lost sight of the moon for whole stretches of the path and had to feel my way along the trees to continue walking. I heard just enough sound to make me feel isolated: the buzzing of the only mosquito still awake in the forest and the lazy *drip-drop* of a stream trickling through a nearby ravine.

My walk took longer than I originally estimated. After an hour, I had hiked barely a quarter of the distance up the mountain. No way could I reach the summit by dawn. A false sunrise had already pushed aside the night. So I paused to look out over the city, to watch it vanish before my eyes as all the street lamps fluttered and dimmed.

A world without color surrounded me until a slender mauve line rimmed the dark sky. I perched on a rock to watch the pink gold sun slip through that fissure in the horizon. Shadows poked up from the earth. Powdery russet clouds rolled over the flag-blue ocean. Lazy waves wrinkled the water. I could have sat there watching forever. Then the odor reached my nostrils: oil from the tankers crowding the docks in the harbor below.

I resumed climbing. A twig cracked loudly close to the path. Just a few feet ahead, a bush rustled though I could not detect a breeze. *Oh, no. Banditos. Of course not, dummy. What respectable bandit would be stupid enough to lie in wait up here? Not enough trade.* But that bush shook again.

Something alive hid on the other side of the leaves, pressed close to the ground. I could hear him breathing in short gasps. Was he winded from tailing me? My imagination talking, of course.

So why were those eyes blinking in the shadows?

I backed away, searching for a weapon. The rocks looked too small, the fallen branches too short and thin. I remembered leaving my Swiss Army knife back at the apartment. What could I do? Calling for help would be useless in such an isolated spot. A line from the ad for that movie *Alien* came to mind: in space, no one can hear you scream. Whoever hid behind that bush must have sensed my fear and decided to make his move. A figure darted through a thicket, dove for my legs, and scurried down the path. My murderous pursuer was Porky Pig's Latino cousin, a wild black swine who had been foraging for his breakfast when this rude American invaded his home.

Climbing higher made it harder to breathe. I entertained the idea that the dense foliage had sipped oxygen out of the atmosphere rather than carbon monoxide, a theory that collapsed when the forest became a microdesert in the clouds. The landscape shifted from green to beige. Dry, stunted shrubs replaced the trees. There was no sign of moisture, and the air thinned so much, my lungs struggled to inhale enough of it. The sunburned rocks reminded me that I had neglected to carry water. Now you know why I never made Eagle Scout— you can count on me to arrive unprepared.

Halfway up the mountain I could not continue any further. My back ached, my legs had gone spongy. I felt sticky. I felt tired. I felt thirsty. I felt one hundred years old. A weird clicking noise nagged at my ears. I could not identify the sound at first. Something slowly opening and closing. Then I got it: the valves of my heart working overtime.

A little switchback trail cut away from the path and continued along the side of the mountain. The day before, a villager had told me that it led to a wealthy German community hidden deep within the rocks. Outsiders never visited the town. No one knew who had built it or how the inhabitants brought in supplies, though some locals reported seeing helicopters hovering in the vicinity.

Stereotypes offend me, but I conjured this image of a futuristic metropolis filled with blue-eyed blondes in steel helmets driving Mercedes. On their dashboards: pictures of Laurence Olivier playing that lethal Nazi dentist from the movie *Marathon Man*. What did he keep asking Dustin Hoffman's character? *Is it safe?* Don't think so, tiger. I had no intention of going near the place.

Instead I sat on my haunches and waited. Dawn had long passed. The event I had come to witness had to happen soon. My mind entertained no doubts.

I knew the world would end that morning.

Sounds crazy, huh? Not to this left-hander. George Orwell's *1984* had made a profound impression on me in high school. It seemed probable that something momentous would occur on the first day of that year, so I imagined the ultimate disaster. Just my nature, though I rarely reveal it to anyone. An anonymous fear colors my perspective of everything and has haunted me nearly all my life. At the age of four, my favorite TV program was *Kukla, Fran, and Ollie*. One of the characters was a fierce, fire breathing dragon. Whenever it appeared on-screen, I ran to hide behind the living room couch. I have hidden behind that couch ever since.

A strict Catholic upbringing exacerbated my childhood anxieties. My first memory of church is of a priest fulminating from a pulpit during a sermon. He resembled a fierce Moses with his long beard and flowing white hair. Every syllable thundered when he spoke. Lightning flashed behind him and blood dripped from his eyes as he warned the congregation of the penalties God extracted when sinners incurred His wrath. I spent the entire service cringing behind a pew.

That priest's god was a tyrant who ruled with threats. If that was religion, I wanted no part of it. When the time came to attend First Holy Communion practice, I locked myself to a bedpost with my Roy Rogers handcuffs and hid the keys. My mother could not release me until long after Communion practice had ended.

I escaped the church's influence for only a day. My parents enrolled me in a catechism class where nuns taught small boys and girls about the devil, original sin, the nature of evil, and eternal damnation. The stuff of nightmares. I hated the course but my marks ranked among the best in our grade. The teachers could not take credit for that. No, someone else provided the motivation—that guy nailed to the cross on the wall above the blackboard. One look at him and I knew those nuns meant business.

I grew up thinking of God as something other than a benevolent deity. To me, he roamed heaven as a snarling Minnesota Fats playing celestial snooker with all the planets. I figured one of these days he would muff that bank shot and send a gigantic asteroid toward Earth to crash somewhere near me. So once I decided the world's demise was imminent, I climbed the mountain to grab a ringside seat for the cataclysm. I did not want to spend my last hours hiding behind another couch.

◆

Pam and I had flown to Caracas after Ozzie Virgil invited me to play for the Tiburones de La Guaira, a team he managed in the Venezuela League. Ozzie had coached third base for Dick Williams when I pitched for the Expos. He was a shrewd baseball man who acted as liaison between the players and their manager. Williams could not have functioned long without Ozzie's assistance. Dick possessed all the talents of a great manager. He knew how to utilize the strengths of every player on his roster and was a master at getting the advantage during key pitcher-hitter matchups in the late innings of a ballgame.

What he did not know was how to tactfully deal with people. When a player screwed up, Dick thought nothing of humiliating him in front of the entire team. I remember a game during the 1980 season when John D'Acquisto, a relief pitcher the Expos had just acquired from the San Diego Padres, could not find his control. He fell behind in the count to nearly every batter he faced. We lost that day, and Dick raged for hours afterward. He berated John in the dugout, in the clubhouse, on the team bus. I think he tailed D'Acquisto into the bathroom to remind him of his shortcomings.

John sat mute throughout the roving tirade, and his passivity galled Williams all the more. The Expos had to catch a flight following the game for the start of a road trip. As we boarded our plane, Dick intensified his attack. "Jesus Christ," he growled in a voice that carried down the aisles, "you come out of the bullpen, you're supposed to throw strikes. You afraid to put the ball over the plate? We should have traded for your fucking wife. She's probably the only one with any balls in your family."

He called John "Mrs. D'Acquisto," a taunt he continued until the pitcher ran to the rear of the plane to escape. We found John in the galley a few minutes later. He refused to return to his seat. If he could have opened a door, I think he would have stepped out. We were only thirty-two thousand feet in the air at the time.

Whenever Williams reamed a player that ferociously, Ozzie commiserated with the victim afterward and applied a much-needed ego massage. We could bring our grievances to him knowing he would present them to Dick without creating a rumpus or inviting retribution. Ozzie also kept our team entertained during games with his singular style for flashing signs. He would sashay down the coach's box, his hands flowing with all the rhythm of a mambo king. Ozzie would finish his signals by swinging his hips and tossing his arms to the side like Jackie Gleason exiting from the stage with "Away we go!" Our coach exhibited so much versatility, he could call for a bunt while simultaneously flirting with any attractive women sitting in the box seats.

Ozzie and I respected each other, and he knew what a stint in the Venezuela League could mean for me: a way back. Many top players from the American major leagues competed in the VL. If I could distinguish myself pitching against them, perhaps some freethinking general manager in the States would ignore my past and offer me a contract. My next birthday would make me thirty-six. This would probably be my last chance.

Pam and I arrived in Venezuela the third week of November 1983. The Tiburones had agreed to pay me $2,000 a month plus living expenses. We should have asked the team to include air-conditioned clothing among the perks. Our plane left Montreal in an ice storm. When the passengers disembarked in Maiquetia Airport on the north shore of Venezuela, we stepped into a microwave—104 degrees that pressed down on the city with the force of 140. A column of heat trapped the jet fuel fumes close to the ground; I could smell the threat of combustion. Whole sections of the tarmac had puddled into black ooze. If you did not watch where you stepped, you could wind up glued to the runway until nightfall. No breeze comforted us. The sunlight seemingly pierced through solid objects, leaving no shade.

The heat thickened when we exited from the cool of the arrivals building. Sweat saturated our clothes in seconds, and my legs buckled low until I was walking on my knees. Could not catch my breath. Our driver had to carry me to his car.

Ozzie had scheduled my first start for the following afternoon. I asked the driver if the forecasters thought it would still be this hot at game time.

"Weatherman says hotter."

Oh, boy.

He saw the concerned expression on my face and laughed. "Just kidding," he said. Oh, yeah? The next day I stood on a pitching rubber that could have doubled as the devil's anvil. A professional ballplayer becomes accustomed to competing in every kind of weather; he should never offer the elements as an excuse for poor performance. After all, the climate is the same for both sides in any game. But the heat in Caracas did not compare to anything I had ever experienced. Hot in North America is you laboring to adjust while pitching in the meantime until that first big sweat flops over your collar and your breathing slows down to the rhythm of your windup and your heart settles and the temperature joins you as an ally, keeping your arm loose and whippy.

Hot in Venezuela behaved like another breed of hound entirely—a competitor. When you adjusted to the torrid clime, he fired up the grill until you bubbled on all sides—his signal to toss on another bag of charcoal. Our cotton uniforms, lighter than those we wore in the States, hardly relieved the discomfort. I might as well have played in an angora jumpsuit.

The configuration of our home ballpark also disturbed me. In the United States, architects align most major-league stadiums so that a pitcher faces west when he works on the mound. That means left-handers frequently throw out of the south into a westerly wind. I believed that made my ball move more.

In Venezuela, the trade winds blow in the opposite direction. I was throwing in a vortex. Every pitch in my repertoire arrived at home plate clothesline straight, without a bit of movement to confuse the hitters. For someone who relies on deception rather than velocity to retire batters, you could not have chosen worse conditions. I tried compensating by throwing a spitter. Bad idea. The ball kept drying before it reached home plate.

I started overthrowing, trying to put too much on the ball. The faster I threw, the harder they hit. In our dugout, the clubhouse boy served the players demitasses of espresso. My teammates sipped the dark beverage all through the game for extra energy, and it worked. Our hitters ran to the plate, pumped their arms, ground their bats into sawdust, and sprinted full out on the base paths. I drank a cup, but it didn't help me. I needed to go in the other direction. Tone down. Find a balance. I asked the kid to bring me a cup of chamomile tea. That didn't help either.

The wind, the ballpark, the heat, the humidity . . . none of these factors hampered the opposing hitters. I retired the first batter of the game on a line drive that nearly decapitated our third baseman, Luis Salazar. Had the hitter uppercut that pitch just an inch higher, the ball would have crashed through the window of some cottage in Nova Scotia. Hard singles from the next two batters put runners on first and third. Then the wolf whistles and chanting started.

Andres Galarraga had yet to play an inning of major-league ball, but we had all heard about him. Scouts considered the twenty-three-year-old first baseman the top prospect in the Montreal Expos' minor league system. Galarraga was a right-handed power hitter, six foot four and 230 pounds of muscle and sinew. He displayed so much athletic quickness and grace for such a large man, South American sportswriters had nicknamed him the "Big Cat."

Tiburones fans used another name for him. As soon as he stepped from the dugout, they shouted, *"El grande maricon!,"* a phrase that translates into English as "the big faggot." They pinned this label on Andre in reaction to his habit of vogueing whenever he came to bat. Galarraga rhythmically rolled his hips and swung his shoulders as he strolled from the on-deck circle to home plate. Once he settled in the batter's box he stuck out his high rear end as though offering it for someone to pinch.

Had Andre hit .200 with popgun power, he could have turned pirouettes on the dugout roof in a pink frou-frou without arousing the slightest reaction from our fans. But he was one of the most dangerous sluggers in the league and regularly pounded our pitching staff.

The team had not provided a scouting report on Andre; I had no idea how to pitch him. He displayed the batting stance of a dead pull hitter. Galarraga crouched far off the plate, as if he wanted us to challenge him inside. My catcher, Bruce Bochy, noticed the same thing and called for a hard sinker, low and away, just off the edge of the strike zone. Perfect. We both assumed Galarraga could never reach that pitch and hit it with authority. Until he swung. That's when we discovered the Big Cat's arms stretched nearly as long as his legs. His bat covered so much plate, he tagged that ball on the sweet spot and smacked a double deep into the right centerfield gap. Two runs scored.

When Galarraga batted with runners on first and second two innings later, he set up closer to home, as if he again anticipated that sinker away. I started him with two fastballs high and inside. He refused to bite at either. With the count 2–0, I threw the Cat a changeup away, figuring he would still be looking for something hard and low. He kept his hands back and popped the ball up, four hundred feet over the fence in dead centerfield for a three-run homer that knocked me out of the game. *Damn,* I thought while trudging to the showers, *that bush-leaguer decoyed you into choosing that pitch. That will teach you to throw him anything soft. Should have just zitzed the son of a bitch with your ninety-four-mile-an-hour fastball.*

Which is when I remembered I didn't have one.

I walked back to our apartment after the loss. Dusk had fallen and the temperature had dropped all the way down to 101. Not far from the ballpark, I passed a high, gray concrete wall perhaps two hundred feet wide. A row of rectangular apertures had been carved into the stone and what I saw in those openings drew me closer: outstretched arms, clutching fingers, and hands waving frantically to catch anyone's attention.

I peeked inside over the flailing limbs and discovered that the wall fronted the courtyard of an asylum. Slack-jawed patients in hospital gowns plodded through an open garden. Some of them mumbled incoherently to themselves. Others bellowed at phantoms. And I noticed the silent ones with Thorazine eyes who just sat and stared without moving a muscle.

I shook every hand along the wall, thinking that even the slightest contact with the outside world might offer the poor souls some comfort. Your heart would have to be stuffed with dead mercy not to feel for these people. But after pitching so badly that afternoon, their plight also struck me as a cautionary tale. Far as I knew, this could be the place Venezuelan teams sent aging pitchers soon as they starting hanging too many curveballs.

4

DON'T CRY FOR ME, VENEZUELA

Pam and I lived in an apartment building right off the beach near a neat, middle-class neighborhood on the outskirts of La Guaira. Most Americans visiting this area stayed at the Hilton in downtown Caracas, where the staff pampered them twenty-four hours a day. The Tiburones offered us rooms there as well, but I had come to Venezuela with a purpose and preferred staying away from the distractions of the city even though it meant a longer bus ride to the ballpark.

Though our digs featured few amenities other than the basics, our bedroom window afforded a magnificent view of the ocean, and the area was free of the foul-smelling smog that continually hid the sun in much of Caracas. We lived like natives. I bathed in the ocean first thing every morning and picked oranges for lunch. The day after our arrival, one of the local beachcombers taught us how to snare lizards. We weaved strands of grass into nooses and lassoed the creatures around their necks. He would take the catches home to cook them for dinner.

When Pam and I walked the streets at night after visiting the local bistros, our eyes continually glanced upward. We were not looking for the moon or constellations, but at the fruit bats with their two-foot wing spans who regularly swooped out of the trees in aerial assaults. These miniature stealth bombers would splatter unsuspecting passersby with payloads of guano. We also kept watch for the feral dog packs that silently glided through the neighborhood every evening. Women and children ran indoors at their arrival unless men were around to chase away the strays.

We had to walk up six flights to reach our place; the building's elevator ran only on Thursdays. Gates and bars covered the doors and windows of every apartment. These barriers let in any cooling breezes drifting off the water while keeping out the bandits and revolutionaries. I wondered about the effectiveness of those protective measures. Sure, the bars looked sturdy enough to stop most large objects. But they could not stop small-caliber bullets.

Caracas was a city of guns. You could not help noticing that when driving into town. We saw soldiers hefting assault rifles or machine guns on practically every corner. SWAT teams made no attempt to disguise their presence in front of banks, corporate high-rises, federal buildings, and other structures the government deemed important. Well-dressed young bloods partied in restaurants at night with bulges under their jackets. Politicos and the wealthier businesspeople rarely traveled anywhere without their armed bodyguards.

Politics provided the primary reason for so many people to tote so many guns throughout Caracas in 1983. There was a national election scheduled for the end of the year. The economy had grown shaky, and the ruling elitists expected trouble. I saw evidence of how high tensions had risen when our team returned from a road trip to Valencia. The bus pulled into the parking lot at the side of our ballpark around 2 a.m. While waiting for the driver to open the baggage compartment, we heard someone softly moaning in the shadows. My teammates found a naked man, his back crisscrossed with whip marks, strung to the ballpark fence with thick rope. Someone identified him as a political organizer and dissident. Whoever had inflicted this punishment had left the victim in this public place as a warning to others.

Despite that incident and all the guns, I never felt threatened walking the Caracas streets. The locals we met were friendly people, slow to take offense and quick to party. Many of the nightclubs in the area never closed, and hardly a day passed without someone inviting us into their home. The baseball fans were passionate yet restrained, nothing like the soccer zealots we read about who started riots anytime their favorite team lost a match.

The Tiburones—Spanish for "sharks"—played their home

games in an oval concrete stadium that we shared with the Caracas Leones. The ballpark seated thirty thousand. Management reserved one small section of the stands for a salsa orchestra composed entirely of any fans who arrived at the stadium carrying instruments. On some nights there could be as many as thirty musicians in this hodgepodge band, and their rousing, audacious improvisations kept the joint jumping from the first inning on.

That nonstop carnival atmosphere took a little getting used to. In North America, major-league baseball fans applaud and shout encouragement throughout a game, but they generally wait for crucial moments to rise from their seats and get thoroughly engaged. When an American home team is down by five or more runs, you often see its supporters sitting on their hands.

The people who attended our games would rise to their feet screaming and clapping before the umpire called, "Play ball!" As soon as the opposing players took the field, our fans serenaded them with some taunting song, a tune they repeated every inning. Their cheering never let up, even if our club fell behind by ten runs.

Whenever a Tiburone homered, the fishermen among the spectators showered the diamond with freshly slaughtered baby sharks. Players brought the fish back to the clubhouse and cut them up for steaks. I learned something the first time I stuck a knife into one: when you slice a shark that died only five hours earlier, the pieces throb in your hand. I took some steaks home for dinner after one game. Tasted just like swordfish, only with a little more twitch.

During the seventh-inning stretch, ushers allowed as many

as a hundred fans down on the field to dance along the base paths to the driving salsa beat. One night I saw two men shimmy from first base to home plate while carrying the carcass of a seven-foot shark over their heads. These celebrations never grew unruly except when we played against Caracas. Class distinctions and political differences added more edge to these games. Venezuelans considered the Tiburones the port team, a working-class franchise whose fans wore cutoffs, T-shirts, and sandals.

The Leones billed themselves as the city club, more blue-chip than blue-collar. Their loyalists arrived at the park dressed in Armani linen and Gucci shoes. Fistfights between the two factions would break out around the fifth inning, after patrons had guzzled all the sangria from the concession stands. Management maintained extra police on hand to stop the combatants before anyone suffered serious injury.

For weeks after the Galarraga game, my pitching stagnated. Ozzie finally yanked me from the starting rotation and relegated me to the bullpen where I languished in a Catch-22. My sinkerball needed work to remain effective; it dropped more sharply when my arm was tired. In order to pitch better, I had to pitch more, but Ozzie saw no reason to pitch me more until I pitched better. So those few times he did fetch me into a ballgame, I pitched worse. And so he pitched me less. And so it went.

Bruce Bochy did all he could to help end my slump. He spent hours catching me on the side and analyzing my delivery. Bochy had played with the San Diego Padres back in the

States, and when he flew down to Venezuela he needed a separate ticket for his batting helmet. He had the biggest head in baseball. I don't mean Bruce was an egotist. I mean his head looked physically immense. Picture an Easter Island carving. You could have used his catcher's mask to net a school of salmon.

In fact, everything about him loomed large. Bruce stood six foot five with shoulders as broad as a cornerstone on a cathedral. His long arms enabled him to set a low target perfect for sinkerballers. You could not throw a ball past him in the dirt. Bruce's hands were so big, his catcher's mitt nearly filled the entire strike zone. He could catch a ball six inches off the plate in the webbing of his mitt and the umpire would still call it a strike.

Like most tall catchers, Bruce had difficulty throwing out base stealers. A catcher cannot release a ball until his feet are set under him. It took Bruce an extra second or so to raise all that body from his crouch and plant his feet. By the time he threw the ball, even the slowest base runners needed only a few steps to reach the bag. But that was Bochy's only defensive weakness.

I appreciated how Bruce constantly studied the opposing hitters so he knew what pitch to call in tight situations. His zany sense of humor was also a plus. And when my pitching deteriorated, I needed someone who could make me laugh. One morning as we spoke at his locker, our sixteen-year-old bat boy, Luis, approached to ask if one of us would teach him English. Bruce worked on a phrase with Luis for several minutes and suggested the boy try it out on Ozzie Virgil.

Our batboy proudly walked into the manager's office while mouthing the words to himself. Two minutes later, we heard a commotion. Luis came tearing through the clubhouse with Ozzie chasing after him. Turned out Bruce had instructed Luis to say, "Your dick in my ass feels good." A cruel joke? Not in a baseball clubhouse, where everything is fair game. Our catcher's wordplay kept the entire team—including Luis and Ozzie—howling for days.

◆

The crisis occurred during the first week in December: we ran out of pot. I had entered the country with a small stash—two dime bags—in the pocket of the plaid shirt I had worn during our flight. Customs officials did not even look. So many drugs come out of Venezuela, it never occurred to them that anyone would bring any in. The country was like Mexico in that regard. I could have walked through the checkpoint sucking on a joint with Pam wearing slabs of hash as earrings without attracting attention.

You did not have to look for hard drugs in Caracas. Dealers sought you out. One afternoon a slender middle-aged man in a tailored suit, tasseled loafers, and Foster Grant wraparounds approached me outside the ballpark. The Rolex on his wrist looked so heavy, I was surprised he could lift his arm to shake hands. He might have been an Anglo or one of those fair-haired, blue-eyed upper-crust Venezuelans. Could have been from anywhere really. His speech was unaccented, uninflected. A drone without a country. His business card introduced him as an importer of "fine objets d'art from the Orient." In Venezuela that could have meant anything. Whatever he did, it must have kept him indoors much of the time. He was the only person walking around the city without a tan.

The gentleman had once lived in Montreal and introduced

himself as a close friend of my former tenant Alex. Which meant he had something to sell besides jade Buddhas—a pound of top quality cocaine for $10,000. I asked why he wanted to unload his product for less than a quarter of its street value. He explained the coke came from a kilo he had planned to send to New York until the seal on its container broke, making it impossible to ship. Many small-time drug dealers operated in Caracas. They did not wear tailored suits, or thick Rolexes, or tasseled loafers, or Foster Grants. They did moonlight as informants. He feared the police might hear about his stash if he did not transact a sale soon.

Curiosity did not move me to find out why he couldn't repair the seal or replace the entire container. His story sounded too fishy, and he looked CIA. Anyway, what would I want with a pound of coke? With a stash that large, I would be up and wired every evening, and there is just not that much to do in Caracas after a certain hour. The nightclubs held no allure for me. Had I wanted to party past dawn, we would have stayed in Montreal. All the TV shows broadcast in Spanish without subtitles. The only diversion left at five in the morning was watching dogs screw in the alley behind our building. How long could that keep anyone entertained? I guess quite a while if you're one of the dogs, but the act gets old quickly when you are only a spectator.

The dealer suggested I could sell the coke to my teammates at a hefty profit. Wasn't interested. When it comes to drugs, I am a consumer, not a retailer. Besides, I was trying to get back to the majors and wanted to keep my mind and body sound. Hard drugs, most hallucinogens, and liquor, except for the occasional beer, were out.

I excluded pot from my abstinence program. I needed the

occasional joint to slow down the thoughts racing through my brain, to relax after a frenzied game. To help maintain focus. I asked one of my teammates where I could acquire a few bags. He recommended two young men who grew marijuana on some land just outside the city.

The next morning I rented a car and drove deep into a canyon and up a short hill until I reached a bluff overlooking the ocean. I found a small farm with only two buildings: a four-room shack and an empty barn with gap-toothed walls. The pens on the property needed new planks and wiring, and although the air carried a whiff of dried manure and urine, I did not see any animals.

A Mutt and Jeff team worked the place. The tall one with the long inky hair pulled back into a ponytail beneath his baseball cap and the silver wire-rimmed spectacles introduced himself as Jorge. He wore the tied-dyed regalia—tank top and jeans—of a Deadhead. His short, stocky partner, Ramón, had the same ponytail, but he dressed in heavy Levi's work pants with a flannel shirt and a suede John Deere hat. Just looking at all that dense fiber under the glaring sun almost gave me heatstroke.

We sat at a wobbly pine picnic table on the back porch of the shack. Both men appeared to be in their early twenties, political science majors who sold weed on the side to help pay for college. They admired Castro, despised Ronald Reagan, hated the upper classes everywhere, and thought the Venezuelan government thoroughly corrupt. In other words, these two men practiced Marxism while using their black-market enterprise to exploit the same capitalist system that they claimed exploited them.

I wondered where they stood in the ongoing dispute

between Great Britain and Argentina over the possession of the Falkland Islands, the hot political topic in Venezuela at the time. Jorge immediately revealed his sympathies when he emphatically declared, "You cannot call it the Falklands! That is an Anglo name. It is the Islas Malvinas!" He stomped into the barn. Ramón explained that his friend was sensitive about the Falklands. They both had reached draft age and feared the dispute would soon erupt into a full-blown war between South America and Europe. Neither wanted any part of the conflict.

A few minutes later Jorge returned from the barn lugging a swollen forty-pound gunnysack. He wrestled the bag to the table. His right arm arced high in the air, and the blade came down so swiftly, I had no time to react. The metal stuck deep in the wood near my elbow and vibrated for seconds like a tuning fork at high pitch. A machete. Very large. Extremely sharp.

Jorge smiled. "And what do we call the Falklands, *amigo?*" he asked.

"Islas Malvinas."

"*Sí.*"

He sliced open one end of the bag to remove a two-foot-square bale of pot about eighteen inches deep. You will not find that much grass covering an eighteen-hole golf course. I bought a pound for $100. While Ramón wrapped it in brown paper, Jorge scraped the gummy cannabis resin from his blade, rolled a joint, and passed it around.

This joint did not hit me like giggly-fit marijuana. They had slipped me Bertrand Russell weed, the kind of herb that turns you introspective at the first toke. My bones melted into the bench. Jorge and I sat side by side engaged in profound conversation. Neither of us uttered a word. Every now and again he waved his hand in some subtle gesture. I nodded. He shrugged. Each of us understood exactly what the other meant. I kept glancing at the pocket watch he wore on his belt. I could hear it ticking. The second hand swept around the numbers unimpeded. Yet an hour passed before 10:00 became 10:01. I finally left with my senses so dulled, it took twice as long to drive back down the hill as it had to come up. Great pot.

◆

I emerged from those mountains on New Year's Day and wandered into a small bar at the edge of a Venezuelan fishing village. Fishermen just off the bay crowded into the place. They had risen at dawn to fish these waters in ancient, creaking boats using hand lines and nets. Now they celebrated their catches with sandwiches made of crispy deep-fried sardines on hard-crusted, doughy rolls washed down with ice-cold beers.

When I walked in, a young fisherman clapped me on the back and handed over a sandwich and a brew. He did not know my name, or what I did, or why I had come there, and it did not matter. Anyone who passed through that door instantly qualified as a friend. I took one bite of the sandwich and started laughing, the taste gave me that much pleasure.

A few moments later I stood on the dock watching the tides froth under the sun. Giggling children chased each other up the white beach. An old man stood waist-high in the surf whistling something carefree while he trailed his fishing line through the water. A young boy and girl sat arm in arm at the end of the pier, dangling their legs above the waves. He sang softly in her ear. I licked the salty oil dripping from my fingers and realized my mistake. The world could never end on a day as glorious as this.

Then I went to the ballpark and surrendered another three-run homer to Galarraga.

Wrong again.

◆

The Tiburones competed for the Venezuela League championship against clubs from five other cities, Caracas, Maracay, Barquisimeto, Maracaibo, and Valencia. All of the towns were reasonably close by, so I never found the road trips grueling. We rode in a wide-bodied, air-conditioned bus with plush leather seats and plenty of leg room. It resembled a motel room on wheels, a vehicle built to accommodate large men.

While traveling to Maracay one afternoon, our driver pulled into a gas station on a highway intersection. My teammates and I saw as many people riding burros as driving cars. We left the bus to eat lunch in a diner next door to the station. I sat down in a rickety truck stop constructed from desiccated driftwood. No booths, just a dozen or so wobbly wooden stools in front of a long cracked Formica lunch counter. In the outdoor kitchen, white-hot coals purred in a large open barbecue pit. A deep fryer bubbled next to it.

Farmers carrying live pigs, goats, rabbits, chickens, and iguanas lined up at the cash register. They had come here to sell, not buy. Each farmer handed his animals over the counter to one of the cooks in exchange for a few bills or coins.

"What's good today?" I asked the waitress.

She pointed to a freshly killed, skinned rabbit roasting on a spit. I had seen it only moments ago, vibrant and kicking, in the arms of its owner. Now it stared back at me with lifeless eyes. Oh, no. I refused to eat Bugs Bunny.

"Can you crack open a can of Spam?"

That item did not appear on the menu. I settled for a grilled chicken sandwich but waited outside until it finished cooking.

I saw a familiar deep yellow logo emblazoned across posters and billboards throughout this region. Shell Oil maintained a heavy public profile in all the cities we played in. Something poetic in that—hitters shelled me in every one of them. Ozzie started me in Maracaibo, where the air stank of burning petroleum from the nearby oil refineries. I walked around that city blind for all the smoke. My eyes burned. I gagged with nearly every breath. The wind blew hot off the lake near the ballpark, and the high humidity made pitching in a day game unbearable. The Maracaibo hitters scorched my best stuff and drove me to the showers in the third inning. I wanted to thank them for removing me from the heat.

My pitching did not revive until the closing weeks of the season, after the weather cooled, my arm warmed, and Ozzie started using me out of the bullpen as his primary left-handed reliever. I surrendered only two runs in my last eighteen innings pitched. The Tiburones finished the season at .500, a record just good enough to earn the last berth in the Venezuela League championship playoffs. We had to win three out of five games against Barquisimeto to advance past the first round.

Barquisimeto opened the series with two wins. We took the third game, but our opponents led 3–2 in the eighth inning of game four when Ozzie brought me in from the bullpen.

Runners on first and second, nobody out. Willie Upshaw, a left-handed hitter, stepped to the plate.

Bruce Bochy called time and joined me for a mound conference with our third baseman, Luis Salazar, first baseman, Clint Hurdle, and second baseman, Ozzie Guillen. Upshaw had played first base with the Toronto Blue Jays in the American League. Neither Bruce nor I had ever seen him hit, so we could only guess how he might approach this at bat. We knew Upshaw had driven in more than a hundred runs for the Blue Jays in 1983. That told us he might look for a pitch to drive deep, to break the game open. Guillen disagreed. He had played against Willie many times and believed the first baseman would lay down a bunt to move the runners along.

I told Bruce we would feed Upshaw a hard cutter away. Willie could bunt that pitch fair in only one direction, down the third base line. Since my motion pulled me that way, I would field the bunt and throw it to Salazar. After stepping on third for the force out, Luis could complete the relay to first for a double play.

We could not possibly screw this up as long as no one dropped the ball and the batter did not cross us by swinging at the pitch. If Upshaw bunted the ball hard enough to push it past me, Salazar could start the double play at third without moving more than a few inches. If the bunt left the bat so softly it took me an extra moment to reach it, we would still get the force-out at third, leaving runners at first and second and the double play still in order.

I threw the cutter outside, just as we planned. Upshaw bunted the ball between third base and the mound. I gloved the ball in an instant and turned to throw to third. No one there. That's when I noticed Salazar standing next to me. He had forgotten his assignment. I smacked him on the bill of his cap with my glove and tossed the ball to first to retire Upshaw, our only play. Willie's successful sacrifice changed the complexion of the game. Ozzie took me out for a right-handed reliever who allowed both runners to score on a bloop single. We lost by three to drop out of the playoffs.

I stalked into the clubhouse and packed my things. Pam had already flown out the day before. The team bus would be leaving for the airport in an hour. *Screw the bus,* I thought. I felt too upset to sit still for even five minutes. I threw my duffel bag over my shoulder and started walking to the airport, two miles away.

The neighborhood near the Barquisimeto ballpark looked like money: well-tended houses with two-car families, white pavement spotless as a new linen tablecloth. Nothing green, though. The sun had baked everything golden brown. Children laughed as they chased each other in a nearby park, but the sound could not touch me.

Four blocks into my walk, I thought the heat and bright sun had conspired to produce a mirage. In the near distance, two shimmering dark objects suddenly sprouted up from the pavement. They resembled twin monoliths rolling my way in a slow robotic motion. As they advanced, I realized these mechanical creatures were two flesh-and-blood men, each nearly seven feet tall, dressed in black Brooks Brothers suits, and wearing ties, of all things, in that sweltering heat. We met in the middle of the avenue. They were both blond, in their early twenties, with peach-fuzz faces. One had recently cut himself shaving.

"You lost?" I asked them.

"No, sir, you are the one who has lost."

"Right, six to three. You guys at the game?"

Silence.

"You guys sure are tall. Basketball players?"

"We've played basketball, yes."

"That right. So what happened they have you walking around in those hot suits? Coach punishing you for missing a few foul shots?"

The boys introduced themselves as Mormon missionaries from Brigham Young University. They had just arrived in Venezuela to work for their church and wanted to start with me, right there, an on-the-spot conversion that would deliver another sinner to the bosom of Jesus. One of them opened his Bible and began quoting scriptures while the other stuck a pamphlet in my hand.

Any other time I would have listened to their spiel just to amuse myself. Not that day. I turned my back on them and walked away pissed. Pissed over losing, pissed the season had ended, pissed at my 5-plus ERA, pissed at Salazar for botching that play, pissed at myself for blowing my shot back to the major leagues. Pissed at the world.

"No, sir, You are the one who has lost."

Amen, brothers and sisters. Amen.

◆

Or perhaps I wasn't lost. After leaving Venezuela, Pam and I stayed at my parents' home in San Francisco. I needed to regroup, to consider all my options—if I had any. Three days into our visit, my former manager Dick Williams called and invited me to join the San Diego Padres for a spring training tryout. I told Dick what I had gone through in '83 with Tom Haller and the Giants. Williams assured me that this would be different; his team wanted my services.

"The people here want to win," he said, "that's all that matters to them. Our club needs another left-hander in the bullpen, someone who can come into a game early and throw strikes. If you can still get people out, you'll get a fair shot."

The next week Pam and I drove to the Padres camp in Mesa, Arizona. As I lugged my bags into the clubhouse, I bumped into Ballard Smith, the San Diego general manager, and his assistant, Jack McKeon.

"What are you doing here?," he asked.

"Dick asked me down to try out for the club. Said you were short on left-handed relievers."

"Oh, he did, did he? Well, we'll have to see about that."

Tom Haller's words all over again. The two men stalked off to find their manager. Five minutes later I sat in Dick's office. He shuffled the papers on his desk, fiddled at the water cooler, and looked everywhere but right at me. When he finally spoke, he sounded angry. Apologetic. Embarrassed.

"I'm going to tell you the truth," he rasped in a low voice. "I've never had this happen before. You look as if you're in shape, and I want you on this team. I just told our general manager I think you can help us and we should at least give you a look. But he said we cannot touch you. Not that we don't want you. We cannot touch you. Now, that's how it is. If you tell anybody I told you this, I'll have to deny it. But you know what's going on, right?"

Yes, I knew. I thanked Dick for his honesty and left. His

revelation hardly surprised me, though it did disappoint. As I walked through the parking lot I realized that my professional career had just ended. How could I say goodbye to fifteen years of my life? Wave to the ballpark? Burn my glove in front of the clubhouse entrance?

The answer came when I opened the door to our car. This pungent odor assaulted my sinuses, an instant reminder that Pam had eaten a McDonald's hamburger during our drive. Big Macs had this strange effect on my wife's gastrointestinal system—they passed right through her. With no bathrooms in sight, my poor wife had no choice but to relieve herself in a takeout bag. The Kroc family owned McDonald's and the San Diego Padres. As a longtime supporter of recycling, I could think of nothing more appropriate than flinging that bag of shit over the left field wall of the Krocs' ballpark as we pulled out from the lot. My farewell to the major leagues.

"Don't bet on it," the man in Montreal had said. Son of a bitch was right.

5

INTERLUDE

I kept my arm in shape playing for the Moncton Mets in Canada's New Brunswick Senior League from 1984 to 1987. Pitched in forty-five games and won forty of them while giving up less than a run every nine innings. Winning that easily becomes monotonous, but that was fine with me. Sometimes you need a touch of monotony. I craved peace and wanted to escape the hugger-mugger of urban life with all its beguiling excess. No more cocaine. No more pounding the pavement through several rotations of the planet. A little pot? Yeah, never hurt. Couple of beers at the end of an evening? Could handle that. But the party hardy days? I consigned those to the past.

Picked a funny place to do it. Coming to Moncton to get reasonably sober made as much sense as moving to Brazil to give up sex. Temptation lurked everywhere. Moncton enjoyed a reputation as a good drinking town with a serious fishing problem. Happy hour in that burg started around 9 a.m. and lasted well past midnight. Few Monctonians drank sarsaparilla; nearly all the best restaurants doubled as taverns. This was the home of the four-beer lunch, and you must keep in mind that the beer of choice in those parts—Canada's own Moosehead—contains 50 percent more alcohol than your standard brews.

Perhaps the sudsy glow Moosehead imparts after only a can or two accounts for all the mellow Monctonians I met. No one in this town ever moved in a hurry. You rarely heard drivers honk their horns or saw cars jockeying to pass each other. People greeted strangers on the street with a wave and a big hello. If your vehicle broke down on the road, it would not be very long before a local pulled over to offer assistance. Another driver would soon come to your aid, and then still another. Someone would pull a few cases of Moosehead from the back of his pickup, and next thing you knew a party would break out that could last until the next morning.

Even with the prevalence of alcohol, my intoxicant intake plummeted all the way to a joint and a six-pack a day. An oak. A rock. A paragon of willpower. Phrases that defined me. Pam and I settled into Moncton life. We tucked in early every night in our summer cabin on the side of a stream as the loons sang us to sleep. On Saturdays we would join other Monctonians on Magnetic Hill, a point in the center of a gravitational anomaly. We'd park our cars in neutral in the center of a grade and watch them roll uphill. Could kill a whole day doing that.

We spent another weekend in Grand Falls, a town not far from Moncton in the western portion of New Brunswick. Turned out the place did not have a falls, but it did have lots of potato farms. One farmer told me with great pride of a recent study that had ranked Grand Falls as the largest potato producer in the world. He taught me the names and distinguishing marks of every grade of spud known to man, knowledge I have not used since, but you never know when it might come in handy. Pam and I later took a vacation in Shediac Beach, renowned throughout New Brunswick as the Bahamas of the Maritimes. We found it under ice.

Living laid back suited us now, but one afternoon that old wild and crazy feeling overpowered me. I went for walk in a cemetery overgrown with weeds and wildflowers not far from Moncton. There I found the headstone of Ronald McDonald. *Oh, how sad,* I thought, *no one told me he had died.* It occurred to me that I had stumbled upon the lost Cemetery of Clowns. I spent the next three days searching for the graves of Bozo and Emmett Kelly. Never did find them.

Nothing else happened in Moncton during our stay there. Nothing much ever does.

All right, that's not quite true. For instance. One afternoon the Mets played a game on the Wanderer's Ground, the only true hardball field in Halifax. In the sixth inning of a scoreless tie, I hit a home run that soared over the fence, over the trees lining the fence, over the street behind those trees, and into a park, where it rolled to the lip of a pond. Must have traveled more than 450 feet.

Afterward, an eighty-year-old man approached me as we packed up our equipment and said, "The only hitter I ever saw hit a ball that far on this field was Babe Ruth during an exhibition game back in the thirties. He hit his shot to the exact same spot you did." I played throughout Saskatchewan two weeks later. An elderly local said I was the first major-league pitcher to appear in that area since Satchel Paige.

Babe Ruth and Satchel Paige! Wow!

I'm not going to tell you that I ever forgave McHale and Fanning, but the praise I received tempted me to write them thank you notes. Let's face it. If those two had not exiled me from the majors, no one would ever mention my name in the same sentence as the Bambino or the mighty Satch.

Oh, and this happened too: I conducted a clinic for the Mic-Mac Indians at their reservation near the town of Sillicers on the northern branch of the Little Southwest Miramichi River in central New Brunswick. This is where Ted Williams spent many summers refining his salmon fishing technique. Eight young braves sat around me on a mound while I demonstrated the basics of pitching. Midway through our lesson, the tribe's chief walked up to home plate carrying a bat and announced that he wanted to hit against me. He was maybe thirty, a tall, long-muscled man with leonine features and long silky indigo hair. The chief carried himself with the quiet arrogance many great athletes exude. He looked as if he could strut sitting down.

Sadly, he did not own a dime's worth of hitting talent. I tossed him one lollipop after another. He either swung over pitches or nubbed weak foul balls to the right of third base. I called time for a moment and said to my students, "Boys, you see how the chief drops his hands and lifts right before he swings? He is trying too hard to elevate the ball instead of driving in on a line. There is only one pitch he can hit taking that approach, a changeup down and in."

I threw a change to that very spot on the next pitch, and the chief pulled the ball over the left field fence for a home run. He ran around the bases, whooping and stomping his feet in a war dance while the braves high-fived me for hitting his bat. Afterward, the chief shook my hand and presented me with a thirty-pound salmon. I hate surrendering homers and never much cared for anyone besting me in front of a crowd, but deliberately laying that meatball in his wheelhouse that day made me happy. I had made a friend, and, perhaps for the first time in my life, that satisfied me more than winning some mano a mano contest. Guess the Maritimes really can mellow a man.

We returned to Montreal not too long after that episode. Had no choice. The laid-back life may suit accountants or clergymen, but I make my living playing a game in which they keep score.

6

THE UNNATURAL

There was this fellow from Lumsden, Saskatchewan, nicknamed the Beast, don't know his real handle, but on the day we met he wore his shoulder-length brown hair parted down the middle like a rock star Jesus, a tied-dyed shirt so wildly patterned you lost your balance if you stared at it for more than thirty seconds, prewashed jeans, and vintage cowboy boots. You know the look, like someone who thought Hendrix was still splashing lighter fluid on his guitar in Woodstock. A great guy—the Beast, that is, though I suppose Jimi was a hell of a person as well—and a baseball diehard to boot.

The Beast had seen me pitch many times with the Expos and had followed my career after I left the major leagues. One day he ran into a group of players from the New Brunswick Senior League team, and they told him how I had recently shut them out in a playoff game while pitching for the Moncton Mets.

Now, the Beast had a brother, also a nice guy but his total opposite, a real buttoned-down, bottom-line type and one of Lumsden's most successful businesspeople. Their town was about to celebrate a holiday, not sure which one exactly, and the locals had scheduled a gala weekend of events culminating in a charity hardball game between the Lumsden Cubs and their archrivals, the Regina something-or-others.

The Beast's brother—his name will come to me, I swear—wanted to hire a celebrity athlete to stoke interest for the big game, and when the Beast told him how I had beaten that Saskatchewan team, they called to offer me room, board, round-trip air fare, and $600 to represent Lumsden on the mound.

I accepted, not out of financial need, although an extra $600 would come in handy, and not out of any great desire to visit Lumsden, a place friends described as divine. I was not even particularly eager to pitch that weekend, since my arm still felt tender from throwing so much during the previous months.

No, I went for the ducks.

The brothers had told me about this annual duck race that was scheduled for the day before the game. About two hundred ducks wearing numbers would swim against each other down the river that ran alongside the town all the way past the ballpark. To wager on the race, you bought a numbered ticket, and if the number on the duck that crossed the finish line first matched yours, you won a thousand bucks.

The concept fascinated me. How on earth, I wondered, could they ensure that those wild ducks would all head in the right direction, since their natural swimming patterns can be so random? I pictured a starting gate lined with saddled ducks, ridden by mice wearing miniature jockey silks and caps and carrying riding crops. Damn, no way I could miss that!

On the way to Lumsden, we passed through the town of Bigger, Saskatchewan, where a local hunter had recently killed a record-sized white-tailed deer. The deer was a male, which means the biggest buck ever brought down in North America was bagged in Bigger.

The Canadian government waxed so proud over this accomplishment, the Treasury engraved a figure of the whitetail across a thick commemorative silver dollar. So now the biggest buck from Bigger resides on Canada's biggest buck. And what is the town of Bigger like? Rather small, actually.

(This anecdote has nothing to do with the rest of the chapter. I just relished the way all those killer B's tripped off my tongue while telling it to my collaborator and we could not find anyplace else in the book to fit it.)

We reached Lumsden on a Friday. One look around the place told me why many consider it to be the most beautiful spot in the entire region. The surrounding countryside resembled a Shangri-la, with the Qu'Appelle River coursing through, a weaving cocoa-colored serpent. Along its banks, a visitor could get drunk off the fragrance of fresh silt and wild roses. The wheat fields gleamed golden even under a moonless night sky, and the air smelled so clean, every breath bathed your lungs pink. And you will not find a more level landscape anywhere on this planet.

How flat was Lumsden?

This flat. A local told me he had once stood on a chair at the edge of town and watched his dog run in a straight line for five days. He did not lose sight of the pet until it dropped into the Grand Canyon. I myself strolled through one field that looked like God's bowling alley; any ball rolling down it would not strike a bump until it reached the Rockies just outside of Calgary. On the Lumsden plains, we did not see a tree, boulder, or any other protuberance large enough to obstruct the wind. Which is why a town ordinance prohibited the people who live there from growing taller than six feet. Anything beyond that, the first stiff breeze could blow them clear to Manitoba.

If you are a Lumsdenian, you will be pleased to learn that those are all the flatland jokes I know.

The commercial heart of Lumsden stretches for only a few blocks with a general store, a feed lot, a real estate company, and a few small businesses. In the street, I saw a lot of pickup trucks, their chassis pitted by all the gravel spinning up from the roads. Men in plaid shirts and overalls walked with that determined step you see in people who know they have a hard day's labor awaiting them and welcome it. Most of the women in town wore jeans and boots or gingham dresses for a chic cowgirl look. Everybody I met acted friendly, not just courteous but genuinely warm. You stopped feeling like an outsider the moment one of them smiled.

We could not find any high-rises in this town. The tallest building of any kind sat near the railroad tracks, a grain elevator with LUMSDEN painted across the top of it in letters so large you could read them through a haze from half a mile away. In a field near the ballpark someone had whittled a wide dirt track about a quarter mile long with two sharp curves. When I asked a customer in the general store what the town used it for, she replied, "Why, for the chuck wagon races, whaddaya think?"

"My god, who uses chuck wagons anymore?"

"Nobody," she answered. "That's why we have so many of them to race."

Well, of course.

That was one of the things I most loved about the Lumsden people—their surprising taste for the absurd. Like the farmer who constructed his own unique take on the traditional scarecrow. Instead of a rag-bag figure hoisted on a pole, he dressed a mannequin in denims, a thermal undershirt, heavy work shoes, and the pointed wool cap northern Canadians call a tocque. The famer stuck a can of beer in the dummy's hand and placed him on a worn vinyl couch in front of a TV set in the middle of his wheat field.

This bizarre figure did not frighten many birds. But the ones that lighted on the farmer's property never even peeked at his wheat. They just sat next to the mannequin on the couch and stared at the television while waiting for the Heckle and Jeckle cartoons to start.

As I walked through town a dry, blustery wind chapped my face. A woman in the motel coffee shop mentioned that nearly two months had passed since the last good rain. Nothing unusual about that in the region, everyone at her table agreed. During the winter, Lumsden farmers maintained a heavy wheat stubble throughout their fields as insurance against dry spells. Those shoots could hold the moisture from the winter snow for a long time. But it had snowed lightly that year, and now the land lay dry and brittle. Farmers could not plow or plant the arid ground without the wind sneaking up behind them to carry off the broken topsoil.

Everywhere you went people discussed the drought, and who could blame them? Lumsden's economy revolved around agriculture, with wheat and canola the primary cash crops. About 70 percent of the people living in this region worked as farmers; the other 30 percent made their living supplying goods and services to the farmers. Once the fields withered and died, it would be like the steel mills shutting down in Pittsburgh.

Government subsidies would give the farmers enough money to replant. But a delay in aid or an early frost would make replanting impractical. Lumsden would suffer a trickle-down tragedy, with businesses closing and jobs lost. The drought even threatened the ecosystem, something I realized while golfing with several townspeople. Newly hatched goslings covered the course we played on. We noticed how thin the chicks looked as they waddled in a yellow line behind their mothers from one sparse water puddle to another. Life was coming into this prairie, but without rain anytime soon there would be no food to support it. The goslings would starve, and the farmers would have to butcher many of their cows since there would be no healthy grass to feed them.

As we neared the end of our round, I told my golfing partners not to worry, that my coming to town was a visit from Henderson the Rainmaker. Precipitation just seemed to follow me. No one laughed. That's when someone mentioned how they would lose their entire wheat crop if it didn't rain in the next few days. Made me feel like an ass with my cheap comment.

To be honest, though, I had been only half kidding. Climate can exert such a dramatic impact on a game, ballplayers develop an instinct for the weather. I noticed the wind blowing out of the south and felt a warm front upon us. The air thickened with the promise of rain. Mentioning that, though, failed to boost anyone's spirits. "They've said that on the news now for four weeks and we haven't seen a drop," said one local.

"Those weathermen," a friend of his huffed, "couldn't forecast wind if they stood in the middle of a tornado."

They did not appreciate my flatland jokes either.

That night, in a bar near my motel, the dry talk of weather continued. Only the beers were wet, and did they keep coming. Everybody, it seemed, wanted to buy the Spaceman a drink. The Oliver Stone in me suspected a conspiracy and figured all the Regina players in the room had paid for most of those rounds, hoping to pound Old Style lager into me that night so that they could pound on me during the game the following day.

Oh, had they only known! I perform better with alcoholic toxins circulating through my bloodstream. Whenever I come into a game nursing a hangover, I pitch economically and concentrate on throwing strikes so that I can get my head under that ice pack in the dugout as soon as possible. Why else do you think David Wells surrenders so few walks? Focusing on the hitters also provides a distraction from the pain. My brain shuts down and instinct takes over, freeing me to fall into a natural pitching rhythm. I don't feel any pressure on the mound because . . . well, because I don't feel anything at all. So when I woke the next morning, my itchy tongue, fuzzy teeth, and cotton-stuffed skull told me the Regina club was about to pay for those beers one more time.

As the game started, a churning, gagging dust blew across the field, reminding me of those goslings and my silly remarks. The atmosphere did not hold the slightest moisture. My hangover notwithstanding, the Regina batters hit me hard in the first few innings; I had forgotten what weird hitters Canadians are. They do everything backward up there, such as throw right-handed but hit from the left side.

Instead of pulling inside pitches, even the burliest Regina hitters took everything to the opposite field, a good approach against someone like me, who at the time did not throw hard enough to jam batters. Took me a few innings to analyze them. These men only played once a week, so they were overeager and prone to swing at balls outside the strike zone. But by the time I started working them off the edges of the plate, my opponents had already scored five runs.

A tall right-hander started for Regina. His cutting slider complemented a mid-eighties fastball, but he did not display a curve or change of any kind. He did not need them. His pitches moved so much, you could not hit them squarely if you made contact with them at all. But we did finally score after he tired, and Regina carried only a one-run lead into the bottom of the ninth.

While I searched for my batting glove—there was a chance I might get up that inning—this noise swept down over me, a rumbling percussion that could have passed for thunder, but no, it was the ballpark crowd chattering among themselves.

The sky had suddenly turned overcast.

Our first two batters quickly made outs, but a pair of base hits brought me to the plate in a position to win the game with a long ball. I reminded myself not to commit my swing too early, to stay back and wait for a pitch I could drive over the outfielders' heads. With the count one ball, two strikes, the pitcher chose that moment to throw his first breaking ball of the day. It hung in the middle of the plate, just begging to be nailed.

I whacked that pitch on a high arc deep to centerfield, and, swear to god, just as it leaped over the fence for a game-winning home run, lightning zigzagged overhead and the clouds overflowed.

I dashed double-time around the bases, laughing my ass off, eager to reach shelter from the wet. That movie *The Natural* played in my head with me as Roy Hobbs rounding those bags in slow motion while Randy Newman's majestic soundtrack swelled in the background.

Now you know. Young boys all over the world dream about becoming ballplayers. But once you've grown up to play in the major leagues, you must look elsewhere for the fantasies to keep you hopeful and young. So I pretend to be Robert Redford.

It rained in Lumsden for the next three days, a downpour that saved the wheat crop and the goslings. A few townspeople connected the cloudburst with the home run, but no one made a big deal over it. Sad. There are no miracles in today's society. Technology has robbed us of our wonder. But a thousand years ago, had I hit that sky-splitting bolt in a stadium in some Aztec village, the natives would have declared me the wheat god and the chief would have rewarded me with my own grain concession behind the bleachers.

Does this mean I think my homer broke open those clouds? A numerologist might say so, what with the perfect symmetry of a three-day downpour following a three-run blast. If this truly counted as cause and effect, those farmers should consider themselves fortunate I did not hit a grand slam, or it might have rained for four days. The rivers would have overflowed, flooding their fields and sweeping away their crops.

Instead, they got just the right amount of water, so maybe I was in touch with the elements. On the other hand, it was probably going to rain no matter what, and I just happened to be there. Woody Allen had it right—half of life is just showing up.

P.S.: Almost forgot. The duck race. Big disappointment. Turned out there were no rodent jockeys on miniature saddles. The ducks were made out of plastic, so they just floated downriver, and the meandering current reduced the race to little more than a crawl. Never did find out who won.

7

TO RUSSIA
WITH GLOVE

Nothing of consequence occurred during my 1988 trip to Moscow. All right, there were the three incidents with the police, but those could have happened to anyone. Besides, the cops would never have confronted us that last time if our catcher had not persuaded the Russian girl to come to his room. So, damn it, you cannot entirely blame me for the fracas that followed. True, the incident at the Kremlin wall could have resulted in our permanent detainment had we not made such a quick getaway, but . . . hold on a moment. Let's back up. I don't want you to feel as if you entered during the middle of this story.

If anything, we should place all the blame on Tom. After all, he organized the trip. Tom Nickerson worked as a professor at the University of California at Davis, a tall, slouchy, soft-spoken man with a solid left-wing pedigree. His father had taught sociology at the University of Southern California while I attended classes there and had achieved some political celebrity on our campus as an expert on the Soviet Union. He was also the only faculty member with the guts to admit membership in the Communist Party at a time when the House Un-American Activities Committee still conducted witch hunts. I admired him profoundly for that.

Tom and I played college ball against each other back in the day. He impressed everyone as a heady competitor, well schooled in baseball fundamentals. I was delighted when he invited me to join a baseball team he had assembled for a series of goodwill games against opponents behind the Iron Curtain. After spending the six previous years pitching in every province of Canada and winning 90 percent of my starts, I needed a fresh challenge. Russia intrigued me; political differences had kept the country closed to most Americans for years. I wanted to discover just how much of what we had read and heard about the Soviet Union was true and how much was propaganda—ours as well as theirs. I also hankered to see just how much progress the Russian baseball program had made in the two years since its inception.

Tom gathered a team from a diverse mix of scholars, writers, lawyers, and other professionals. I was the only former major leaguer on the roster, but several members had competed in some form of organized ball. John Lehr worked as a high-octane California attorney who also owned the Visalia Oaks, a Class A minor-league team. He fit the role of our team's Cary Grant, a bon vivant dripping with nonchalant charm and fashion savvy. Glowing skin, perfectly even tan, manicured fingernails, never a hair out of place. On him, the Gap wore like custom-tailored Alan Flusser. John had played some college ball as a left-handed catcher. He could not throw from here to there or hit your grandmother's limping slider, but he proved himself a smart receiver who called a great game.

Bob Wagner, a land surveyor, had pitched for several minor-league clubs during the 1950s. He had recently turned sixty-five, a tall, gray-haired man who walked with the loping strides of a natural athlete. A hard, round beer belly held the only fat on him. Bob wore jeans and hand-tooled cowboy boots with all the panache of a San Joaquin rodeo rider. He came across as a serious, focused man, but he also had these effervescent blue eyes that never stopped searching for a good time.

I took an instant liking to Jay Terwillinger; his name sounded so baseball. You could just hear it stretching from the lips of a stadium announcer: "Now playing shortstop for the Toledo Mud Hens, Jay Terrrrr-wil-ling-er!" At six foot one, Jay was lanky and rawboned and probably hadn't gained more than a pound or two since playing baseball in college. He looked to be in his mid-forties, a high school counselor from northern Georgia who also worked with convicts in the local prisons. This probably made him better prepared than any of us for our journey into the land of the gulag.

Jay spoke in a slow, thoughtful drawl fresh out of a country hollow, and he continually demonstrated a knack for putting things in perspective. For example, one day during lunch in a Moscow restaurant, he noticed that most of the Russians in the place ate caviar. This was at the height of a severe food shortage, which prompted Jay to remark, "You see, here is the problem with this country in a nutshell. Everybody over here eats bait. Now if they just put some of that bait on a hook and went down to the river, they might catch themselves a real meal." I loved the way his mind worked; we immediately became each other's sidekick.

Then there was our twenty-year-old catcher, Jim Nelson. Lean and broad-shouldered with a full head of curly goldilocks, Jim possessed a movie-star smile that he flashed at full wattage whenever a female ventured near. Did not matter if she was nineteen or ninety, single, married, or a Carmelite nun. All that racing testosterone made Jim a Molotov cocktail itching for a match. At the start of our journey, we voted him the player most likely to be found dead in his hotel room. Everyone figured some KGB operative would ice him after finding the kid rolling around on a mattress with the agent's wife, his daughter, and the family's prize heifer.

A loud, blustering New York businessman was the only team member who did not fit in. During conversations, he gave the impression that he never heard anything you said; he just waited for your lips to stop moving so he could continue his monologue. He sat in the Kennedy Airport bar before we embarked, boring anyone who listened with travel stories obviously meant to reveal his worldliness. Talk about karma. After our plane touched down in Russia, whom do you think the Soviet customs officials detained on the spot? That's right, the global traveler himself. He had forgotten his passport.

Three days passed before any of us saw him again, and he remained relatively quiet for the rest of the trip.

Our group stayed at the Olympic Village, a concrete-and-steel complex of lowdown high-rises overlooking a Moscow train station. My small room resembled a monk's den, sparsely furnished with just a table, a few chairs, and a slate-hard metal cot. The mattress on that bed was less than three inches thick and barely six feet long. My toes hung over the end even when I assumed a fetal position.

Freight elevators provided access to every floor of the building, but we rode them with trepidation. Power outages regularly occurred on that side of the city; the odds of getting stuck in an elevator increased every time you stepped into one. I could not shake the feeling of being constantly watched while we lived in the complex. Perhaps it was my American paranoia. Or perhaps I was just spooked by the continuous presence of the KGB agents in the front lobby, humorless men whose eyes narrowed whenever you passed as if they could scan you right down to your shorts with X-ray vision. Their constant surveillance played on the dark side of my imagination. Our apartments overlooked an atrium dominated by a large white wall. I remember thinking what a dandy spot it would make for a firing squad. Now that *was* my paranoia talking.

On Saturdays a flea market operated in a soccer field across the avenue from where we stayed. Most of the tables and booths offered an inventory of forlorn items that sold for only a dollar or two: old military uniforms and medals, broken rhinestone jewelry, statues whittled from pine, secondhand clothing, and watches that ran backward.

We did find one man whose goods looked extraordinary.

He was a pale, emaciated artist with a runny nose and a hacking, tubercular cough. He had rescued the gray woolen coat on his back from a garbage bin. Some tailor had cut it for a much broader frame. His fingers disappeared beneath its floppy sleeves, and when he stood up, the coat's hem scraped the ground. You could have wrapped the garment around him three times over.

He moved slowly, an old-timer at twenty-six. There was no vitality to him except for the dark, intense eyes that peered from beneath the bill of his grimy black linen cap. You could guess his vocation if you noticed how he observed the life around him. He never casually glanced at anything. Instead, his eyes absorbed people and objects as if he could store every aspect of their appearance for future reference. Nothing escaped his gaze.

A beige leatherette portfolio lay open on the table in front of him. As I turned the pages, my own eyes welled. This man lived in the direst circumstances, but he had retained an appreciation for beauty. I have seen Dürers and Rembrandts that could not match the exquisite black-and-white etchings in his collection. My favorite depicted a Russian forest blanketed under snow. The rough-textured bark on the trees rose off the drawing paper and the snow layered on the branches actually seemed to be melting.

In the bough of one tree, he had drawn a lone partridge no more than half an inch tall, yet so detailed we could see the notch on its head and follow the sweep of its feathers. This artist could not afford any sophisticated etching tools to produce these remarkable effects; he accomplished them with nothing more than a sewing needle dipped in ink. I gladly paid him $150 for the etching. It hangs on the wall of my Vermont home today.

◆

We did not play any games during the first two days of our visit, so a matched pair of cultural attachés took us sightseeing. Our guides resembled Soviet espionage agents straight out of central casting: blond flat-tops, opaque gray eyes, broad features, broad shoulders, broad everything. Neither of them subscribed to *GQ*. They dressed in ill-fitting black suits, too tight in the chest and too slack at the waist. Fresh white shirts but no ties. The cuffs of their pants stopped an inch shy of their ankles. They wore heavy white athletic socks with sandals. I had seen this look before, on undercover cops working the streets of South Boston during the seventies. They wore the same white socks and short pants, then wondered why drug dealers vanished before the police could get within a mile of them.

The Moscow our hosts showed us appeared dreary, a city in monochrome. Nearly every modern building fit the same mold, a gray concrete rectangle as inviting as any dungeon. The gilded church spires, the crimson walls of the Kremlin, and the bright murals depicting the workers' revolution provided the few splashes of color. On the Moscow streets, vendors sold cigarettes, milk, bread, vodka, and flowers in glass-enclosed kiosks, some no larger than cubicles. Everywhere the city felt cramped.

You will never see a place so crowded yet so bereft of life. Most Russian passersby appeared grim-faced and slow to smile at strangers. We detected no giddyap in their steps. They dragged themselves along the avenue, which made us think they had little enthusiasm for wherever they were heading.

Arbat Street, a five-block-long commercial district, resembled Rodeo Drive with staid upscale stores and the only McDonald's in town. Unlike Manhattan, Moscow had no hot strip, no Forty-second Street with its looming, intrusive brand names and all the frenzied neon that makes that stretch of town resemble the inside of a demented jukebox. I missed that kitsch. When I want the utterly unadorned, I have Craftsbury, Vermont, and other quiet rural spots. Every big city, though, needs a touch of the garish and the outsized to balance its more refined side. Otherwise no matter where you'd go, you would always be in Des Moines.

We moved about freely, but the attachés had structured the tour so that the team had little chance to interact at length with the average Muscovite. Our guides took us to art museums, cathedrals, an armory, and a bustling communal store that had far more customers than inventory. At one counter, seven customers jostled against each other while competing to buy the same pair of tweezers.

On the second day, we traveled nearly an hour into a rural setting east of Moscow to visit a crumbling Romanov fortress. Terwillinger and I had seen enough of icons, armor, and other inanimate objects. Longing to meet some typical Russians, we split from the group at lunchtime to explore the countryside.

We found a time warp after a quarter-mile hike to a village with a name so long I cannot pronounce or spell it, in a place so obscure Anastasia could have been hiding there. No one would have known to look. There were no asphalt streets, no pavement of any kind. Only a muddy dirt road lined by neat clapboard houses and wooden cabins crowded close together and wrapped in chimney smoke.

The village looked like it had been deserted long ago. We did not see a single passerby. Goats snacked on scraps in a narrow alley. We came upon some cars, sorrowful heaps long past running. A horse-drawn milk cart missing its driver sat on the side of one road. The only modern vehicles were unattended tractors or pickup trucks. Not one of the houses wore a TV antenna.

Jay and I decided to rejoin our team. Just before heading back, we heard the sound: muffled chanting somewhere at the end of the road. We followed those voices to a dingy white wooden church. Inside, dim candlelight cast an amber glow over the pews jammed with townspeople. Painted wooden icons of the Virgin Mary and the saints glimmered on the walls. The unmistakable fragrance of incense drifted over us, but we smelled another odor beneath it, something dusty and fetid.

We stood in a hallway behind the pews. As the bishop spoke, members of the congregation sobbed. Since we did not understand the language, neither Jay nor I had any idea why the parishioners had gathered. Terwillinger leaned over to whisper something in my ear when suddenly his eyes grew large and his body turned rigid. He nudged me to look at the table to my right.

That was when I saw the corpses. Someone had stacked them like so much cordwood one on top of the other in a corner. We had stumbled on a funeral; the deceased had passed away during a coffin shortage. Ushers came down the aisle to carry the bodies to the altar. As they loaded the dead on plywood planks, Jay and I tiptoed out through the door. The scene so unnerved us, we said nothing to each other during the entire walk back to the fortress. We would not stray again for days.

◆

When my teammates and I finally played baseball, we faced the Russian national team. The squad's roster included many of the country's top young players, and they expected to steamroll us. Imagine how stunned they were when our motley group beat them 7–0 in the first game.

I picked up the win even though the Russians put seven runners on base with two squib hits and five walks. But none of the players scored, and with good reason—I picked off every one of them. Obviously, these players had never seen a left-hander with any kind of move to first base. No one had taught them how to time a pitcher's motion. The moment I raised my front foot, some Russian player would blithely take off for second without even noticing that I had not yet started my windup. A quick toss to Bob Wagner at first, the relay to second, another runner erased.

The defeat and those baserunning blunders humbled the Russians, but they positively freaked when I removed my cap for a joint team photo. All that gray hair got the whole team howling. These twenty-somethings could not believe that this old American guy had just shut them out. They badgered one of their coaches to ask for a second shot at me in the game we were scheduled to play two days later. I agreed.

Pitching on short rest, the old American guy pitched another two-hit shutout, walking only a pair this time. And once again I picked off every Russian who reached base. Obviously we had stumbled upon a glaring vulnerability in the Soviet attack that even the Pentagon had yet to uncover: Russians could not back up.

This shortcoming was symptomatic of their economy. Most Muscovites spent their lives waiting on long queues just to buy the basics such as meat, bread, canned goods, or toothpaste. In some cases unpredictable distribution made it difficult to obtain even abundantly produced items. We saw a group of testy Russians flip over a car in a Moscow street and set it on fire after the local state-run retail outlet ran out of cigarettes.

The cigarette company had plenty of tobacco to produce more packages. But the trade union that manufactured the filters had staged a work slowdown, and the truckers who carried the products to market had refused to drive in sympathy. The retailers could not guarantee when the next batch of smokes would arrive. Not what an angry, twitching group of nicotine addicts wanted to hear.

A Russian player told me how he repeatedly had to stand on line for six hours or more just to purchase a bag of sandwich rolls. *Boy,* I thought, *those must be some rolls!* I love the glazed chocolate doughnuts they sell at Krispy Kreme—would practically kill for them. But if I have to wait more than five minutes to buy some, I'm off to the local deli to grab a box of Yodels.

Those lines trained the Russian ballplayers to move in only one direction—forward. They regarded shifting in reverse as an alien concept. If you took just one step back in a Moscow line, it added at least another hour to your waiting time. Given the shortages in this country, those extra sixty minutes could reduce you to using *Pravda* as toilet paper for a week. Of course, that alternative was considerably more comfortable than using the regular Russian toilet paper. Don't get me wrong—it was a first-rate product if you needed something to sand down the grout in your bathroom.

So it never even occurred to the Soviet players to just reach back and touch first base with their foot before my throws arrived at the bag. I swear, had Czar Nicholas been a left-handed pitcher, Russia would still be an autocracy. He would have picked off Lenin and Trotsky long before the revolution gained any momentum. They never would have seen his move. Of course, the Communists could have countered that by sending Josef Stalin to the mound. Iron Joe, after all, had earned a reputation as the ultimate lefty; he picked off five million people in just two purges.

◆

In subsequent games against a Red Army squad and other local teams, we found the Soviets poorly schooled in every aspect of baseball. These players could not bunt. The hit-and-run was too complicated for them to execute, and they continually played out of position on defense.

The Russian outfielders—most of them converted tennis players—exhibited excellent speed and wide range. Yet they muffed easy fly balls by closing their gloves too soon. None of them could throw. The best arm we saw belonged to an eighteen-year-old gymnast who arrived at the ball field wearing a Los Angeles Dodgers warm-up jacket. She gave her name as Katerina.

When I first met the Red Army manager he gushed, "Wait

until you see our star first baseman. He has power like that big slugger you played with. You know, Jim Rice." And, son of a bitch, the guy did hit like Rice.

Anne Rice.

During batting practice, we watched the first baseman and his teammates helplessly flail at one mediocre fastball after another. They lacked timing, balance, and plate discipline. But at least four of them had marvelous singing voices.

Most of the Russians were as powerfully built, tall, and thick-bodied as Barry Bonds. However, they took such long, slow swings, even a junkballer could blow the ball past them inside. You could get them to lunge at balls six inches off the ground or a foot over their heads. Not one of them had ever seen a breaking pitch. The first time I struck out a Russian with my curve, he stayed at the plate for two minutes with his mouth agape in shock while his teammates demanded that the umpire frisk me. They thought I had smuggled a trick ball out to the mound. None of them could comprehend how anyone could make a ball bend that way.

When the manager asked us to assess his batters' skills, honesty compelled me to reply, "Your guys could fall out of a boat in the middle of the Moscow River without hitting water." He finally agreed that the Russian baseball program would never progress unless the People's Sports Committee imported American coaches to teach players the rudiments of the game.

I gently pointed out that the committee would also have to improve their teams' dismal baseball fields. We played the national team at Lenin University on a diamond designed by Yugoslav engineers. These were the same people who had constructed the Russian perimeter to resist Nazi Panzer attacks during World War II. Our first clue that these engineers had applied to this project many of the construction principles they had developed during the war came when we saw the base paths. They were recessed. Like trenches.

Cheesy Astroturf covered the infield. Base runners between first and second had to dash up a pronounced grade. We found so many holes—each the size of a miniature crater—gouged into the turf around the pitching mound, it looked as though the engineers had deliberately dug them as tank traps just in case the Panzer division returned.

To their credit, the Yugoslavs had installed modern outfield fences complete with protective vinyl padding. They'd made one small mistake, though. The engineers had anchored the fences backward, so the padding faced out. Any player who crashed into the flat, hard panels on the field side while racing after a fly ball risked permanent brain damage. And this turned out to be Yankee Stadium compared to the other fields we played on. Baseball is hard. You cannot learn how to play the game properly on inadequate diamonds. Our group finished the tour undefeated, and the thing is, we were not that good. Any half-assed American saloon team could have demolished us.

◆

Now about that first brush with the Soviet police. My teammates and I were taking a cab to dinner in a downtown Moscow restaurant. Halfway there, our driver made a sharp turn around a corner and cut off a spanking-new silver Mercedes with tinted windows as it darted from a driveway.

Within minutes, the wail of police sirens deafened us. Russian traffic cops waved the cab to the side of the avenue. The Mercedes pulled up, its windows rolled down, and this man, his face as cuddly as a stone gargoyle's, began jawing with one of the officers while jabbing his finger toward our driver. The Mercedes owner clearly carried weight. After he flashed a card on the police, they fined us two hundred rubles (about ten dollars) without even bothering to hear our side of the story. Not that we had one.

Ah, the Soviet judicial system! Whatever it lacked in even-handedness, it made up for in expediency. Back in the States, when the police pinched you for a traffic violation you paid your fine in court or through the mails. Russian police eliminated the middleman. They did not issue a summons or schedule a hearing. Instead, we settled our penalty with the cops on the spot. In cash.

I don't mean to imply that they pocketed this money, though I did notice later that Russia has the best-dressed police force in the world. Its officers appeared in the top Moscow night spots sporting Rolexes, Brioni suits, and Sulka ties while smoking foot-long Havanas. Expensive items, but over 325 million people lived in the USSR in 1988. That's a lot of cars to pull over.

We arrived at the restaurant, located in a pockmarked but elegant brownstone, only to discover that it doubled as an art gallery. The owner had put in a few tables and offered a menu of black-market food to augment his declining profits. One look at the artwork on the restaurant walls revealed the reason for the tepid sales. Most of the paintings resembled bad imitations of Salvador Dalí and Paul Klee, dull splatterings without an ounce of perspective or passion to make them interesting. The least expensive of the lot cost over $100, a bit too pricey for the average Russian in 1988.

As a waiter led us to our table, my eyes shifted from the abstracts to a ravishing young woman munching caviar and pâté at a corner table, a dead ringer for the model Christie Brinkley. Guess who sat next to her? That guy with the Mercedes.

He stared at us while we ordered, and mumbled something about "pushy Americans." What followed was not my best moment. I shot back with a retort—something clever constructed around the word *fuck* as both a noun and a verb—and the Cold War suddenly flamed hot. The man jumped to his feet and growled, "To my chin you say that, why don't you?"

No one could tell us how this fellow made ends meet, but his reply immediately ruled out English translator as a possibility. Judging by his slick wheels, the runway looker on his arm, and the tailored Bond Street duds covering his mushroom-squat frame, we had him pegged as either a commissar or the head of Russia's lingerie black market.

Whatever his profession, he did not appreciate my laughing off his question. He kneed his table aside and bulled forward, so angry the chef could have fried pierogies on his forehead. We met for a dueling rant at the center of the restaurant. This is the stupid way many men respond when they think someone has challenged their manhood in front of a beautiful woman. Even while I reveled in telling him off, a part of me knew I was making an utter fool of myself.

We stood nose to nose, so close the waiters could not wedge between us. His breath stank of vodka and garlic. I noticed escargot drippings on his lapel. His hair appeared to be dyed with shoe polish. An old man trying to hide his age from his much younger date, he could not back off. When he jabbed his finger into my chest, the Clint Eastwood in me grew incensed. "Put that down," I yelled, "or I'll bite it off, you no-good son of a bitch. Point at me again, I'll come back to Moscow in my BMW and drive it straight up your ass."

So much for my diplomatic skills. Luckily for détente, the man's girlfriend intervened. She whispered something soothing in his ear, and they immediately turned to leave. I never should have let it get that far, right? Sorry, there is this immature side to me, the eternal frat boy who cannot resist getting in one last dig. But give me some credit. As the couple stopped at the coat check, I did stop myself from asking Mr. Mercedes if he would translate *pussy-whipped* into Russian for us.

After we finished eating, Tom Nickerson suggested we visit Lenin's mausoleum for the midnight changing of the guard. To my surprise, the Russians had not buried their former leader in a cemetery. His corpse rests in plain sight under glass in Red Square. Lenin wears a peaceful, near saintly look on his face, but his remains have lain in state for over sixty years and his leathery skin has taken on the greenish tinge of Gumby.

The four soldiers guarding the display case gave the appearance of crackerjack troops: khaki greatcoats, gleaming brown calf-length military boots, crimson epaulets with gold braid, and squared-off red caps bearing the black hammer and sickle insignia. Each bore a rifle. Their show began when the bells in a nearby tower tolled midnight. Four relief guards appeared out of the mist, marching in lockstep across Red Square. As they came within a few yards of Lenin's body, the guards on duty stepped forward to join their comrades in an intricate drill of turns, shuffles, and stops. Their choreography flowed so smoothly, the eight soldiers exchanged places without any of us detecting how they did it.

Watching them march through their paces gave me an idea. Russia desperately needed capital investment; its economy was teetering on the brink of implosion. I wanted to buy Lenin's body, ship it to New York City with the display case, and make it the centerpiece of a disco. We could call the club Lenin's Tomb. Guards would stand point around the corpse just as they did in Red Square, only they would be go-go girls in hammer-and-sickle thongs and pasties. I imagined Lenin spinning in his grave over the idea. But that could be one of the club's prime attractions, provided we could time his rotation to a hip-hop beat.

I had just finished explaining my concept to Terwillinger when a teammate nudged me from behind. "We have to get out of here," he said.

"In a minute . . ."

"No. Now. I just shit on the Kremlin Wall."

"Jesus, you're kidding. Where?"

"Right behind the blue spruces," he said over his shoulder as he walked away, "while you two watched the guards change. I figured the crowd wouldn't pay any attention to me."

Our friend's act did not represent a political protest of any kind. He just had to go and there was a shortage of public latrines in Moscow. Anyone who has experienced that situation could understand why he did it. Anyone, that is, but the armed Kremlin guards stomping our way from across Red

Square. For a moment I thought we would be playing our next inning of ball for the local gulag. A car pulled up in front of us. "Hey, Americans, come here! Come here! Let's go for a ride!" A gypsy cab driver named—what else?—Yuri sat behind the wheel of a battered black Lada.

For those Westerners who have never seen the vehicle, a Lada is a midsized compact roughly the size of a Volkswagen Jetta, only perfectly square. Soviet designers chose that shape for its practicality. Once the car's forward gears burned out—something that routinely occurs in many Russian-made vehicles within a month of purchase—the owner could simply turn around the seats and drive in reverse. No one would notice the difference.

Yuri's Lada showed some mileage on it. Springs had pushed through the backseat cushion. Baling wire held the rear bumper in place. He had to arm-wrestle his balky stick shift whenever he changed gears, an isometric exercise that gave him a right forearm nearly twice as large as his left. His car did not appear to conform to any known safety standards, but we had no time to wait for something better. Those guards were almost on top of us and we were standing downwind.

Jay and I climbed into the backseat and asked Yuri if he knew of any pool halls nearby. "Oh, yes," he replied, "Great. Pool. Know just the place. Beautiful. You will love. Guaranteed." He passed over a bottle of Russian cognac he had hidden under his seat. "Only the best, straight from a vineyard in the Ukraine," he assured us.

You know that book, Wine for Dummies? The authors wrote that for me. I have never claimed to be a connoisseur of anything. When Tom Seaver and I played for USC, people said that if you looked at Tom, you could tell he was destined for a long life of vintage brandy, expensive cigars, and stretch limousines. On the other hand, if you looked at me, you saw a future of filterless Camels, six-packs, and canoes. And clearly one day I would smoke too many cigarettes, drink all those six-packs, fall out of that canoe, and drown.

Yet even I knew that true cognac comes only from France. The concoction Yuri served tasted of boiled muscatel and turpentine distilled in a sugary syrup. Even so, it sure packed a wallop. Two sips and my brain melted down into a runny yolk sliding from my ears. My tongue blistered, and I could feel the enamel peeling from my teeth.

It took all of my willpower to maintain equilibrium. Yuri drove with the same regard for personal safety that Mad Max on a bender might exhibit. Did his car have brakes? Perhaps but he sure used them sparingly. Whenever we approached a red light, Yuri decelerated to a crawl, then floored it just as the light turned green. If he timed the signal wrong, he simply spun around the corner whether we needed to or not.

Our cab careened through city streets, swerving from one curb to another. I expected a traffic cop to pull him over. Drivers seldom sped in this town. Only commissars or gangsters owned the few Russian vehicles that could exceed fifty miles an hour. Moscow police did not even need radar to keep tabs on most drivers. They could have assigned a squad of elderly women in babushkas to sit on street corners and clock the cars with sundials.

Somehow Yuri managed to keep the pedal to the metal without attracting the police. He drove us to a bleak neighborhood of shuttered factories and warehouses just outside the center of Moscow. Our cab swooped under an elevated train station and barreled up a dead-end street.

The pool hall stood in the middle of the block, a white brick warehouse with a corrugated aluminum pull-down door. Yuri never exactly stopped in front of it. Instead, the car crept along while we slithered out from the backseat. He nodded toward a side entrance halfway up a dimly lit alley littered with broken beer bottles. We could hear rock music blaring from inside. "That's where you go," he called out "Very tip-top. You will see."

Soon as our feet struck pavement, Yuri shifted into overdrive. His tires squealed, his muffler belched. He rode off swilling that cognac without looking back to see if anyone even let us into the joint. Hey, I could understand that. The man was in a hurry. He had places to go. People to run over.

A sinewy bouncer with the lantern jaw and rampant facial acne that said steroid abuser ushered Jay and me inside. The pool hall was a recently converted garage with a high ceiling and a naked concrete floor. It had an industrial smell, the odor of motor oil and antifreeze. Low-hanging domes of bad fluorescent lighting illuminated eight tattered pool tables. Young Russian men and women crowded the place, many of them dressed in second-rate knockoffs of American designer jeans and T-shirts.

We bought a pitcher of beer for twenty cents to wash out the foul flavor of Yuri's cognac. No improvement. That Russian brew tasted yeasty, warm, and flat. Rather than stay at the bar, Jay and I walked over to a pool table for a little kibitzing.

We immediately noticed that all the balls rolling across the green felt surface were white. These kids played each other with nothing but cue balls. During the game we watched, a young man hit one white ball to sink another. When they both dropped into the pocket, he bunny-hopped around the room to high-five all his friends.

In America and the rest of the planet, that double dunk counted as a double scratch. You deducted both balls from your score and forfeited your turn. In Moscow it passed as a trick shot worth extra points. Watching the shooter and his mates celebrate brought to mind all those Russian base runners I had picked off over the previous few days. "Well," I said to Jay, "here's another sport they haven't quite got the hang of yet."

When someone identified us as Americans to our bartender, the celebration started. Drinks were on the house. Two men invited me into a back room where a group of Russian university students were rolling hashish. Not Jay's scene at all; he stayed at the bar. I smoked several bowls while listening to a local punk rock band's bootlegged cassette, music that the government prohibited. It is difficult to describe the singer's high, slurring, ragged voice. Imagine listening to Jiminy Cricket with his larynx trapped in a high-speed blender. The music behind him played slow but hard-pushing, a funeral march set to rock rhythms. I was thoroughly into it.

Perhaps it was that hash we smoked. As the music grew louder, the floor undulated beneath us. My pupils enlarged so wide, the fluorescent light became a cool, liquid sun pouring past my eyelids. Suddenly we stood inside the Tower of Babel. Everyone in the crowd seemed to be chattering at each other in some foreign language. I wanted to scream in panic. Then I remembered: this was Moscow, not Hoboken. They *were* speaking in a foreign language.

My mind got further blown when a woman I danced with introduced me to two brothers. Not only were they identical twins dressed in identical suits, their parents had named them Sergei and Sergei. This is not something you want to hear while tripping your face off on ersatz cognac, hashish, vodka, and beer and the hazy world already resembles the set of a David Lynch film. The brothers worked as black marketers who traded in caviar, bonded scotch, Genoa salami, Cuban cigars, and marijuana. They suggested we jump into their car and continue our party at a nearby disco.

Whichever one of the twins sat at the wheel must have been shitfaced. He could not drive a straight line. The car weaved through traffic and nearly sideswiped several vehicles. Before long, Soviet police cars surrounded us. An officer gave our driver a Breathalyzer test and detained us on a DWI.

We did not reach the disco parking lot until two hundred rubles later. My leg muscles had cramped. Manufacturers did not build the Lada for anyone much over six feet tall. I was in such a hurry to get the blood rushing back into my limbs, I opened the car door without looking and banged into a black van parked alongside us. A van owned by a Russian plain-clothes policeman. The officer jumped out of the vehicle screaming and flashing his badge.

We tried to explain that it was an accident. There was not a single light in the parking lot; the dark had practically cam-ouflaged the van. I probably would not have seen it even if I had been looking. Or sober. He did not want to hear it. All right, we knew the drill. I reached for my wallet, but before I could hand over more rubles, he jabbed the point of his night-stick into my chest.

Indian Thugees smoked hashish to buttress their courage

before embarking on strangling raids. The drug will give you brassballs, which is probably why I had the audacity to yank the nightstick from the cop's hands. Did that get his eyes bulging! He started backpedaling at sprinter's speed across the parking lot. His performance riveted the twins until they collapsed in a fit of giggles. "Omigod, look," one of the Sergeis said, "he is moonwalking! Just like Michael Jackson!"

Lord knows what the cop's partner was doing all this time but when he came out of the van, all laughter ceased. This officer was a six-footer, wide as a hunk of rock from Stonehenge and built so hard you could ice-skate on him without leaving a mark. Anyone with that much size gets your attention right away. He made even more of an impression with his jacket. Probably because when he parted the front of it, we saw the butt of a pistol peeking over his waistband.

He motioned for me to return his partner's nightstick and asked to see my papers. I handed them over with none of my usual smartass commentary. There is something about the presence of a .44 Magnum that dampens my wisecracking skills.

"So you are an American," the officer said in a metallic Terminator monotone. "We do not want to make this an incident. I suggest you go back to your hotel and stay there till morning."

I do not know what happened after that. The hash and vodka had combined with sheer exhaustion to sledgehammer my brain. Everything turned black. Someone must have driven me to the Olympic Village. The next thing I remember is stumbling into my room on rag doll legs, tripping over my feet, and collapsing into bed.

I awoke an hour later with my head banging. No, that was the door. Someone yelling too. Terwillinger. "We've got a big problem," he blurted soon as I let him in, "It's the kid. You have to get to his room or we might not see him again."

Jay led me to an apartment down the hall. Inside, I found Jim Nelson, our young buck catcher, shivering in a corner. He was red-eyed and bare-chested, wearing only a pair of pants he had obviously just thrown on; his belt was missing and his zipper was undone. No shoes or socks. On his bed sat an eighteen-year-old Russian woman, a porcelain-skinned brunette dressed in a sheet and god-knows-what under it. She was pretty but had that sunken-eyed, not-fed-enough look we had seen in many young women around Moscow.

Two KGB agents stood at attention in the middle of the room. I signaled the one who guarded the lobby to join me in the hallway.

"You were told before you came here," he reminded me, "no bringing women up to the rooms for sex."

"How do you know he brought her up here for that? It probably started innocently."

"So your friend claims. I am supposed to believe she came up here to play Scrabble?"

"Why not?"

"She doesn't speak English."

"Good point. That would make the game a tad one-sided. Look, you know things like this are going to happen. Haven't you noticed that when American men visit a Communist country they walk around with perpetual erections? They confuse spreading capitalism with spreading their seed. You have two kids here, practically teenagers. What else are they going to do in this town on a Saturday night? They are not going to spend the night drinking your cognac, I can tell you that."

"We have to take him in, unless . . ."

Oh, sure. About eight hundred rubles' worth of unless and they let off Superstud with a reprimand.

We left the next day, which was fortunate since the team had run out of Russian money. As we checked through customs, officials rummaged through my bags looking for any merchandise I might be trying to sneak through without paying the duties—one last shot at a gratuity. They never found the sable hat I had purchased on a Moscow street corner for $20, I guess because it sat on my head.

A few months later, the Berlin Wall fell. We were nowhere near it at the time. Honest.

8

STUMPED ON THE STUMP

I did not know Charlie Mackenzie when he first phoned in September 1988. A mutual friend had given him my number. Fans called our house all the time to talk baseball or invite me to some event. So it did not seem unusual when Charlie asked me to meet him on Duluth Street in midtown Montreal.

"I have a proposal I'd like to put before you," he said in a slightly southern accent.

"Can't we discuss this over the phone?" I had not planned on going out that afternoon.

"No. There are other people involved. I promise we won't take up too much of your time."

He described a place that was only a ten-minute drive from my home. Charlie had mentioned free beer and eats. I went without having any idea what he wanted.

We met in a dark tavern that straddled a street corner in a working-class French neighborhood of sidewalk bistros and three-family houses. Nothing fancy about this establishment—a beer-and-shot joint without the shots. L-shaped bar, a few tables, a row of wooden stools without cushions, one pool table in the back, and a lot of plywood paneling. A clock on the wall said it was just past 4 p.m., downtime between lunch and dinner. I walked into a room empty save for Mr. Mackenzie and his crew.

Charlie stepped forward to greet me. He had come to Montreal some years earlier, an American expatriate and Vietnam War vet with light brown, shoulder-length hair parted down the middle and a straw cowboy hat tilted back from his head. He had strung hippy beads around his neck, the kind I had not seen since visiting Haight-Ashbury in the late sixties. When Charlie spoke, his frames of reference indicated he was no more than fifty, but he appeared to be older. I noticed a lot of miles grooved into that face.

The men who accompanied Charlie introduced themselves as professors from the University of Montreal. They resembled a gang of Trotskyites. Most of them wore the same uniform: short beards, peaked berets, rimless glasses, and black jackets with no ties. One beetle-browed man with bushy gray hair sat apart from the group, looking off into nowhere while puffing on a Gauloise Blonde cigarette carrying four inches of ash on its tip. He was too lost in thought to notice.

Charlie explained that they all belonged to the Rhinoceros Party, an alternative political organization that had attracted a large following throughout Quebec in recent years. During the last election, several Rhino candidates had run strong, competitive campaigns, and one woman had even won a seat on the Montreal city council.

I had read several articles describing the Rhinoceros Party as a progressive, even anarchistic organization with a political philosophy based on Dadaism. A USC professor once told me all I knew about Dada, which is this: as soon as you understood what Dada was, it became something else. That logic sounded just quirky enough to appeal to my bent brain.

Charlie was the Rhinoceros Party coordinator for all of North America. Under his direction, over a hundred thousand Canadians had registered as members. Now he and his colleagues wanted to expand. When I asked how I might help, one of the professors, a tall, thin fellow with a thick French accent, said, "Every time the United States sneezes, we up here catch the cold."

"Yeah, and what does that mean?"

"Just that when something small goes wrong in your country, we pay the price for it. It is time that we exerted some influence on U.S. politics."

"You want me to introduce you to some congressmen?"

Charlie responded, "No. We want you to run for public office."

I had worked with political activists before. While playing

in Boston, I campaigned in favor of school busing, handgun control, and the Equal Rights Amendment. But no one had ever put my name forward as a candidate for anything. I mean, this was me we were talking about.

"What office did you have in mind, Charlie? Alderman, councilman . . . ?"

"We think you should be aiming higher."

"Congressman?"

"Uh-uh. We want you to be the American Rhinoceros Party's 1988 candidate for the White House. Bill, we want you to run for president."

"Cool."

To be honest, I didn't say "cool." Truth is I just stood there, waiting for the punch line. They were serious. No one in the room believed I could win a single vote unless they held the election in an asylum. They did think, though, that my candidacy could generate enough publicity to make their party known throughout the United States and help them to register more American voters as Rhinos.

Peck's Bad Boy wanted to jump in, to pull the ultimate prank. I asked what issues we would run on. A member handed me a sheet of paper outlining a party platform that one Rhinoceros candidate later described as being "two feet high and made of wood." Included among the planks:

- A proposal to abolish the environment rather than protect it on the grounds that it took up too much space to keep clean.

- A law that banned companies from pumping oil from the ground. The reason: the party believed that oil bubbled below the surface to keep Earth running smoothly on its axis. Withdrawing any more of the lubricant might cause the planet to grind to a halt.

- A plan to bulldoze the Rocky Mountains so that Alberta could receive a few extra minutes of daylight.

- An alternative plan to move the Rockies one meter to the west as a make-work project.

- A motion to sever Montreal from the rest of Canada, declare it an independent island state, and tow it down to Florida during the winter months.

- A law that required car companies to put outsized wheels on the back of every vehicle so that drivers would always be riding downhill and conserving energy.

- A proposal to paint the White House pink and turn it into a Mexican restaurant.

- A ban on guns *and* butter, since they both killed.

- A plan to conserve energy by lowering the boiling point of water. Not by any scientific means but by simply declaring that the boiling point had been lowered.

I only had to read the document once before agreeing to sign on. After a round of handshakes and beers, one of the professors marked the occasion by presenting me with a geo-desic girder. He had lifted the artifact from the American Pavilion, the futuristic dome Buckminster Fuller had designed for the Montreal Exposition back in 1969. Welders had forged the steel link into an L shape. Nine prongs emanated from its center, like the points of a starfish, and the piece must have weighed seventy-five pounds. The professor strained to budge it off the floor.

The gift touched me, though I had no idea how anyone in the room knew of my affinity for Fuller. Made me wonder if they already maintained a Bill Lee dossier in their files. One thing about the girder troubled me, though. Most political parties handed out key rings, banners, pencils, or T-shirts as souvenirs. This bulky item struck me as a tad extravagant. I immediately made my first vow as a candidate: to economize on all future campaign spending. That would not be a difficult promise to keep, since we had no campaign funds to spend. The Rhinos made it clear that raising money for the presidential run would be one of my chief responsibilities.

At the end of the meeting, Charlie asked whom else I wanted on my ticket. "There is only one person for the job of vice president," I told him. "Hunter S. Thompson, the original gonzo journalist. He knows more about vice than anyone in the world, and if you read his book *Fear and Loathing on the Campaign Trail,* you'll see he understands the inner workings of America's corrupt political system like nobody else. He's our man."

A few days later the Rhinos issued a press release announcing Thompson as my running mate. Without asking him. Oh, they tried to contact Hunter, but either he did not return Charlie's calls or someone had given the Rhinos a wrong number. There is no time to lose when you are trying to foment a revolution, so rather than wait to find Thompson, the Rhinos declared him the party's vice presidential candidate in absentia.

We kicked off the campaign the following month in Boston. Mackenzie sent a group of volunteers to assist me, a crazed bunch, former Nam vets who had clearly absorbed way too much Agent Orange. They dressed in paramilitary-style black T-shirts and fatigues and acted as though we planned to over-run some enemy position rather than capture the White House. These men did not do advance work; they ran reconnaissance. They did not set their watches; they synchronized them.

They never mentioned their war experiences. But you could tell Nam had not ended for many of them. I heard the sense of betrayal in their voices when they railed against the U.S. government and its policies. These men expressed joy over the end of Reagan's presidency, but they did not trust Bush or Dukakis or any other representative of the major political parties. They would have supported Daffy Duck had the Rhino Party designated him as its candidate. Most of them just wanted change, any change—a chance to rattle the establishment and challenge the status of the status quo.

We drove through the heart of Boston in an open-air limousine. Several drinking buddies, acting as Secret Service agents, ran alongside my car. My campaign manager had selected brawny linebacker types dressed in Bermuda shorts, black tuxedo jackets, and wraparound shades. I asked their leader if any of them would be willing to take a bullet should some crazed assassin try to end my campaign prematurely.

"Don't see how we could," he confessed. "We'd be too busy ducking."

"But you guys are supposed to be my bodyguards."

"Right, and if something happens, we will guard your body until a reputable undertaker shows up to claim it. And don't forget there are six of us. You won't be lacking for pallbearers."

That thought comforted me.

As our limo slowly rolled from the Bull and Finch Pub to my old Red Sox haunt the Eliot Lounge, we handed out plastic rhino noses to the nine or ten people who lined the streets to cheer me on. At least two of the spectators mistook the rhino noses for pig snouts and thought I was Jimmy Dean on a promotional tour for some new sausage.

A crowd of fans waited for us at the Eliot Lounge. Our volunteers sold Rhinoceros T-shirts, buttons, and party membership cards to raise cash for the campaign. We also solicited contributions from everyone in the bar but I limited each donation to a quarter. I considered the presidency a two-bit office and therefore deemed it unfair to accept more than that. This was some ten years before Senators McCain and Feingold introduced their campaign finance reform bill. It is obvious they stole the idea from me.

Our efforts raised about $36.45 in three days. Since $25 of that went for beer, this left very little for advertising, transportation, staffing, office supplies, or other necessities. We could not buy anything in volume so buying smart became the key to our campaign. For instance, we had no funds to promote voter registration. The Democrats had already launched a mammoth campaign to register drivers who applied for licenses at motor vehicle bureaus across the country. The Republicans employed a similar strategy only they restricted their efforts to Ferrari and Maserati dealerships.

I decided to outwit both parties by pursuing a bloc of the electorate neither side courted: voters who could not vote. We scheduled a series of no-cost campaign stops at several New England prisons. That may sound strange, but if you examine the Florida results for the 2000 presidential campaign, you will see that soliciting votes from people who could not cast ballots because they were either felons or dead was another strategy way ahead of its time.

At one prison, we heard about a convict who had created a corporation that sold no products, performed no services, employed no people, and annually took in nearly a million dollars in pure profit but paid no taxes. I told my aides to get his name. He sounded like just the man we needed to head the Treasury Department.

As the campaign progressed, I followed the speeches and press conference of the other candidates to probe for their weakness. I finally found an opening. Whenever journalists asked Bush or Dukakis about the deficit, both candidates responded with long-range plans they claimed would balance the national budget in eight to ten years. Yet I knew how to erase the shortfall in less than a day. Since the government owned the printing presses and currency plates, we merely had to print more money in large denominations. Bye-bye deficit. Seeing as how neither of my opponents could figure out a solution as easy as that, both men were obviously too dense to be president. If I could just entice them into a nationally televised debate, the American people would recognize that.

Too bad our party had no means of publicizing my message or getting out the vote. Two months into the campaign we still had no funding. No brochures. No posters. No advertising of any kind. We could not finance any petition drives, so my name would not appear on the ballot in a single state. I ran the race as the ultimate stealth candidate.

We also still lacked an in-the-flesh vice presidential candidate. Hunter Thompson had eluded every attempt to reach him. One of my volunteers pressed me almost daily to find another running mate.

"You can't have a vice president who doesn't show up," he insisted.

"Oh, yeah? Have you looked at the job description for VP? Seems to me someone who doesn't show up is perfect for the position."

"But Dukakis has Bentsen, Bush has Quayle . . ."

"You're making my point."

Charlie Mackenzie called in late September. He had worked the phones every day trying to wangle an endorsement for my candidacy from some major political figure. Now he thought we had one. The man was a well-known political and social activist who had founded a counterculture political party of his own during the sixties, one of the leaders of the American antiwar movement during the Vietnam era, the author of a best-selling anarchistic manifesto, the dissident prankster who once led a peace demonstration in which over fifty thousand people tried to levitate the Pentagon using psychic energy, a recent fugitive from justice who only the year before had been arrested for the forty-second time after leading a demonstration against CIA recruitment on the University of Massachusetts campus, an alumnus of the Chicago Seven.

Abbie Hoffman wanted to meet me.

My hero.

The two of us sat down at a table in a bar just outside of New Hope, Pennsylvania. Abbie was shorter than I expected. He had arrived dressed in T-shirt and jeans. His dark hair was tangled and longish, receding at the crown and streaked with gray. He looked ill. His face was drawn, his body frail. Yellow tinged his eyes. But I could see the flames dancing in them.

We shook hands. He asked if I still played baseball and seemed pleased when I told him about my career on the semi-pro circuit. Turned out the revolutionary grew up a Red Sox fan. We talked about the Rhinoceros Party, and he agreed to give me his blessing. He broke into a belly laugh when he read our lunatic platform.

Suddenly, though, Abbie's mood turned somber. He told me fighting the establishment, even as part of a fringe organization, nurtured the soul but that the corporate culture in the United States had become so deeply rooted, so institutionalized, little we did would ever make a real difference nationally.

The Vietnam vets who had accompanied me to New Hope didn't want to hear that kind of talk. They formed a dissenting Greek chorus at the next table and mumbled how we could still "beat those bastards, just wait and see." Abbie wanly smiled at the background noise. He still worked as an activist, opposing injustice and supporting environmental causes on the grassroots level. He also saw life realistically. Abbie told me he admired my associates' passion but that our shot had come in the sixties with Berkeley, the civil rights marches, and the antiwar demonstrations. That had been our chance to overturn things. "And you know what happened," he said.

Yeah. Bobby. Martin. Nixon. We all knew what had happened.

I hugged him and left for home. We campaigned little after that meeting. After talking to a real revolutionary, someone who had spent his life putting everything on the line, the joke had lost its humor. I just wanted to get back on a ball field and shag fly balls in the sunshine. My writers prepared a speech for election night in case we won. I had planned to immediately resign and turn over the reins to Hunter Thompson. You never heard that address; those twelve write-in votes I received left us just short of reaching the White House. Next time I'll figure out how to fill out the ballots faster.

Hunter Thompson and I never did get together. My friend Jim Nowik met him in New York City in 1992 and learned the journalist had known of our ill-fated candidacies. Jim later wrote to me describing the encounter. We close this chapter with a portion of his letter as evidence that my vice president and I would have made a perfect match:

> I ran into Hunter Thompson at the bar of the Pierre Hotel in NYC, around the first week of November. He was in town for *Rolling Stone's* twenty-fifth anniversary bash at the Four Seasons restaurant. . . . I had caught him alone, though I'm sure he would have been happy to find something with two legs and a dress. . . . [A]fter treating him to about four pint glasses of Chivas Regal over ice in about half an hour . . . he treated me to some barely intelligible bursts of conversation (not to mention a bar bill of $100).
>
> I brought up your . . . run for the White House on the Rhinoceros ticket with him as VP. I can't quite remember his mumbled words exactly, but I did catch "mutant," "pig-fucker," and "I'll gnaw on the bastard's skull." . . . I could tell immediately you were still intimate running mates.

9

ALMOST A GOOD IDEA

In 1989 I signed on as player-manager for the Winter Haven Super Sox in the newly formed Senior Professional Baseball Association. The league offered an opportunity to test my skills against clubs composed entirely of my peers. Jim Morley, a Colorado real-estate developer, had founded the eight-team league as a haven for retired pro players thirty-five or older (the league made an exception for catchers, who could be as young as thirty-two). Our schedule called for teams to play seventy-two games from the first of November to the end of January. Each player received $9,000 a month.

My teammates included several former Boston Red Sox such as Ferguson Jenkins, Bernie Carbo, Butch Hobson, Darrell Brandon, Mario Guerrero, and Gary Allenson. We played our first game on November 1 against the St. Petersburg Pelicans in Winter Haven's Chain of Lakes Park. Mitchell Maxwell, the Super Sox owner, had assured us he would run a first-class operation, but the opening-day ceremonies convinced me I had returned to Port Hawkesbury with the Hockey Legends. A singer from *Les Misérables* began the festivities by belting out an off-key rendition of "The Star Spangled Banner" while the balky sound system slapped our ears silly with feedback. A twenty-one-gun salute followed the performance. I swear at least six of the rifles misfired.

Maxwell chose some celebrity for the traditional throwing out of the first ball, a celebrity no one in the crowd of over three thousand had ever heard of. He jogged to the mound in near silence. After he completed his tosses, the players on both teams were forced to wait before assuming their positions while the Winter Haven High School band promenaded across the field and treated us to their entire catalogue of marches, each of them sounding like a high-velocity variation of "99 Bottles of Beer on the Wall."

For the finale, the stadium loudspeakers blared a fight song that ended with the immortal phrase, "It ain't over till it's over, that's Super Sox baseball!" I still own a tape of that ditty and play it outside whenever we want to chase rodents from our property.

Jim Bibby started for us that day. The right-hander had won

nineteen games with the Texas Rangers in 1974 and had only left the majors three years earlier. He pulled a hamstring in the fourth inning, forcing him to retire to the clubhouse. My original plan called for Mike Cuellar, a Cy Young Award winner with the Baltimore Orioles in 1969, to enter the game as the first reliever out of our bullpen. The left-hander could not spell Bibby or anyone else. Mike had come up ailing before the game and was unable to hoist his leg high enough to complete his pitching motion.

In the fifth inning, our catcher, Gary Allenson, fell with a pulled hammy of his own while sprinting to first base on a groundball. One inning later, our backup catcher, Doug Simunic, stumbled as he chased a bunt and grabbed the back of his thigh. Another hamstring pull. So many of our players dropped on the field, I looked into the palm trees across the street from the stadium expecting to find snipers perched on the branches.

Our first baseman, Pete LaCock, bravely offered to sub behind the plate. Reliever Pedro Borbon took the mound for us, and he threw his sinker down and in against the Pelican's predominantly right-hand–hitting lineup. Not an easy ball for even the most experienced receiver to handle.

LaCock took a unique approach to his new job. He did not consider it important to actually catch any of Borbon's sharply breaking bastard pitches just so long as he got his mitt in the general vicinity of the ball. So many sinkers eluded LaCock, I finally said to him, "If you mix in a catch every now and again, you might be able to confuse the opposition. On second thought, don't even set up a target. Just let the ball hit the backstop. You can grab it on the rebound."

We lost the opener, 9–2. The good news: only four of our

players left the game injured. The bad news: our roster carried just twenty names, and at that rate the team would go under in less than a week. After the Pelicans recorded the final out, every light in the stadium dimmed until darkness enveloped the field. Players had to grope their way back to the clubhouse. We all thought power outage until that first explosion behind the centerfield fence ripped through the night. Fireworks.

Oh, sweet Jesus, I thought, *can't this team do anything right?* The concept was simple enough. The home team does not ignite rockets and flares unless it wins. What part of that sounds difficult to grasp? The fireworks display troubled one other person in Winter Haven besides me. A woman who lived across the street from our stadium owned a poodle. The sonic boom from the display so panicked the dog, it ran through a plate glass door, and the falling shards sliced the animal in half. Within days, the distraught owner threatened the team with its first lawsuit.

After that, things started to go bad for us.

Fergie Jenkins, a 284-game winner during his major-league career, took the mound for the second game of our series against the Pelicans. He pitched strongly and allowed only one earned run in five innings before collapsing to his knees. The forty-five-year-old right-hander crawled around the diamond, dry-heaving and gasping for breath. We thought he had suffered a heart seizure or a stroke. Turned out Fergie had swallowed his chaw of tobacco.

I had to relieve him with little warm-up, and the Pelicans made me pay. They scored four runs before the inning ended. They hit so many hard line drives down the left field line, our third baseman, Butch Hobson, tried to call time so he could go into the clubhouse and strap on catcher's equipment for protection. A dismal first outing. The Winter Haven fans impressed me, though, by yelling their support even while the Pelicans pummeled every pitch I threw. "Take the pitcher out!" they gleefully chanted. Had I been sitting in the stands, they could have added one more voice to that choir.

We lost that game 12–2 and dropped four more before notching our first win. As the defeats continued, the Winter Haven troops started grousing. Several players complained to Mitchell Maxwell that I was too disorganized to manage a baseball team. They claimed I had no set time for infield practice, no set time for batting practice, no set time for running or stretching. I offered Maxwell a perfectly good reason for the casual schedule: I did not own a watch.

As morale drooped, I tried to rally the team with a rousing locker room speech. Spent all night writing it, trying to create the right tone. I understood which qualities a manager must exude during such a critical presentation. Compassion. Empathy. But above all, tact.

"We are horse shit," I announced while striding to the center of the clubhouse. "We are supposed to be an egalitarian group of rebels here to have fun, to play hard and support one another while winning a few games. But we cannot beat the Pelicans. We cannot beat the Legends. Gentlemen, we cannot beat our grandmothers. Most of you sons of bitches are down here stealing money,"—a line Jim Fanning might have proudly uttered—"You guys know who you are. You are not in shape. Get in shape. I keep the key to the pool in my desk. Use it. I swim there every day. Getting my work in, doing my cardio. My body fat is down 30% and I feel great."

I did everything but tell them about my boxing gloves.

From the back, a voice—I don't know whose—piped up, "Yeah, you look great but you're getting your ass kicked out there too." In the face of such blatant insubordination, Patton would have cut off the balls of the offending soldier and grilled them on a kebab spit. But this man had a point. I promptly brought the meeting to a close.

My soliloquy did make its impact, though. Mitchell Maxwell was powerfully stirred by my eloquence, my command, my overwhelming clarity. He fired me two days later. As several sportswriters soon pointed out, Maxwell's pink slip made me the first manager eighty-sixed by a SBPA team.

That failed to bother me. I am used to breaking records wherever I play. Besides, even my closest friends realized that hiring me to manage anything stretched the Peter Principle far beyond all sustainable limits. Ed Nottles, a minor-league skipper from the Red Sox organization, took over the club, and Maxwell agreed to retain my services as a pitcher. For a short time we did play better. But the Super Sox finished last in the standings and rarely drew more than 250 people to any of our home games.

Despite the adversity, the season presented its share of memorable moments. Like the night one of our starting pitchers sat at the bar of a Winter Haven nightclub and tied his penis in a knot to entertain the crowd. His performance amazed and amused most of the patrons, but it shocked at least one witness, a journalist who asked me why on earth my teammate would do such a thing.

Dunno, Ollie. Because he can?

A personal highlight occurred during a game against the Port St. Lucie Legends. Bobby Bonds—Barry's dad and one of the best baseball players from my generation—patrolled right field for the Legends that afternoon. I sat in the bullpen behind him. We chatted until one of my teammates hit a line drive deep over his head. Bobby galloped into the right-field corner, picked up the ball on one bounce, and tossed it. To me. "My arm is shot," he yelled, "throw that to third." It did not matter that Bonds worked for the enemy. Instinct took over. I threw the ball on a clothesline back to the infield and just missed nipping the base runner sliding into third. That throw nearly extinguished my own team's rally, but dang, it turned out to be the best play I made all year.

◆

During the brief time I skippered the Super Sox, we maintained an open door policy regarding tryouts. Anyone ambulatory could audition for the team. It did not matter if you had any prior baseball playing experience, I would look you over. Six or seven amateur players approached us; none of them could cut it. There was one man who tried out that I wanted to add to our roster, but I knew management would not allow it.

Tom slinked into the Chain of Lakes clubhouse dressed in a green short-sleeved T-shirt, frayed black sweatpants, black cap pulled low as his eyelashes, black socks, and black sneakers. Silver streaked brush cut under the cap. A cigarette pack rolled up in his left sleeve. His face was a topographer's map, rutted and grooved. Nicotine had left his teeth a stained row of ancient piano keys. Pained eyes. Upper torso cut into a body builder's V, but short. His head ended at my chin. He reminded me of James Dean, an older model gone to seed. Said he was forty-eight. Looked sixty. Claimed he had signed a contract with the Yankees back in 1954 ("Would have made them too but the army drafted me and I was too old when I got out"), which would have made him at least fifty-three.

"I'm a pitcher, a right-hander," he told me in his heavy Brooklyn accent while avoiding my eyes, "and I'm also an inventor. I can help your ball club in more ways than one if you give me a chance." He rattled on, spilling his life story, how he had tried out for numerous teams but never got the break he needed and how he should have made it with the Pittsburgh Pirates and how Whitey Herzog almost hired him for the Kansas City Royals but didn't for reasons he would explain later and how he had driven over a thousand miles in a Toyota held together by nerve and spit and airplane glue and spent over $500 to get here and how this was his last chance after fifteen years of playing semipro baseball for teams whose names I did not recognize since I only half listened to all of that.

No disrespect meant; I just immediately knew Tom lacked the goods. All that talking gave him away. One minute after he introduced himself, I told him he could pitch to me in the bullpen, show me what he had. He just kept jabbering. I needed no more evidence. Pitchers want to pitch. If you offer one the opportunity to take the mound and he hesitates, insists on first reciting his résumé, he is stalling for a reason— fear of being found out or fear of finding out or both.

We walked to the bullpen. In one hand Tom carried a bat- tered brown leather suitcase covered with stickers from places no sane person would ever want to visit. In the other was a black duffel bag. Stored his gear in that, a baseball glove and a pair of spikes so traveled they curled up at the toes.

Tom's first pitch hinted that I might have misjudged him. He displayed a pro's presence on the mound. Smooth, compact windup that allowed him to consistently hit the same release point on pitch after pitch. A nice, relaxed motion. Never muscled the ball. He threw with precision, hitting the target wherever I placed it. One problem: I could have caught him barehanded, his velocity was so spare. He claimed his repertoire included an unhittable screwball. I asked him to throw it. He pleaded for more time to "loosen up." When he finally unleashed his screwgie, it did drop as it crossed the plate, but only in surrender to gravity. The pitch lacked teeth. He had nothing.

I tried to reject him gently. "Look, you might not be able to pitch on this level, but you can play somewhere this summer. There are lots of semipro teams. . . ."

Tom had heard that before. "I don't have to start on your regular roster," he said too eagerly. "Taxi squad would be good enough. Let me throw on the side for a while. When you need a replacement, I'll be ready." Taxi squad members received $2,000 a month just to stay in shape in case we lost a player to injury. He lacked the skills to fill even that role, but he sounded so desperate. "We'll see," I said.

"All right. Well, thanks for looking at me." He knew. I started off the field; he would not let me go. "Look," Tom pleaded, "maybe I can't pitch for you yet, but I invented this slide, see? Nobody in baseball uses it. If you put me on the taxi squad, I can be an extra coach and teach it to all your players. I guarantee they will never get tagged out again. You've got to see this. Let me get my special shoe."

Tom unzipped his bag. It resembled an ordinary baseball

spike except for the long leather flap that extended down from the top of the laces to his shoe tip. "You play third," he told me, "and I'll run in from second. I won't swerve to either side but you still won't get me." At the count of three, he sprinted straight toward third. I dropped low to prepare the tag, but before he reached me Tom somersaulted and landed with his foot just short of my glove. The leather tongue unfurled from his cleat, snaked over my wrist, and landed on the base. "Safe!" Tom yelled.

He acted so pleased with himself, I could not tell him that the rules required you to touch the bag with your body before an umpire could call you safe or that his shoe violated our league's uniform regulations. He could not wear that flap during a game.

Nearly dark. I put my arm around Tom and walked him to his car. As he pulled out I thought, *There goes the real spirit of this league, another guy who does not want to grow old, hooked on a dream, hooked on the game.* Ability stood as the only difference between him and us.

◆

As the season entered its final weeks, the Super Sox played a game in Bobby Maduro Stadium in northern Miami. Another loss. During the bus ride back to Winter Haven, we stopped at a 7-Eleven to pick up beer and soda. Dalton Jones, a utility infielder with our club, and his wife, Barbara, parked behind us in the Mercedes Dalton had bought with his 1967 World Series share. We had just entered the store when we heard Barbara screaming in the parking lot. Some teenager had reached through the car window and grabbed her purse.

The thief ran through a gauntlet of players while making his escape. Not one of us former world-class athletes could put a hand on him. We chased the boy down the road, but he outdistanced the entire team without exceeding trotting speed. As we dragged ourselves back to the bus, tongues hanging, I realized the Senior Baseball Players Association was a tad too senior ever to succeed as anything more than a curiosity. The league folded midway through the following season.

10

THE CURSE

I sat at my kitchen table enjoying a tasty country breakfast on the morning of April 1, 2001, when a houseguest handed me the sports page. My stomach somersaulted. An interview Boston pitching ace Pedro Martinez had given after throwing a spectacular game against the New York Yankees two days earlier caused my distress. One of the Boston beat writers had asked Pedro if he believed in the so-called Curse of the Babe, the legend that the Red Sox will never win a World Series because the baseball gods had damned the franchise for selling the sport's greatest player to the Yankees back in 1918.

Pedro scoffed at the superstition. "Bring back the Bambino," he said, "and have me face him and I'll drill him in the ass!" That comment elicited a lot of laughs in the clubhouse but none in my home. I immediately tried contacting Martinez, but the Red Sox refused to reveal his phone number or convey my message. Big mistake. Somebody had to warn him about the danger.

Several weeks passed before one of my sportswriter friends offered to contact Martinez. Too much time had elapsed. Pedro was no longer Pedro. He had become Venus de Milo. The right-hander's pitching arm had practically fallen off, and he would not throw another inning for the rest of the season. Losing him effectively ended Boston's pennant hopes. Martinez had only himself to blame. He had forgotten that Babe Ruth had not only played the outfield when he wore a Sox uniform. He had also starred for the team as a great left-handed pitcher, one who relished coming inside on anyone who crowded the plate. That arm injury was the Babe dusting off Martinez with a slider at the chin.

In 2003 Ruth sent him sprawling once more. Pedro was pitching against the Yankees in the deciding game of the American League Championship Series. He looked dominating that night and carried a 5–2 lead into the bottom of the eighth. But Boston manager Grady Little failed to remove Martinez even though everyone else in Yankee Stadium could see that the exhausted pitcher could not face another batter.

New York tied the game against Pedro and won in extra innings on an Aaron Boone home run to advance to yet another World Series. It was, in the minds of many Red Sox fans, the worst defeat in the franchise's history. Had Pedro spoken to me, I could have shared my one experience with the Curse; perhaps he would have recanted in time to save his arm or win that championship game.

◆

Wednesday, September 26, 1990 gave us one of those glorious Vermont fall afternoons that make you feel as if you could work outside forever. A high blue sky, no clouds, and just enough nip in the air to keep you moving quickly. Friends and I were finishing the window frames and cedar siding on my Craftsbury home when the phone rang.

The voice at the other end of the line belonged to the sports director for WZLX, Boston's most popular music station for anyone with a taste for heavy, butt-thumping rockers like Led Zeppelin or the Stones or Pearl Jam. He invited me to attend a ceremony the disc jockey Charles Laquidara would be hosting near Fenway Park the following Saturday. The sports director offered $500 for my time along with a box seat ticket to that afternoon's game between the Red Sox and Toronto Blue Jays.

"What sort of ceremony would that be?" I asked

"An exorcism."

"Come again?"

"You know the Sox and Jays are fighting it out for the American League East title. Whoever wins two of the three games they are playing next weekend will probably go on to the playoffs with a good shot at the World Series. Sox fans are tired of Babe Ruth jinxing their team. We are going to exorcise the curse and ask Babe to let Boston beat the Jays. Charlie wants you on stage to help cast the spell."

I recalled that scene from *The Exorcist* in which Linda Blair levitated above her bedroom with her head a roulette wheel spinning on her shoulders while she vomited pea soup on a pair of priests. Not often you get offered a front row seat for a show that entertaining, so I agreed to participate.

Three days later I drove to the Twins Souvenir Shop, a sports memorabilia emporium located just across from Fenway Park on Jersey Street. Over six-hundred fans, many of them wearing Boston caps and jackets, crammed the nearly block-wide store for the event. Posters of great Red Sox players—Ted Williams, Carl Yastrzemski, Dwight Evans, Wade Boggs, and Roger Clemens among them—stared down from the walls at this odd collection of people carrying voodoo dolls, crosses, and other icons.

I shook hands and signed autographs while Charlie led me to an upraised platform in the center of the store. He introduced an exotic-looking woman with long dark hair tufted white wearing a form-clinging black dress and a tall, tricornered hat. She carried a broom. Laurie Cabot listed her occupation as professional witch. We had met before. In 1975, Laurie danced on the roof of the Red Sox dugout during a rain delay in Cleveland. After that, our team won fifteen out of seventeen games and went on to meet the Cincinnati Reds in the World Series; I considered her magic potent.

A warlock from Salem stood at her side. Paul Poier, a towering man in his late thirties, resembled Eddie Munster all grown up with his pointy ears, pointy eyebrows, and prominent fangs. He wore his licorice-colored vinyl hair slicked back from a high forehead and dressed in a black suit and flowing dark cape that dusted the floor wherever he walked.

The two witches joined hands in front of an effigy of Babe Ruth and began speaking in fluent mumbo jumbo. While the pair shouted incantations, members of the audience clapped, stomped their feet, and filled the room with a more familiar chant:

"Yank-ees Suck!"

As the ceremony drew to a close, Charlie Laquidara asked me to step forward. The Red Sox had sent over a Louisville Slugger broken only the afternoon before during batting practice. A clubhouse attendant had heavily swathed the handle in electrical tape to keep it intact. Laurie, Paul, and I held the bat aloft while the witches asked the Babe to forgive the Sox and help them triumph over Toronto. Then they presented me with the bat.

I tossed the lumber into my car trunk and walked to the ballpark. The Red Sox began the day in first place, one game ahead of the Blue Jays with five games left to play. Roger Clemens started for the home team that afternoon. He must have been throwing a hundred miles an hour when he first took the mound. The Blue Jays could barely make contact with any of his pitches.

After Boston took an early lead, the game looked as good as over given the way Rocket was throwing. I left in the third inning. My softball team was playing that evening, and it was vital that I return home in time for the first pitch. A butcher sponsored our team. He paid us in steaks.

It was 250 miles to Craftsbury and I had only three and a half hours to cover the distance. I lined the dashboard with autographed pictures of me in my Red Sox uniform. These were Get Out of Jail Free cards, to be handed out to any highway patrolman who might flag down my car for speeding. Worked every time.

I followed the game on the radio. The Blue Jays rallied against Clemens for a tie, but just as I turned out of Boston, Tom Brunansky hit a home run to put the Sox ahead. A few innings later, Tom hit another homer to increase his team's lead. Spooky. Brunansky had come to the Red Sox in a trade with the Minnesota Twins earlier in the season. He played right field. Babe Ruth's old position.

My car rumbled through Franconian Notch along a foliage dense road that brings you through New Hampshire into Vermont. I listened as Toronto tied the Sox and put the go-ahead run on base. The broadcast faded into white noise. The mountains in this region rose so tall and thick they silenced the radio transmission out of Boston; I scrambled to find another station carrying the game.

Twenty minutes passed before I could barely make out the voices of the Red Sox announcers through the static of WTIC out of Hartford. No idea where the score stood or which team was batting. I stopped the car and shoved my ear tight next to a speaker just in time to hear an announcer yell, "It's a high fly ball out to deep left field . . . way back . . . will it go? . . . Yes! . . . it's out of here! . . . unbelievable! Brunansky has hit his third home run and . . ."

The world went mute. I sat alongside the road for five minutes, staring at nothing. Un-fucking-believable was right. We exorcise the Curse of the Babe in the morning and that very afternoon the guy playing his position hits three home runs to help Boston win this important ballgame. A player who wasn't even on the team at the start of the season? Who would believe it?

It got better. The following Wednesday Clemens pitched again, this time against the Chicago White Sox. A Boston victory would clinch the division title. In the top of the ninth inning, Red Sox closer Jeff Reardon arrived on the mound with his team ahead 3–1. He retired the first two batters, but Sammy Sosa chopped a clean single through the infield, and Reardon hit Scott Fletcher to put the tying run on base. My old Tiburones teammate Ozzie Guillen walked up to the batter's box.

Reardon poured two quick strikes past him. Then he threw a fastball that moved away from the left-hand-hitting Guillen but stayed up over the plate. Ozzie hit the ball solidly, high and far down the right field line. Brunansky had not expected the slightly built shortstop to pull the ball with so much authority. He had been playing Guillen toward center. Tom sprinted far across the Fenway outfield. As he neared the ball, he stumbled to his knees and slid over the grass. Double. Tie score, with the potential winning run in scoring position. Except Guillen's hit never made the box score. Somehow Brunansky had kept his glove open and upright and the ball nestled into its webbing for the game's final out. The Red Sox had won the division championship.

They failed, however, to advance to the World Series. The Minnesota Twins beat them in the playoffs. "Damn," I said to one of my neighbors, "those witches balled it up. They only asked for the Babe to let Boston win the American League East rather than the World Series. Typical Red Sox fans, afraid to demand total victory." I was joking. This was one ballplayer who did not believe in fate or God or magic or talismans or any other superstitions, only in action, reaction, and chance. My presence at the exorcism was nothing but a lark. I knew that ceremony had not influenced Brunansky's heroics. Coincidence had played its hand in those games, nothing more.

The next morning Pam and I decided to go shopping. I cleared out the car trunk to make room for all the packages. Stuck in the rear under the jack, I found that taped bat the witches had given me. I was about to toss it in the garbage bin when I noticed the name inscribed across the barrel of that C243 Louisville Slugger.

Tom Brunansky.

Now you know why I do not take the Curse lightly. So here is the advice I would have passed along to Pedro had we spoken. If you want to win a World Series with Boston, grab a yellow pages. Look under *W* for warlocks and witches. Cross-reference *S* for sorcerers. Stay away from illusionists; Red Sox fans have seen enough of them over the years. Whomever you hire, make sure he or she removes the entire curse this time. And never, ever screw around with the Babe again. He'll deck you in the batter's box every time.

11

REVELATION IN MAINE

I n November 1994, I drove to a high school gym in Rockland, Maine, to play in a charity basketball game that pitted several Red Sox alumni, including Rick Miller and Bob Stanley, plus some local talent against members of the town's fire department. I got there moments before starting time only to discover that half the players had not yet arrived. A snowstorm had stranded many of them on Route 1 near the Shawshank Prison.

With each passing minute the crowd grew more restless, stomping their feet in the bleachers and whistling for the event to begin. As I suited up in the locker room, the promoter poked in his head and asked, "Think you could entertain the spectators with a pitching exhibition until we have enough people to field two teams?" He handed me a glove and ball.

"Great," I said, "but what are we going to do for a catcher?"

"We'll pick someone."

"It's not an easy position to fill if you really want me to throw with any kind of speed. Could be dangerous."

"Don't worry."

They picked a chunky kid, barely twenty, built low to the ground with dangling simian arms. We moved to the center of the basketball court and stood sixty feet apart. "I used to be a catcher in high school," he assured me.

He assumed a catcher's crouch, quite professional-looking, and set up a target with an oversized mitt. The boy did everything right. Until I unleashed my first high fastball and he ignored one of the basics of catching. He forgot to raise his mitt. The pitch crashed right between his eyes and ricocheted some twelve feet into the air. He dropped boneless as a jellyfish and lay spread-eagled on the floor with all the breath gone out of him.

"Jesus," I yelled, the only voice in the place, "that kid's dead!" Spectators screamed, several dropped to their knees in prayer. I stood paralyzed. Two men ran to my catcher's prone body. Before they could reach him, the boy sprang to his feet, a potato-sized knot bulging from his forehead. He blinked at me through glazed eyes, raised his arms up toward the rafters, and ran a victory lap around the gym floor. You could tell he had no idea where he was, but at least he was moving. Later on, a doctor pronounced him fit. The young man had not suffered even a slight concussion.

That was the day I discovered whatever fastball I once had was gone.

12

FLYING WITH THE
GOLDEN JET

Bill, would you like to drink some cognac?" Bobby Hull sat next to me in a lounge chair on the back porch of an inn on the northern shore of the St. Lawrence River. Across the water, a bruised moon rose from the cliffs of the Monts Chic-Chocs to cast deep shadows across the yard. I could barely make out Bobby's face, but whenever his mouth opened, moonglow gleamed off his perfect white teeth.

Sports fans knew Hull as the Golden Jet, perhaps the greatest National Hockey League player of his generation. It was July 1996, and we had seen little of each other since I last appeared as the halftime show with the Hockey Legends in 1984. Hull had been that team's biggest attraction and he knew it. When some amateur assigned to cover Bobby tried to show off his fancy skate work, the Golden Jet would tell him, "Don't wear yourself out, son. The crowd came here to see me score, not you." We were both nightcrawlers who enjoyed each other's company. Too much, perhaps. We had a tacit understanding that getting together more than once a decade would remove five years from our life spans. Now he and I had signed to play on a softball team sponsored by the Molson Brewing Company. Time to catch up.

"No, Bobby, cognac isn't for me. The last time I drank that stuff, Pam found me slumped over the backyard fence naked at five in the morning. Neighbors say I danced under the moon for hours before passing out. Gave me a hangover that lasted the rest of the summer."

"You don't know how to drink it right. Just hold on and I'll show you."

He went inside for a moment and emerged carrying a bottle of Courvoisier, a pitcher of ice-cold spring water, and two shot glasses on a tray.

"Here's the trick," he said. "You drink some ice water first, sip your cognac, and chase it with two more shots of ice water. The water dilutes the alcohol in your system so you don't get too high, and it also keeps you hydrated so you won't wake up with a hangover."

"We do this bottle, I won't wake up at all."

"Try it."

While we drank, Bobby talked about his family, recalling how they used to fish together on this very waterway. One day his father and sister motored out to the middle of the St. Lawrence, where she hooked a forty-pound muskie minutes after dropping her line into the water. A muskie is a monster freshwater fish with the jaws of a crocodile and the torso of a snake. After Mr. Hull and his daughter struggled to reel her catch into the boat, the fish refused to die. That muskie flopped from stem to stern snapping at both of them.

Mr. Hull grabbed a ball peen hammer from his tool box and started pounding the fish. The muskie squirmed and rolled every time Mr. Hull brought down his weapon. Bobby's father could only land one blow out of every three; the others cracked through the boat bottom. He finally killed the fish, but the craft filled with seawater and they just made it to shore without sinking.

That muskie stretched out so long, Bobby's sister could not hold the fish by its tail without its head scraping the ground unless she stood on a stool. Turned out to be a world-class catch. Most people would have mounted such a prize on their wall. Bobby told me his father paid the local butcher to slice the fish into steaks, which the Hulls feasted on for weeks. What you have to realize is that no one eats muskie. The fish tastes like pure grade pig iron and comes with bones the size of an NFL linebacker's forearms. That story revealed much about why Bobby grew up to be such a tough competitor.

He was a bruiser on the softball field, a man who still liked to make hard contact in what is essentially a noncontact sport. Bobby was an excellent defensive catcher even though his knees had gone gimpy after years of abuse on the ice. His reflexes remained sharp, and few could match his hand-eye coordination—he could catch any ball you put near him.

Bobby proved particularly adept at blocking the plate. He was tall and chiseled, solid as one of those muskie bones. In baseball, everyone wants to go home. Thing is, Bobby didn't want you going home. At least not in one piece. When the Golden Jet planted himself in front of the plate with the throw coming in and a runner bearing down, those last ninety feet from third to home became the Bataan death march.

During a game we played in Saskatchewan, one opposing player tried sneaking in headfirst under Bobby on a close play. Hull came down on him with so much force, we ended up using the poor bastard's flattened skull as home plate for the rest of the game. Another time a runner tried to bowl over Bobby with two men out in the ninth and our team only one run ahead. The runner collided with Bobby at home plate. For a moment I could see only Hull's glittering blue eyes in the swirling dust. Bobby tossed the ball to the umpire and trotted off the field. Game over. We followed, and so did the opposing players, except for the runner. He remained prostrate in front of home plate. Nothing on him moved. I heard his teammates buried him on the spot. He was not a regular member of the club, just a traveling bowler who had agreed to sub for a sick player at the last minute. No one knew the man's name. So they called his grave the Tomb of the Unknown Bowler. It is the only mausoleum in North America with two self-serve bowling lanes.

Yes, I made up that last part. Couldn't resist.

In between drinking and talking, Bobby entertained me with his version of a stupid pet trick. Mr. Hull is blessed—

there is no other word for it—with the longest tongue in the known universe, and not just among humans. Few aardvarks can match Bobby for length or width. I watched him stretch the tip of his tongue all the way up to the top of his forehead. He spread the tongue across his nose until it covered his face like a snug pink baseball glove. I could barely see his eyes under that slab of meat. He finished the demonstration by licking down his eyebrows. I am sure this is the reason his wife lets him out only once a month.

Okay, that is the last joke I make at Hull's expense. Bobby is among the most congenial of men, and I love him dearly. I would hate to offend him with an errant word. But it is not just respect that keeps me from throwing another jibe. Fear also motivates me. When angered, Bobby is not the sort of guy who will chase you. No, it's much worse. He will catch you. And in a fight the Golden Jet would undoubtedly display all the delicacy of Mike Tyson coming off a six-month steroid jag. First Bobby would cut the boxing ring in half on me. Then he would cut it in half again. Then he would cut it in half one last time. Then he would cut me into ribbons.

Bobby and I followed his drinking regimen until nearly dawn. We downed that entire bottle of cognac—on top of two carafes of wine—and two pitchers of ice water. I stayed drunk out of my gourd for two straight days, most of which I spent crawling over bathroom tiles barking. But Bobby was right about the hangover. The prolonged stupor carried me right past any traditional morning penance.

Bobby, on the other hand, rose early the next afternoon to devour a large lunch without showing any ill effects whatsoever. Muskie eater.

Our slow-pitch softball team developed as an extension of

the original Hockey Legends. I still played hardball in several senior leagues around New England, Arizona, and Florida, but there were never enough games to feed my habit, and softball kept me in shape. The Legends let me take an occasional turn on the mound, but I usually played first base or the outfield. I was the only former pro baseball player on the roster. Among the hockey greats who traveled with us were Jimmy Mann, Eddie Shack, Frank Mahovlich, Marcel Dionne, Maurice Richard, and Jean-Guy Talbot. Angelo Mosca, the Canadian Football League Hall of Famer, rounded out the squad.

Molson paid each athlete $500 a day plus expenses to compete in charity games against the police and fire departments throughout the Maritimes and upper St. Lawrence region. We played thirty games in thirty-five days and spent a good deal of our time watching movies on the team bus. Our driver, Gilles, was a lovely man with a gentle manner and more endurance than your average mountain climber. He could sit at the wheel of that bus for twenty hours straight without taking a break.

One thing about Gilles worried me. He had no sense of direction whatsoever, a handicap for any bussie. One evening we were traveling to a tavern in Hamilton, Ontario, to eat dinner with a team of local policemen we had played earlier in the day. Gilles drove through the city for nearly an hour without finding the place. He stopped to study the map before turning onto a road he guaranteed would bring us to the tavern in no time flat. Five minutes later, farm country surrounded us. "Hey, Gilles," I called out, "look in your rearview mirror and tell me what you see."

"Nothing, Bill. Just lots of lights."

"Now look in front of us. See any lights there?"

"No."

"Right. That's a clue, Gilles. When you see lights behind you and none ahead, that means you are heading out of the city. Not going toward it."

"Oh, yes, Bill. I get it now."

He turned around, and we reached the dinner just in time for dessert. A few weeks later Gilles drove us to a game in Saskatoon. Or tried to. As we entered the village of Yorktown, I looked out the window to my right and saw a golf course with grass greens. That was unusual. Most of the courses in this region had sand greens. Which means they were not green at all, but beige or brown or off-white or whatever the hell the color sand is. So why do they call them greens? Don't ask, these are Canadians.

Gilles pulled into a PetrolCanada to stop for gas while we ate lunch. A few moments after we resumed our journey, I looked out the window again and saw another lush green golf course. Only this time it was on my left.

"Hey, Gilles, do you know how many golf courses they have in this town? It's kinda small."

"I am not sure, Bill. I don't play golf."

"Well, maybe you should take it up. Unless they have two only a block apart, we are heading back the way we came."

Had I not glanced out that window, Gilles undoubtedly would have driven the bus to the tip of Nova Scotia and possibly beyond.

Frank Mahovlich and I occasionally sat next to each other on the bus and talked to pass the time during long rides. The Big M had visited the Soviet Union years before to compete in the Hockey World Cup and understood the paranoia that had nagged me during my own trip to that country. His entire time there, he believed the KGB was following him. One day he combed his hotel room looking for electronic bugs and other spying devices. Frank cleared out the closet, flipped over the mattress, unscrewed the lamps, and checked under the toilet. He finally pulled up the carpet and found a metal plate bolted into the floor. Aha! A listening device, cleverly hidden. Frank unscrewed the bolts. Soon as he finished, a loud crash resonated from the room below. He had unfastened a chandelier.

Our team was an offensive juggernaut; we often scored twelve or more runs a game. But we gave them right back on defense. Few of the hockey players could field with skill. Jean-Guy Talbot split catching duties with Hull, and he had this habit of trying to stop every ball thrown to him with his feet—an old hockey practice he could not abandon. After one week of playing, his toes ulcerated. We thought about sewing baseball gloves to his shin guards, but he retired midway through the tour, probably to ensure that he would be able to walk long into old age.

Players told me that if you ever prayed to God for a bigger prick, Eddie Shack appeared on your doorstep the following morning. He displayed surprising range for a 250-pounder whenever he played third base. Too bad Eddie had Jennifer Lopez's throwing arm. Our other infielders were content to block balls with their bodies rather than make clean catches. Massive Angelo Mosca turned his back on hard-hit grounders and let them ricochet off his stonewall behind to another fielder for an assist. I finally called a meeting to tell the boys those leather things on their hands were gloves, not oven mitts, but they never quite got it.

These men were tough competitors, grittier than any ball-players I knew. We had just started a game in Winnipeg when the tail end of a hurricane deluged the field. I asked the umpire to call a rain delay. The hockey players overruled me. They thought we'd be wimping out if we let "a little drizzle" make us quit. None of them cared that every base rested under six inches of water.

In the fifth inning, I hit a grounder that was waterlogged by the time it reached the second baseman. The ball squirted out of his hand as he pulled back his arm to throw. He picked it up again and threw past the first baseman into right field.

As I ran toward second, the shortstop braced himself on the bag to catch the throw from his right fielder. I dropped into a slide that carried me through a foot-and-a-half-long bog. They should have nailed me. But the right fielder threw the ball a foot over the shortstop's head. And the pitcher's head. And the catcher's head. The ball did not touch ground until it banged off the backstop and rolled to home plate.

Before I could touch third base a mud hole sucked my spikes deep into the ground, and I fell five feet shy of the bag. The catcher retrieved the ball and threw toward the pitcher, who was covering third. The pitcher would have caught that toss had his arm been just six feet longer. Instead, the ball carried so far into the outfield, I recovered my balance, touched third, and scored the game's go-ahead run on a jarring hook slide that raised a tsunami at home plate. A spectator who also served as a judge for Canadian water sport competitions gave me a 6.4 for time but a 9.2 for form and execution.

When I stood up to run into the dugout, no one could see me for the mud. My uniform blended into the environment. After a few minutes the mud caked, leaving me with all the defensive range of a Frederic Remington statue. I could not catch any balls hit more than an inch or two to either side of me for the rest of the game.

We won that day and quite a few other days, but not nearly enough to satisfy our promoters. When the Legends played hockey, they won 99 percent of their matches. The softball team achieved victory little more than half the time. The promoters thought we could do better and called me in to ask how we could improve the club.

"I know this might sound crazy," I told them, "but instead of putting hockey players on your softball team, why not try stocking it with baseball players?"

Now there was an idea. The promoters put me in charge and we invited former major leaguers such as Tony Oliva, Rico Carty, Ferguson Jenkins, Willie Wilson, and Rick Miller to join the club. I insisted on retaining Hull. Bobby was a top-notch softball player, and besides, I didn't want to lose his services until we had that cognac-drinking thing down. Luckily for both us, I am a slow learner.

13

BABES IN THE WOODS

Not all California males grow up longing to be surfer boys. Oh, I do love the ocean, but prick me with a pin and you will discover river water flowing through my veins. Whenever some team I play for visits a town near a river, I make it a point to rise just before dawn to walk alongside its currents. In many places, I arrive so early water from the evening tides still covers the paths alongside the banks. As this water recedes, its continual rise and fall creates the impression that the river breathes. And, of course, it does.

My grandfather Paul Hunt passed on this love for streams. He owned a farm on the Stanislaus tributary of the San Joaquin River near Sacramento, California. Granddad taught me to fish those waters soon after I learned to walk. Most of the time, we used poles, but he also showed me how to improvise when rod and reel were unavailable.

First we filled the bottom of a fishing net with salmon and trout heads. My grandfather would attach a rusted wagon wheel rim to the net to weight it down. We dropped the contraption into the water. A large cork at the top of the net kept its four corners open and suspended so any passing fish could easily enter. Grandfather would have me tie one end of string around the cork. Then he would fashion a miniature lasso out of the other end and loop it around the neck of the empty Clorox jug we floated on the river's surface as a marker. We would leave the net there unattended and go off to fish at some other spot.

To a crawdad, a succulent crustacean that resembles a midget lobster, few meals are more alluring than a pile of fresh fish heads. When we retrieved our net at the end of the day, we frequently found as many as fifty crawdaddies chowing down on their meal.

My family would enjoy a crawdad boil that night. Mom cooked them in a big pot of water with nothing more to spice them than some salt and pepper and Old Bay seasoning. Once they were done, she peeled the crawdads and tossed them in a salad. Eating so good, I still carry the memory of it on the front of my tongue.

My grandfather died some years back. I fish today as a way of staying in touch with him. I'm not much for headstones, and life is too short to waste time indulging nostalgia. But I believe that if you do a thing taught to you with love, the teacher never leaves you. That is not a rod my fingers fold around as I stand at the river's edge—it's my grandfather's hand.

So when the All-Star Baseball Legends pulled into Prince George early one March morning in 1998 for a charity softball game against the local fire department, my nose immediately led me the nearest waterway. Prince George is a British Columbia hamlet located at the confluence of the Frazier and Nechako Rivers.

Clear water feeds the Nechako—we could see straight down to the bottom where it ran deepest—while the Frazier resembles flowing chalk. The two streams mingling produced a color reminiscent of milk of magnesia. We did not notice any crawdads waiting to be trapped in these waters, but several local fishermen told me the river teemed with salmon.

I learned something of the town's history from them. Prince George had once thrived as a lumber town, a place where over five thousand loggers plied their trade. Those men had chosen to settle here as a matter of convenience. They transported the trees they cut by floating them downstream to the local sawmills, but the logs would wedge against each other as the rivers converged and narrowed. So the loggers decided to save time and manpower; they processed the logs where they halted. A few entrepreneurs built large mills near the silty riverbanks, and a community bloomed.

Prince George's fortunes have risen and fallen with the timber market ever since. From the 1950s right up through the

1970s, when peddling timber for profit represented one hard dollar, the town declined into a sort of honky-tonk, with a lot of beer-and-shot bars and strip joints lining the few main thoroughfares.

When we got there, though, it showed all the signs of becoming a modern village. Gentrification had smoothed the town's rougher edges; the new businesses that had opened were strictly Main Street, with a lot of upscale coffee shops, boutiques, and souvenir stores. However, when a town's economy depends so much on one product, the vagaries of the market determine the pace of progress. The tariff the United States imposes on Canadian softwoods had wounded Prince George's economy and hampered investment.

Weather conditions had also slowed any further building. Prince George lies tucked between the Rockies and the Pacific Coast range at a point far north of Vancouver. Winter temperatures regularly plunged to twenty below. Developers and construction crews prefer to tear down and build in warm weather, but you will not find much summer in these parts. The climate offers maybe six hot days a year, and we were lucky enough to be there for two of them.

Rob Myers, the local fire chief, coached the team the Legends competed against that weekend. He stood in front of his station waiting as our bus arrived. From the look of him, Rob would have made a first-class Navy Seal. He was medium height and broad-shouldered, not heavily muscled, but lean and silver-dollar hard. In his dark dress blues, burnished brass buttons, and squared-off chief's hat, he could have stepped off a horse-drawn fire engine from a nineteenth-century daguerreotype.

Rob sounded tickled to be hosting a group of former major-league baseball players. John Tudor, Bert Campaneris, Rick Miller, and Willie Wilson played on our team and he wanted us all happy. The moment Rob learned of my fondness for fishing, he offered to lend his four-by-four to Ferguson Jenkins and me for an afternoon of chasing salmon.

If you follow baseball at all, you probably know all about Fergie. He is that tall, lanky right-hander, a Hall of Famer who pitched from 1965 to 1983 for the Philadelphia Phillies, Chicago Cubs, Texas Rangers, and Boston Red Sox. Bob Gibson, the St. Louis Cardinals ace and arguably the best pitcher of my era, once named Jenkins his toughest opponent. Fergie probably had the best control of any power pitcher who ever toed a rubber. During his big-league career, he walked fewer than two men every nine innings. Fergie could locate pitches with such precision, Gibson said he was the only pitcher he had ever faced who never gave a batter a good pitch to hit.

Before we left, the chief told us the area's lushest fishing holes were set back deep in the forest. To get there, Fergie and I had to rumble out of town over a gravel logging road with potholes so wide in parts you could lose a Volkswagen in them.

We followed a rushing stream filled with spawning salmon for about forty-five minutes. You could actually see the fish, their golden pink skins flashing metallic in the sunlight, skimming the water as they struggled against the current. We also caught glimpses of a few bears and foxes foraging in the dense woods. But none of these scavengers looked any bigger than cubs; they didn't carry enough size to frighten anyone.

We drove until we reached the largest clear-cut in the world, a gap in the forest so wide it appears on most satellite imagery.

The townsfolk had no desire to destroy the woods that had once shaded miles of fertile land, but they had no choice. An infestation of spruce budworms had ravaged acres upon acres of trees. A spruce budworm is one hag of a critter, olive brown and mottled with two spots, sickly white as fungus, on either side of its torso. These pests defoliate acres of strong timber with all the thoroughness of Agent Orange. A spruce budworm will bore so deeply into a tree, all of the sap will run right out of it. After dining on the bark, the budworm uses the tree's needles to floss. The wood quickly dries until all you have left is a tinderbox. A fire had already claimed one section of this forest. The townspeople had to harvest the remaining trees for lumber or risk losing them entirely. It saddened me, the thought of all that beautiful scenery being reduced to ash.

Fergie and I drove past the wreckage and followed a side road to a bridge that a flood had recently washed out. We arrived at the mouth of the stream, a place where, according to one fisherman we met near the fire station, the salmon would jump into your bag without you even nudging them. Fergie parked close to the riverbank, and we unpacked our gear.

The place had a prehistoric feel with its downed, nearly petrified trees and its cloying stink of rotting vegetation. Shattered boulders and splintered logs, remnants left by the river's hard-driving currents, jutted from the water. We immediately saw some forty-pounders flopping against the tide, but I knew they would not be interested in anything dangling from our lines. Large salmon and humans share at least one common trait: when they are set on spawning, no bait will deter them. Even if you attach a live fly, a salmon's favorite delicacy, to your hook and jiggle it in front of them, they will not waste a glance on it. We decided to try catching some smaller silver salmon, the midget chinooks that trail spawning fish upstream hoping to devour their roe.

Fergie chose to fly-fish that afternoon. That is a delicate art. Fergie would have to cast three or four times before throwing out his lines. He had to exercise supreme patience. The key for any fly caster is how slowly he can lead that fly over the water. The idea is to simulate the movement of a live insect struggling against the grip of the stream. I lacked the touch for that.

My preference is to bait a hook with whatever I find at hand, drop it in the water, and wait for the fish to discover us. I considered using a roe sack, a powerful lure albeit hardly a choice for anyone squeamish. To assemble one, you must first find a pregnant female salmon and strip the roe out of her— either push down on her belly to force out the eggs or slice her open to reach the roe cluster. You tie up the eggs in a tight little cheesecloth bag and hook it to your line. The pungent aroma pouring out of that sack will open the nose on any buck fish in the vicinity. Salmon and trout will shoulder each other aside to reach those roe.

Constructing roe sacks is time-consuming. Fergie reminded me that we were playing a game that evening, so I instead baited my line with a grub, one of the cattus fly larvae that attach themselves to the bottoms of streamside rocks. If you want to use grubs for bait, you must collect the larvae before they hatch. Breaking open the cocoon releases a pupa with the tentacles of a miniature squid. Those long legs are what attract a fish's attention. With a little practice, a seasoned fisherman can get a grub to sink low in promising waters with just a little split shot on a fly line.

We fished for hours with only a few bites, but it was so re-laxing neither of us cared. In the solitude of all that green with the water whispering fast over the rocks, the aspen leaves fluttering in the wind, and your focus tight on your line, time stops. You can live forever on a good day's fishing. In that sense, it is a lot like baseball.

I had just started to move upstream a piece when, out of the corner of my eye, I saw a shadow streak behind me. I spun in its direction but saw nothing there. My attention returned to the salmon. Another shadow lumbered behind us, this time closer to the riverbank. The hackles rose on my neck, and I could actually hear a voice in my head saying, *Don't make any sudden moves. There is a goddamned bear walking through the slash.*

We should have known. Black bears will take a hunk out of you, but they are primarily omnivores who love eating grass, berries, and nuts. When you have a slash in a forest such as the one we were fishing near, blueberries, raspberries, and huckle-berries flourish. And with the trees no longer blocking the sun or drawing nutrients from the ground, the grass was free to go crazy. This made it an inviting place for any hungry bear.

I didn't dare shout a warning to Fergie. Instead, I slowly reeled in my line while walking toward him. He stood about a quarter mile further downriver than I, with the truck parked on the road between us. Fergie was fishing his hole so intently he had not seen or heard anything. I quietly tapped his shoul-der. When we both turned around, there he stood, nearly seven feet and a quarter ton of black bear blocking the middle of the road, just looking at us as if we had intruded on his picnic.

That bear stood just as near to our truck as we did. All we carried for weapons were our fishing poles. Canadian wildlife laws prohibited us from packing firearms to ward off any dangerous animals. The rules did permit us to pack pepper spray, which was fine if you faced a particularly vicious squirrel or jackrabbit. A full-grown black bear considers pepper spray a condiment. He will douse his victims with it just to add some spice before eating them.

Most people think of grizzly bears as the most dangerous members of their species. But, given the choice, I would rather go toe-to-toe with a grizzly over a black bear anytime. The grizzly might maul you a bit, but he will more often than not smack you into your grave with one quick swipe of his paw or let you run away.

Black bears? Well, they seldom work expeditiously. Oh, they will kill you as well, but they don't do it all at once. First they want to play with you. A black bear will slowly swat your body shapeless and chew on you for cud over several days. Once you pass on, he will roll in you as if you were dog shit. Now, I've read the works of Joseph Campbell, and animal rituals fascinate me. But this was one rite of passage I definitely was not eager to participate in.

Neither was Fergie. "Walk to the truck slowly," he whispered. "Don't make any sudden moves. We won't start running unless the bear does." Sound advice from the Hall of Famer. Black bears are plodding creatures, but they do this plodding on four legs, so they can cover short distances as fast as an average human sprinter. Once they get going, these bears can motor at about 30 miles an hour. They also don't tire quickly. Your car might run out of gas before they do.

Besides being quick, these animals are smart. If you shoot a black bear on a grade above you, he will drop into a ball and roll down at a violent speed until he's on top of you. When that occurs, you become dough for the rolling pin. They do have one weakness, though. Black bears cannot run diagonally on the side of anything slanted. They can race uphill or downhill in a straight line, but never sideways. Get them zigzagging on a steep grade and their legs tangle. But our bear glared at us from a road as flat as an airport runway.

Fergie led me toward the truck one slow step at a time. That bear stood stock still. Only his head moved, a lazy greased turret, as his eyes followed our retreat. Risen to full height on his hind legs, he resembled Darth Vader on a bad hair day. I tiptoed, too scared to draw a breath. Images flashed through my mind: my children racing through a field with arms outstretched to greet me . . . an early fall purple sun setting over Fenway's Green Monster . . . Nicole Kidman writhing on satin sheets . . . my grandfather teaching me to track and shoot quail . . . the buttercream smoothness of my first baseball glove . . . Nicole Kidman writhing on satin sheets . . . the birth wail of my youngest child . . . all that nervous sweat sopping my uniform during my first major-league appearance . . . Carl Yastrzemski loping back on a fly ball as if he were tracking it with a homing device . . . Nicole Kidman . . .

We got maybe ten feet from our truck when the bear let rip a terrifying roar from deep in its gut. That sucker sounded hungry. As soon as Fergie and I heard him bellow, we dropped our rods and hauled ass. My heart pushed so much blood into my head, I felt top-heavy enough to tip over. To comfort myself, I kept repeating as a mantra some advice a forest ranger had once passed on to me: if a bear is chasing you and a companion, you don't have to outrun the bear, you only have to outrun your friend.

My chances in a footrace against Mr. Jenkins rated pretty high, but I could not take advantage of him. I consider Fergie my brother, and I would have lost sleep—at least a whole night's worth—had the bear caught him instead of me. So we ran in step together and reached the four-by-four just barely ahead of the beast. It was so close at the finish line, I swear that animal's claws breezed past my collar as I hurtled through the car door. We drove without looking back, so I have no idea when the bear gave up the chase.

By the time we rolled into town, Fergie had regained his composure. Now I know how he could throw strikes over a plate the size of a quarter with the bases loaded. The man was just born to be cool, I guess. Not me. My adrenaline had jolted my nervous system. The incident left me so pumped, I smacked three home runs against the firemen that night, the only time I have done that in any game not played with a Wiffle ball.

On second thought, maybe something more than adrenaline added all that muscle. Native Americans place great stock in bear power. They believe that a black bear's spirit can inhabit human form and imbue it with the strength to accomplish heroic feats. This is one river rat who has just enough faith in woodland lore to think that a bit of that black bear's spirit might have passed into me during our encounter. Maybe Fergie and I will visit him again should we ever play another game in Prince George.

If we do, we will arrive bearing gifts for the bear god. We

will also insist that Jon Warden tag along. Jon, a former major leaguer who pitched for the Detroit Tigers, is the All-Stars Legends' catcher. He is great company on any outing, a witty raconteur, a good drinking buddy, and a man who knows how to stay calm in tight situations.

And he possesses one more important attribute: with his build, roly if not actually poly, Jon is at least four steps slower than Fergie.

14

A MAD DASH TO CUBA

One morning in November 1999 Cy Peterson called my house to make one of those offers you can never refuse. Cy headed the loggers' union in Vancouver and served as my catcher with the Spy Hill Canucks. He was tall and flinty, 220 rugged pounds, a social-ist with intense, friendly eyes, deaf in one ear from all the years spent working under the din of chain saws. He and his friend

Tom Robertson had asked members of the National Men's Senior Baseball League to accompany them on a tour of Cuba. The squad would play five games against Cuban senior teams with the idea of promoting friendship first, competition second. They offered me a round-trip ticket with all expenses paid.

Cy had visited Cuba many times and knew the country well. "Just show up with your uniform," he advised me, "Bring a bat, glove, spikes, and as many balls as you can carry. They don't have much equipment down there. Bring a lot of dollar bills, too. You will need them for tips. And be sure to stash a twenty-dollar bill somewhere. That's how much it will cost to process your exit visa. You can't get off the island without it."

Hmm, that sounded ominous. You had to pay customs officials $15 to enter Cuba, but they charged you $5 more to leave? Made me wonder what would happen if you could not produce that sawbuck. Cuban officials probably packed you off to shovel chicken shit in some commune. That did not appeal to me. I preach socialism fluently until the time comes when I actually have to participate in it. Still, the idea of competing against some of Cuba's legendary baseball stars—said to be the best over-fifty players in the world—provided an irresistible lure. I stapled the $20 to the last page of my passport.

Of course, getting out of Cuba would probably not prove as difficult as getting in. As we write this, it is still illegal to travel to the island from the U.S. without State Department approval, something the agency rarely grants. I had already agreed to join members of the 1975 Boston Red Sox for an autograph signing at the Foxwoods Resort in Connecticut on the night before the Cuban series opened. I planned to drive from there up to Dorval Airport in Montreal to catch a direct flight to Havana.

The event ended early enough for me to make my plane with time to spare, except it took the organizers forever to cut our checks and autograph hounds kept besieging us to sign "just one more." When we finally exited Foxwoods, a vicious winter storm percolated outside with swirling winds so powerful, big-wheel trucks rocked on their suspensions in the parking lot. I jumped in my Nissan Pathfinder and opened my travel kit to make sure I had everything before pulling out. Toothbrush, yes . . . comb, yes . . . shaver, yes . . . nail file, yes . . . roach clip, yes . . . passport . . . now how could that have happened?

The reason friends and neighbors in Craftsbury, Vermont, call me Half Cocked is that I always forget something. But for this trip, I had taken the precaution of putting my passport in plain sight on a table near the front door of my home. There is no way I could walk out of the place without noticing it. Unless I left through the kitchen.

All right, I figured, Craftsbury was on my way. Sort of. Veering off the route to retrieve the passport would add only forty-five minutes to my seven-hour trip. Plus I had no choice—there was no leaving without it. So I drove the Pathfinder quickly on roads that already glistened under black ice. Bridgestone had constructed my tires to laugh at treacherous conditions, but they fumbled to get a grip on this frozen highway. A wall of glass would offer more friction.

Riding through the blizzard, I reminded myself not to get cocky. When you can no longer hear your tires racing over the road, you must tread lightly. Stay alert. Keep your car's weight centered. No sudden movements. Do not brake abruptly and, once you are up to cruising speed, do not accelerate. I maintained sixty-five miles per hour, just fast enough to stay ahead of the storm.

The snow fell so thickly it looked like polar bears dropping from the sky. I could see no more than six feet in front of me as the four-wheel-drive slipped from side to side. Nevertheless, the Pathfinder crossed the Vermont border so far ahead of schedule, my flight seemed a lock. Then I saw them. All those rows of creeping red lights, cars backed up for a solid mile.

My car snaked through the traffic jam. I drove along the breakdown lane, passing vehicles until I pulled behind two semis. Everything halted. Those big trucks in front of me had slowed to a squat, blocked by a Crown Vic highway patrol cruiser that had suddenly lurched across the road.

I jumped out of the Pathfinder and approached the cruiser to ask how long this delay might last. Two troopers sat in the front seat of the Ford, a cardboard takeout tray containing three cups of coffee fresh from some diner perched between them.

I drew closer. The cruiser's coffee-steamed window silently glided down. I could see the driver was one of those hard cases. He looked as pale and hollow-cheeked as a cadaver with dark, Dennis Hopper eyes: a no-nonsense squint tinged with the mania of someone peaking after a forty-eight-hour caffeine binge. One look at him sent shudders deep through my soul. I thought I had uncovered the whereabouts of that third gunman from Dealey Plaza. "What the hell do you want sneaking over here like that," he asked in a drill instructor's emphatic cadence.

I had seen his sort before in army boot camp, bullet-happy bastards who got their jollies firing live ammo over the heads of raw recruits shitting their pants as they crawled through the parade ground mud. The slight heft to his right shoulder indicated that the fingers of his gun hand had already coiled around the butt end of a pistol. All that good police training had left this trooper leery of surprise. I raised my hands chest high so he could see I traveled unarmed and answered, "Well, to tell you the truth, I wondered if you had any plans for that extra cup of java?"

That witty repartee—the best I could do considering the late hour and the inclement conditions—dropped his jaw. He bristled, "Oh, yeah, wiseass? And just who the hell do you think you are?"

"My name is Bill Lee, and I live in Craftsbury. Can you tell me how quickly you can get these lanes cleared? I have to catch a flight in Montreal."

His partner perked up at the mention of my name. This was just a kid, the eternal sidekick, so porcine he resembled a rump roast with a mouth slit under a button nose and a pair of Mr. Potato Head eyes. The outline of a meager goatee and the slick oily sheen on his cheeks indicated that his hormones were still Mexican jumping beans slamdancing to some insatiable carnal rhythm. I even detected a hint of Bazooka bubble gum on his breath when he leaned over to scrutinize my face.

"Dear god," he told his grim partner, "that really is Bill Lee." Ah, a stroke of luck. This member of Vermont's finest had rooted for the Red Sox since he had worn diapers. As soon as I explained my situation, the troopers got out to wave both trucks to the side of the road. In a country obsessed with all things famous, even semicelebrity retained its perks.

With the lane cleared, I prepared to gun the Pathfinder and vamoose. But Trooper Drill Sergeant warned me not to move. "You're asking for trouble if you leave now," he said while pointing up the steep highway leading to the road home. "There are cars and trucks jackknifed all along that incline. A snowplow will be here in a few minutes. You can follow him up. It will be a lot safer."

Fifteen minutes passed. I nudged my ears into that frigid wind, hoping to hear the snowplow's comforting rumble in the distance. Nothing but wind whistling. Now I began to feel antsy. The two officers sat back in the cruiser, still sipping their coffee. It occurred to me that if they believed the road too dangerous to travel until the snowplows did their work, neither of them would be eager to follow if I just took off. Which is exactly what I did.

I shifted into third gear and stayed there to keep the weight of the Pathfinder bearing down on the front wheels. This created just enough torque to scramble up the highway grade. My vehicle morphed into a pinball slithering between all the fallen vans, trucks, and trailers.

One minute into the ride, a screaming red light slashed across my rearview mirror. *Oh, fuh-uck*, I thought. *All this deep snow has just turned into deep shit.* I figured the troopers had decided to take up the chase after all. From the rear of my vehicle came a muted thump, the sound of the cruiser's bumper kissing my Pathfinder's ass while that crazed driver drew a bead on me with his Dirty Harry magnum.

But, no, it was all freeze frame when I glanced back. That

cruiser remained parked near the rest stop. The young patrolman stood alongside it, scratching his head as he watched this
demented son of a bitch drive balls out on some clandestine
mission that was obviously too vital to national interests for
even the elements to delay.

Lickety split, I moved up the grade to level ground and
found the whole highway rolled out white in front of me—
buried under more than half a foot of snow, it's true, but without a single vehicle upon it. Clearly, no one else was insane or
wired enough to risk this drive. This did not deter me. Space-
men cruise in where angels fear to tread.

After stopping off at Craftsbury, I broke speed records to
reach Dorval Airport just in time for my departure, only to
learn that the airline had canceled the flight. I spent the next
half hour cobbling together an alternative plan. Mixing and
matching the schedules of several rogue carriers produced an
itinerary. First I had to drive twenty miles north to Mirabel
International Airport. From there, I could fly direct to Mexico
City, catch a shuttle to Cancun for a brief layover, and continue to Havana on Mexicali Air.

I had to avoid any delay getting through customs. My
flights practically piggybacked on each other. Luckily, the
Mexico City customs officials took a casual approach to their
work. As soon as my fellow passengers and I got off the plane,
they herded us into a bar near the main terminal where we
waited to be checked through. I sat in a booth, draining a mug
of beer while reading a book. I forget the name of that novel,
but the plot must have engrossed me. I never heard anyone
call us to the checkpoint. When I finally looked up, the passengers and the custom officials had left.

I scrambled outside and found an information booth. The woman in charge told me the next flight to Cancun would leave in twenty minutes. Shortly after touching down in that city, I found a man who sold Havana visas for $15. With my visa in hand, I could roam all over Mexico, ready to fly into a Communist country without anyone vetting me a single time.

I could have smuggled in a dirty bomb or some other nuclear device. Who would have known? In the pre-9/11 world, security professionals in many countries approached their jobs so casually, it was no wonder terrorists could travel the globe with impunity. Mexican customs officials scrutinized your luggage only if they suspected you of dealing drugs. But when you brought drugs into Mexico City, you were sneaking sand into the desert. Whenever the *federales* caught anyone with pot or cocaine crossing their border, they would slap the dumb bastard upside the head and say, "You're going the wrong way."

As our plane approached the Havana airport, we noticed that the landing strip was not quite as modern as what we were accustomed to in the States. No lights. Okay, I exaggerate. We did see lights, but together they cast about as much illumination as a single 30-watt bulb. The runway resembled an ancient chariot race course with all its ruts, cracks, and potholes. Our plane, a small DC-9, stutter-stepped as its wheels scraped the ground.

Going through Cuban customs offered us a surrealistic experience. Custom officials enacted a ritual as soon as they learned I lived in the United States. First they stamped my visa and handed me an identification card. Then they mimed stamping my passport. No kidding—the stamp never touched a page, so they left no record of my having entered the country. Castro had ordered this procedure. He did not want any visiting Americans to get into trouble with their government for evading the travel restrictions.

We waited a long time at the luggage carousel for our bags. The windshield for a '57 Chevy spun out first, followed by four slightly balding white wall tires, a wounded transmission held intact with duct tape and copper wire, four more frayed tires sans white walls, a grease-caked muffler sporting a large dent, a peeling chrome bumper, a twisted carburetor and a box of vintage spark plugs wrapped in rubber bands and twine. I figured someone was bringing in parts to fix Fidel's car.

Two Cultural Department attachés greeted me in the waiting lounge. We rode off in their new Saab, a vehicle that passed for a Rolls-Royce in that part of the world. The clock glowing in the dashboard read nearly midnight. Not a car on the modern, immaculate three-lane road. With Ruben Blades and Tito Puente blasting from the stereo, I sat in the backseat popping open bottles of Cerveza Cristal, Cuba's most popular beer, from an ice-filled cooler. My companions peppered me with questions about American baseball: How hard did Roger Clemens throw? Was Tony Gwynn as good a hitter as Tony Oliva? Could Luis Tiant really smoke a cigar in a shower without getting the tobacco wet?

Our Saab traveled the 150 kilometers to a mountain town called Vinales in under ninety minutes, but I measured the distance in six-packs. We reached our destination only after the two Cuban attachés and I had consumed so many bottles of Cerveza Cristal, my jaw had numbed. You could have used a hand grenade to extract all my teeth without applying any other anesthesia. I would not have felt a thing.

A spectral moon beamed over Vinales, a secluded spot surrounded by limestone cliffs overlooking a thriving green valley. My hotel appeared as quaint and homey as a bed-and-breakfast inn, but the designers had built it on eccentric angles that closely followed the rolling contours of the hill it sat on. Either that or the hotel was about to slide from its moorings. Someone later told me that a group of Cuban army engineers had constructed the place. My guess is they had used prefab materials to produce a building they could quickly dismantle in case G. Gordon Liddy ever convinced Pat Robertson to finance another Bay of Pigs invasion.

My memory of checking in remains sketchy. After so many beers, an elemental homing device automatically activates to lead me through any alcoholic haze to some safe port. I do recollect waking up early the next morning to a rural paradise.

This part of Cuba could have passed for Craftsbury, Vermont. A cooling sea mist hung over the valley, silent at six a.m. except for the peal of oxen bells. From my window, I saw a Cuban farmer, his face shadowed beneath a sombrero, plowing his field with a team of oxen. A bright winged parrot perched on the back of one beast. Anytime the farmer wanted the oxen to change direction, he released a machine gun splatter of Spanish that made me think of a football quarterback calling audibles. Whatever he said was unintelligible to human ears, but the animals understood and immediately altered their course.

Chickens, tomcats, and black pigs ran wild over the grounds like a squad of drunken USC freshmen gone amok on their first panty raid. The air smelled brisk and sweet, with the fragrance of morning glories masking the gamy underscent of fresh tobacco.

The first rays of the morning sun dazzled me. I had never seen a light quite this luminous, with a color so indescribable it seemed part of a mutant spectrum. As it crept into my room, everything suddenly became starker, more alive. I imagined the furniture had started breathing. My bed and armoire were damn near pulsating. I could not tell if the sunlight had miraculously animated these lifeless objects or if the pure environment had simply hoisted my consciousness to some higher plane.

Then again, perhaps it was nothing more than those psychedelic mushrooms I had ingested while listening to my first Jimi Hendrix album, finally kicking back on me. It sure did look like the sixties in there.

15

THE ROAD THROUGH VINALES

fter waking to the thrilling sight of the Cuban countryside, I stumbled back to bed, still woozy from all those toxic Cristals consumed the night before. Slept so late, my ride to our first game arrived and then left when no one could rouse me from bed.

Cristals will do that to you. The Cuban brew trickles down your gullet smoothly, with no more initial kick than an unusually potent Sprite. Don't let that fool you. Imbibe two six-packs of the stuff and you marinate your gray matter in formaldehyde. When I finally stumbled into the lobby, our concierge offered to call a cab. I declined. Throughout my baseball career, I have maintained a ritual of walking or jogging to whatever stadium my team played in. It's my way of getting a feel for a town, to see how it is laid out, and to meet its people.

A bellhop kindly scribbled directions to the ballpark on a napkin. "Just follow the stream outside," he said, "and you will reach the center of town in half an hour." I took to the road resembling an overgrown Huck Finn, with my baseball cap on backward and a glove dangling from the bat slung over my shoulder.

The concierge had not prepared me for such an arduous hike. That stream flowed beside a dirt walking path for only a few hundred yards before turning into a large overgrown pasture smelling of alfalfa and mildew that proved as easy to negotiate as a minefield. I had to dodge livestock, leap over steaming cow patties, elude wild dog packs, and crawl under barbed wire fences for a good mile or so before reaching the bridge that crossed into urban Vinales.

I dragged myself into the ballpark just in time for the top of the second inning. Our team was playing Pinar del Dio, the newly crowned Occidental League senior champions. Eight hundred diehards sat in the rickety wooden stands, and they cheered our opposing team's pitcher as if he were a matador poised for the kill. His name was Lazlo, and he had once reigned as Cuba's premier power arm, a pitcher who in his heyday could match 100-mph fastballs with Nolan Ryan.

Lazlo was fifty-five years old and carried 240 solid pounds on his six-foot-four frame. His pitching mechanics looked perfect. At the start of his delivery, Lazlo lifted his left foot up until all his weight rested on his right leg. He pushed off the mound toward home plate while his right arm buggy-whipped straight over the top. A long, balanced stride kept his hips down low to the ground, loading his entire mass behind every pitch he threw.

You do not need a radar gun to know if someone is throwing hard. Your ears will tell you. A catcher's mitt emits a flaccid, spongy thump when it receives a pitch light on velocity. A high-caliber fastball, though, will make tough leather scream. I had heard the whack of Lazlo's pitches from outside the ballpark and immediately knew we were in trouble.

Lazlo served his nasty stuff to one of the most gifted catchers any of us had ever seen. This receiver—I never did learn his name—displayed such perfect balance, he could crouch on the very tips of his toes while warming up his pitchers and catch their heaviest tosses without the slightest recoil. His reflexes appeared so sharp, his feet so quick, he would pounce on bunts and come out of the chute throwing to nail runners at second. Base stealers looked helpless against him. The catcher could throw line drives to second from his knees while hardly bringing his arm back. Just a flick of the wrist would send the ball zipping across the diamond. Of course, we knew that only from watching him throw the ball around the infield. Our team put so few runners on base, we seldom found the opportunity to challenge his arm.

None of us could tell whether the catcher called a good game. There was nothing tricky about his pitch selection.

He just let Lazlo rear back to deliver a fastball that appeared smooth and straight as it approached the plate, a real hitter's pitch—until it suddenly swerved late six inches or more to either side. Lazlo brought it home at 86 miles per hour, real heat when you are facing a squad of mid-life weekend warriors. To our aged eyes, he looked as if he could throw dawn past a rooster.

Somehow, though, we pecked away—a bleeder here, a dunk base hit there—to take a 2–1 lead after five innings. Tom Robertson pitched for our side, and he kept the Cubans close. In his younger days, Tom had been a top prospect with the Vancouver Mounties in the Pacific Coast League. He knew how to bear down in clutch situations. Pinar had runners on base in every inning, but Tom slipped out of trouble with a nifty changeup that continually threw those Cuban hitters off balance.

Tom pitched so well, so fluidly, I was stunned when Cy tabbed me to relieve him in the bottom of the sixth. *Sweet Jesus,* I thought, *what madness is this?* My teammates were hoping for a save from someone who had arrived at the park with less than three hours sleep and the previous night's brews still foaming through his gut. I wrote in a previous chapter how pitching with a hangover frequently improved my performance. Trouble was, I had not yet reached the hangover stage; my brain still floated in pickle brine. And, boy, did it show on the mound. Within only a few minutes, all my pitches turned to mud. My breaking ball would not break, my sinker would not sink, my fast ball would not fast . . . oh, it was ugly!

Pinar tallied eight runs on twelve hits before I could retire the side, and they inflicted all this damage with third-rate bats constructed of inferior wood wrapped in masking tape. Baseball equipment comes at a premium in Cuba. We saw young boys near our hotel climb up trees to scrape the sap from the bark and shape it into baseballs for their games of catch. Entire teams might share only one or two vintage bats, a single pair of batting gloves, and a lone batting helmet.

The carnage might have been worse. Pinar battered us bloody even though their best hitter stayed out of the lineup. I had seen Luis Casanova play for the Cuban national team in Parma, Italy, six years earlier. At six foot six and 260 pounds, the right-handed-hitting outfielder resembled Roberto Clemente on steroids, a brutish slugger so strong, no ballpark in Cuba could contain his soaring blows.

Casanova cut an imposing figure in the batter's box. He towered over home plate with most of his weight hovering above his rear foot and his upper torso cocked so far back, the bat head rested on his left shoulder. Whenever a pitch crossed into his hitting zone, he rotated his upper body at the hips and brought all his weight forward in one smooth, ferocious motion that produced a perfectly balanced swing with just enough uppercut to hit the ball for great distance.

During the Parma game, Casanova hit a 440-foot line-drive home run to right center. In his very next at-bat, he smacked another 440-foot bomb to left center. Such awesome power to all fields can render even the most confident pitchers into cowering sops. Lucky for us, Casanova declined to take the field against us once he saw our ineptness. He just sat on his team's bench, sadly shaking his head at our feeble, lunging swings. This served as an excellent example of Cuban sportsmanship. Our opponents did not mind shoveling dirt on our grave, but they refrained from pissing on it.

My afternoon quickly settled into a dull routine: throw the

ball and race over to back up third after some slugger creamed yet another fence-rattling longball. Yes, my pitching reeked, but the line score would have been less unsightly if our defense had not broken down. Cuba's tropical climate extracted a toll from us gringos. The heat proved so debilitating that by the fifth inning it looked as though our team had manned every position with cardboard cutouts.

Except cutouts would have exhibited more range. I suspect Castro used us that afternoon as guinea pigs to test the efficacy of some new secret weapon, a Russian crab grass that wrapped around our ankles and held us fast. We ran after balls as if our legs had taken root. With better D behind me, the Cubans could not have scored so often that inning. They would have plated no more than six, seven runs, tops.

My only highlight for the day came during my first at bat against Lazlo. With the count 0–2, I reminded myself to swing early—to simply guess where Lazlo's next pitch might cross the plate—and smoked a one-hop double off the wall. That was the loudest ball our team hit all day, and it came as a consequence of nothing more than dumb luck. I had closed my eyes before making contact; it was just pray and swing.

Once our team fell far behind, Pinar showed us the killer instinct that marks all championship teams. Instead of sending in a mop-up pitcher to finish the game and offer us some chance of scoring a face-saving run or two, the opposing manager brought in the lethal weapon he had hidden in his bullpen.

The right-hander slowly strode onto the field with the hurry of a lazy monarch accustomed to making his subjects wait. On the afternoon he took the mound against us, ace reliever

Porfirio Perez was sixty-five years old, a tall, light-skinned, angular Cuban with long, dark curly hair, a lopsided grin, and satanic eyes that made him resemble a crazed Mozart. He did not have an ounce of fat on him.

He also apparently didn't have any bones or joints. Pinar fans knew Perez as "the Man of 100 Moves" and it was not just because he was rumored to maintain two wives with two separate families on opposite ends of the island. The first time I saw him wind up, he resembled an octopus unfolding from a coil. Except this octopus changed his form at will. On one pitch, he mimicked El Duque Hernandez with his 'scuse-me-while-I-stick-my-toe-through-my-forehead leg kick. With his very next offering, though, he might bow deep below his waist, bob up, and throw à la Mike Mussina. Or he could rear back to drive his legs down low while coming straight over the top. Greg Maddux to the life.

Flexibility stood out as his primary strength. While delivering a pitch, Porfirio could stretch his leg up toward the sun, throw the ball over his shoulder, catch it with his bare hand behind his back in mid-windup, then deliver a strike to the plate. Read that one more time. It is an impossible move for anyone else to execute, yet this senior citizen performed that routine on top of a double windup.

Tracking Porfirio's pitches called for radar. The challenge for hitters is to read the pitch, gauge its velocity, and anticipate where it will cross home plate. To do this accurately, they must quickly identify a pitcher's release slot. Where does he let go of the ball? But Porfirio had more slots than a mail room; you never had any idea where his next pitch might come from. When I faced him, he spun on the mound like a corkscrew, hid the ball behind one knee, and shot it out of his ass. Or at least that is how it appeared.

Porfirio's graceful ballet on the diamond mesmerized our lineup. We couldn't smell a hit out there. His pitches veered so eccentrically, some of our hitters grumbled that he threw a spitball.

But I recognized Perez as one of those mescaline-eating sages Carlos Castenada wrote about, and knew he was simply teleporting his pitches through thought control. How else to explain my first at bat against him, when the umpire called a strike on a pitch I never even saw? The ball rested in Perez's hand for a split second, disappeared from sight, and poof! it magically rematerialized in the catcher's mitt.

The pitcher displayed all these marvels with an economy of effort that awed our entire team. Porfirio seemingly never threw hard. He just flipped his pitches through the fissures separating space from time. Perez fooled me with one changeup so tardy, it felt as though I took six hacks at the ball while it levitated in front of home plate. Not one of them connected, and the bat ended up wrapped around my ankles. We could not score a run against him.

Porfirio pitched so impressively that afternoon, we enlisted him for our team when we returned to Cuba two years later. That did not work out well. Perez had lost all his velocity by that time, and the Cuban hitters had grown so accustomed to his gyrations, he couldn't bamboozle any of them. They tagged him whenever he came into a game. We still intended to let him finish the tour, he was such a charming guy. Could listen to him talk all night about the great Cuban ballplayers he had pitched against. Sad to say, we had to release him after our first baseman caught Porfirio taking equipment from the team bus.

That was the day we discovered he was really the man of 101 moves.

Perez and Lazlo were not the only pitchers to buzzsaw our lumber that day. Our swings against that pair looked so inept, the Pinar third base coach—a small man well past seventy—inserted himself into the game and tossed two innings. He couldn't equal the speed of his mound predecessors, but he threw his great breaking ball and a heady assortment of junk with pinpoint accuracy. His changeup arrived at home plate light as a spinach leaf; you had to supply all the power to hit it for any distance. The coach moved the ball around on us, altering speeds with each succeeding pitch slower than the one before it. Just when we started timing him, he would rip a 70 mph fastball inside on us that looked like 90 for the contrast. The man was a pitcher.

Pinar won that afternoon, 9–2. The result mildly discouraged us. We should have declared a holiday. As things turned out, that loss would be our best performance on this brief tour. We dropped every game we played against organized teams by a combined score of 76–9. One club drubbed us 15–0.

Those one-sided defeats convinced me and my teammates that everyone in Cuba can hit a baseball. Kids born on that island must emerge from the womb toting fungo bats, a good reason why the attending doctors or midwives never smack them on the rump. The Cuban hitters bludgeoned everything I threw. Even grandmothers jumped out of the stands to rock a few doubles. Our lone victory came when we beat a squad composed entirely of employees from our hotel in a pickup game. Yes, we bullied them 11–3, but we did not want to leave the island winless. And they got their revenge. None of us saw a clean sheet for the rest of our stay.

Aside from the drubbing they inflicted on us, the Pinar players acted as gracious hosts. Paramedics remained on hand in their ballpark throughout the afternoon in case anyone suffered an injury—they forgot to bring bandages for our pride—and the team even assigned several nurses to massage us on our bench while the game progressed.

In our dugout, a Pinar coach hung a papier-mâché figure of the Santeria god Chango, his bulbous torso clad in a baseball uniform. Someone on our team stuck a miniature cigar in the grinning mouth of Chango's large ebony head and slung yellow prayer beads around its neck. Our hitters kissed it for luck whenever they went up to the batter's box. Obviously, this ritual didn't help. Pinar's players also chipped in to supply us with a top-shelf spread of food after the game as well as coolers filled with beer, sangria, and soft drinks. Their generosity humbled us; the average Cuban earned about $17 a month.

We reciprocated by treating our opponents to a banquet at a local resort. Our tables creaked under the weight of all the dishes: platters heaped with sausages and cheeses; deep-fried marinated pork dripping with a peppery red sauce so hot it made your nose run; grilled citrus chicken pungent with garlic; and huachinango à la veracruzana, pan-fried red snapper dressed in a salsa of minced onion, capers, tomatoes, olives, and pickled jalapeños and served on a bed of rice. A treat so delicious it makes me hungry just to read the name.

Despite the succulent entrees, the most popular item on our menu for the Cuban players was the cold beer that arrived at their tables in frosted mugs. Many deprived neighborhoods on the island lacked reliable refrigeration. One waiter told me that some friends of his operated the local black market for ice, but I think he was kidding. Would not surprise me, though.

The Cuban players we partied with displayed an uninhibited physicality among themselves. They greeted each other with powerful bears hugs and kisses, and their laughter emerged from someplace deep within them. Everyone I spoke with stayed completely in the moment, listening intently. When the salsa band opened their set, the American men waited until they stepped on the dance floor before they started dancing, and most of them seemed awkward and self conscious, as if they found little comfort in their own skins. But the Cuban men danced at their tables—sometimes *on* the tables—and moved their bodies with the abandon of Gypsies. My teammates and I had rhythm and none of us stumbled over our feet, but compared to the Pinar players, we each resembled Al Gore trying to get jiggy to some hip-hop groove.

About an hour before the banquet ended, I left to walk back to the hotel with Jake Robertson, Tom's eleven-year-old son. This was my first opportunity to learn how the town was laid out. The narrow sidewalks in the older section of Vinales looked barely wide enough to allow pedestrians to walk side by side. Most people in this village lived in attached buildings of peeling stucco in hues that had undoubtedly looked vibrant long ago but had since faded into dreary pastels of pinks and blues swirling into each other. These simple, boxy structures had shops on the ground floors and residential apartments above. Pigs, chickens, and goats scurried in and out of the stores and sauntered down the avenue browsing the windows.

Billboards along the cobblestone streets trumpeted the glories of Castro's revolution and incendiary graffiti splashed across the walls of many of the buildings. We paused to watch two young artists paint one fence with some slogan for or against Fidel—my Spanish is limited—and they wielded their brushes like machetes, posting their message in angry, slashing red and black strokes.

We could not walk far before encountering reminders that Cuba still ranks as the cigar capital of the world. On one block, an elderly woman sat in front of a bodega rolling cigars, a ten-inch stogie hanging from her lips. Passersby smiled at you with a mouthful of fractured teeth tinted dark by nicotine. Teenagers chewing blunts congregated on every street corner.

Nothing smells like a Cuban cigar store, an aroma acrid but sweet and utterly masculine. If you are trying to quit smoking, shops such as these should never appear on your itinerary. The products sold in these stores smelled straight-off-the-farm fresh; workers finished them on the premises. Shops that catered to tourists sold these smokes for $20 apiece, but in these bodegas you could buy ten cigars of the same quality for a buck. The price discrepancy offered an example of the two marketplaces that coexisted in Cuba, one for the monied foreign visitors, another for the impoverished locals.

In the back room of one store, three women worked at a wooden table. A compressed block layered with tobacco lay in front of the first woman. She rolled the leaves while the woman next to her trimmed them into cigar shapes. The third worker applied the cigar's final wrap, a large high-grade tobacco leaf, before rounding off its tip with an implement that resembled a miniature scythe honed razor sharp.

Some tourists asked the workers to pose for pictures. The women happily agreed but insisted on receiving a gratuity. The teenage girl who cut the cigars was pregnant and she patted her swollen stomach while explaining that the coins were not for her but "for the bambino." With the economy so thin, most Cubans constantly hustled in the best sense of the word. Nearly everyone on this island worked two jobs and cottage industries that attracted extra cash abounded.

Throughout Vinales, Jake and I saw people selling home-made products, mostly clothes such as white cotton blouses, floral print dresses, hand-stained leather belts, and rope san-dals. One vendor hawked baseball bats. He could not afford the lathe artisans traditionally use to mold their bats, so he carved each one by hand. Most of the bats came out too short, the handles too wide, to be useful to any hitter. He fashioned his product from a wood so porous, the bat barrel swerved into an eccentric angle after only a few good whacks. Hardly anyone patronized his little stand.

The sculptor who worked a few doors down enjoyed greater success. He stood behind a table covered with examples of his expert craftsmanship: miniatures of Cadillacs, Chevys, and baseball players which he fashioned out of papier mâché swathed in bright acrylics. These merchants gave the street all the color and air of an exotic flea market. But then I saw a dark side to this underground economy as we passed one alleyway: the teenage girls, with eyes as empty as their bellies, who sold themselves to any man for the price of a sandwich.

As we neared the edge of town, cobblestone gave way to asphalt. We followed this road past the only modern housing in all of Vinales: soulless white cinderblock tenements with peeling faux stucco siding crowded against each other in an industrial-age ghetto, the remnants of the Russian presence on this island.

So much urban drab depressed me but we did not have to

walk much further before it surrendered to the lavender twilight of the countryside. Here we discovered wondrous sights that I had missed while taking that shortcut into town.

In a field to the side of the road, children harvested tobacco, laying it to dry on the aluminum roofs of sheds while cattle bellowed in the near distance. Overhead, the last rays of a fading sun reflected off the quartz shards embedded in the limestone cliffs, transforming dead rock into a magic mountain of glittering jewels.

We passed immaculate clapboard homes with trim gardens set behind white picket fences. Built for single families, they housed twelve or more people. These soon gave way to more primitive housing, huts with palm frond roofs and no glass in the window frames. The owners had elevated the huts to keep them above the damp ground. Their roofs featured unusually long overhangs that prevented the rain from splashing inside. I wondered how anyone could live in one of these houses in cold weather before remembering that Cuba does not have winter.

The asphalt turned sinuous as we moved deeper into the country, a road of small valleys and peaks. Engineers had constructed a chine up the middle of the road as a rain runoff so that it resembled one long black ribbon of continual speed bumps. Your car did not race over the lanes so much as surge. Drive more than 35 mph on it and you risked becoming airborne.

Some Cuban bureaucrat had designated the road for two-way traffic. This official was obviously a city dweller whose phobia of pig manure had prevented him from ever setting foot in these parts. Unless he thought people around here used skateboards to travel. Pavers had left the road so slender that when two small cars came down opposite lanes simultaneously, one had to pull over to the shoulder to let the other pass.

And more than cars clogged this thoroughfare. The road pulsed with life. Jake and I walked behind a farmer leading a flock of billy goats with chickens straggling behind; a cart loaded with damaged furniture an enterprising young man had plucked for resale from the Vinales garbage bins; an elderly man pushing a wheelbarrow filled with tobacco; merchants moving their sacks of spices and other wares on the backs of mules; and large extended families, their arms linked and their voices raised in song, out for their evening stroll. Despite the congestion, you never heard a single car horn honk. No one rushed, no one pushed to get ahead. It looked like the road of the unhurried. The anti-autobahn.

We even saw a camel. No, not the kind that Lawrence of Arabia once rode. *Camel* is the name locals have bestowed on a kind of bus, a double-decker flatbed hauled by a semitruck. It can carry as many as three hundred passengers—a microcosm of Cuban working-class society—and all of them must stand, packed so close that you could faint without dropping to the floor.

Directly behind the camel, a man in overalls and sombrero drove another vehicle you rarely see anywhere else in the world: a horse-drawn cart with a heavy bench nailed to each side to form a pair of wings. Passengers for this funky, primitive taxi sat on those benches six abreast, their fingers clinging to the underside so they would not be jostled off, their feet dangling only inches above the asphalt. The driver did not need a meter to calculate the fare; his passengers paid him in produce.

Two hours into our walk, we stopped at the side of the road

where we found a sack of discarded tobacco. I taught Jake how to clip it and separate the seeds. An old, heavyset woman came running from her home, little more than a shack with a tin roof. She looked any age with her brush of coarse iron gray hair pulled into a bun, her snaggletoothed smile, battered muslin shift smudged with grease, and a face so seamed she could have hidden rainwater in its folds.

We understood enough of each other's language to communicate. Her four-year-old grandson had seen us walking up the road from the living room window and wanted to meet the tall gringo. But when we entered her home, we did not see him anywhere. I thought the boy had left until Jake noticed a frightened pair of large, brown eyes peering out from behind a chair.

After much coaxing he emerged from his hiding place and stood next to his grandmother without saying a word. A shy, fragile little boy, all boney angles and naked except for a pair of ratty briefs that looked a size too large. We sat in a sparsely furnished room without carpeting of any kind, just the dirt floor that was such a common sight in rural Cuba. That floor fascinated me. I expected it to be dusty, but the constant humidity caked down the soil and just walking over it kept the floor packed tight. Our hostess could not afford indoor plumbing.

The woman brought us out back to see her garbage disposal: a pen of pigs feasting on that evening's leftovers. She apologized for having nothing left to offer us. Then something caught her eye. Midway up a wizened tree in the rear of her yard hung a ripe guava, the last piece of fruit on these branches. She grabbed a broomstick and brought it down with a few strong pokes. Then she folded the guava into my hand to thank us for our visit.

When you play major league baseball, people frequently give you things, sometimes of substantial material value. But no gift I have ever received could be more precious than this piece of fruit passed to me with love by a stranger who owned so very little.

We hugged each other goodbye long and hard. Before Jake and I got much further down the road, our team bus pulled over to pick us up. I sat huddled in the back, too moved to speak to anyone. No one could guarantee we would ever play baseball in Cuba again once this tour ended. But as I bit into the pink, sugar-laden flesh of that guava and its syrupy juice ran into the salty tears trickling down my chin, my heart told me I would return to Vinales.

16

THE PREACHER BLOWS A SAVE IN LANDISBURG

August 2001. Rural Pennsylvania is a place that invites you to get lost. Local maps offer no warning of this. They fail to indicate how the landscape is composed of a series of valleys, each one an exact replica of the other. As soon as you cross over the first ridge after Harrisburg, you are traveling through the Appalachians. Here, the old trails tend to run northeast to southwest, so you had better be headed that way as well.

You can drive for some distance without seeing a single house or person. Stop near the edge of a forest and you might hear the rustle of creatures foraging in the distance. Actual sightings, though, are rare. The deer and other woodland animals in this region prefer staying hidden. Nothing moves. Even the tree leaves and branches refuse to let the wind sway them. You are driving through a still life.

Suddenly, you pull up to a large, bustling farm at the center of a junction. Men bellow against the roar of tractors and the diesel fuel fouls the air. Don't let this glimpse of civilization and commerce mislead you. You won't find a single landmark to pinpoint your location.

What will you find instead? More roads. Roads without signs or billboards. Forked roads with only a coin flip to help you choose between them. Roads that lure you deep into the countryside before abruptly halting in a dead end or a graveled yard guarded by a frothing mastiff. Curlicue roads that stretch on for miles only to turn in on themselves, so if you stop paying attention, you keep returning to the place where you started. This terrain can confuse the most hardened survivalist.

My six-year-old daughter Anna and I had been driving for hours around Landisburg, Pennsylvania, and its outskirts, searching for a baseball field. Anna wanted me to stop and request help, but I resisted. You have probably heard how many men loathe asking for directions; that's a cliché, I know, but, it happens to be true. Asking betrays the code. Our genetic code.

Modern males have evolved from hunter-gatherers who eschewed maps, choosing instead to read the stars or observe which side moss grows on a tree to plot their courses. Honor demands that their descendants maintain this innate sense for where they are at all times. A real guy cannot betray his heritage, particularly in front of his youngest daughter, just because he made a wrong turn.

And I didn't see any reason why a dedicated New Age back-woodsman like me should. Not at first. Whenever I am lost, primordial instinct spontaneously takes over. My nose turns wolfen to sniff out the tracks that will lead to our destination, while my eyes become an ancient radar ferreting out lost trails or hidden paths even in the dark.

However, after a decade of sinus abuse—can't even begin to imagine what noxious powders are permanently impacted in those cavities—I found my nose could barely pick up the down-wind scent of a manure spreader only a few yards up the road. We had to ask a passing postman to show us the way to Brad Shover's Doubleday Field.

He pointed down a two-lane blacktop. "Less than two miles up this road," he assured us in a scratchy, singsong voice. "It's just past the Mennonite farm. You slow down and cross the bridge over the Sherman River. Shover's farm is on the other side, tucked up against a ridge."

We followed that road straight through Pennsylvania farm country: ceramic silos hiding under shadows, grain brushing against the wind, the sun glaring off injured chrome, men in coveralls riding tractors and mopping the sweat from their foreheads with speckled bandanas, the perfume of grain mingled with turpentine. Midway through our drive, Anna pointed out the car window. "Daddy," she yelled, "see over there! It's not morning anymore, but that horse is still sleeping in the field. Look how funny his legs look." I slowed to find out what she was referring to and saw four brown legs, dappled white at the hooves, standing upright as poles in the middle of an uncut hayfield.

Horseflies near big as hummingbirds, the kind of flies that don't merely bite but can actually rend bits of flesh from your arm, flitted around the animal's haunches. I noticed a flicker of movement but no hard muscle behind it, just a light breeze gently shifting those limbs. Daddy had to explain that this critter was sleeping, all right, sleeping for an eternity. He appeared to be as dead as King Tut.

This struck me as a bad omen. Brad Shover had offered me $2,500 to pitch that weekend. I figured that after paying such a high fee, he just might feel entitled to work my arm the way someone had worked that stiffened nag.

About a mile further down, though, any apprehension I harbored disappeared. Just the sight of Brad's diamond in the rough sold me. This gentleman obviously loved the game. He had plowed over a thriving corn field to build a dazzling miniballpark with old-fashioned klieg lighting on creosote basted telephone poles, two cozy wooden dugouts, and a backstop featuring a high screen topped by old fishing nets to contain foul pops.

Beyond the outfield fence loomed a hitting background that would delight any major leaguer—the Appalachian Mountains dense with lush, green maples the color of mint jelly. As a bonus, anyone retrieving a home run ball hit just beyond that fence could help themselves to a free snack of wild berries that flourished in a large untended patch. Anna and I visited there after every batting practice, not to gorge ourselves on the fruit, which tasted sweeter than any candy. No, we went because there is something sad about a baseball left abandoned to rot in the damp. It is an image I just cannot abide.

Off to the first base side of the diamond, fans gathered on a grassy knoll to barbecue hot dogs, hamburgers, potatoes, and corn. They sat in the stands catching up with one another or set up lawn chairs on a berm overlooking the field. Most of these people were locals, as many as two hundred of them, gathered to cheer on their friends and family in the big game. One elderly man in farmer's coveralls, his back stooped from a lifetime of bending in fields, proudly passed around a gnarly potato the size of a mature eggplant, a mutant spud he might have acquired from a roadside stand on Mars.

There was nothing homogeneous about these crowds. Their clothes told you that. We saw backslapping executives and their assistants in khaki shorts and pastel golf shirts, their arms in permanent crooks from too many gatherings spent holding cold beers in front of their sliding paunches. Soldiers had driven over from their barracks in Carlisle to watch some baseball and flirt. Just a glimpse of their wiry frames, bulging biceps, and burr cuts turned the knees of the local teenage girls liquid.

Some of the guys who worked for a tool and die company in Lancaster tried to outdo the soldiers by flaunting their own brawn in sleeveless tie-dyed T-shirts topping baggy camouflage pants. When you spoke to these boys, they looked through you with faraway eyes from underneath battered New York Yankees hats. Young wives, almost all of them in jeans and tank tops or midriffs, chased after giggling children, their faces already smudged with chocolate, mustard, and dirt, as they darted across the field.

The men and women who belonged to the Harrisburg banking set flashed yuppie chic in their Ralph Lauren jeans, Donna Karan tees, and stylishly scuffed Kenneth Cole loafers. Anyone dressing down wore spotless Nikes or Adidases. A brand-name crowd.

You could easily spot the car dealers from Harrisburg. Nearly all of them wore polyester double knits and heavy gold necklaces. Good people, every one of them. Quick to laugh, especially at themselves, and generous, the sort of men who would argue long and loud with each other for the right to pick up a check.

These car dealers had come to the field to have fun; winning was a secondary consideration. They brought along two elderly pitchers who, if you put their best fastballs together, could produce one good changeup. A catcher warmed up both of them wearing little more than a Kleenex on his business hand. But they let the seniors play and no one cared how many runs it cost them.

Spectators parked their cars near an old, sun-baked barn where the teams dressed for battle. Players emerged from behind the building's doors like a troupe of swaggering Shoeless Joe Jacksons, sporting turn-of-the-century collarless flannel uniforms with raglan sleeves. Across their chests, a seamstress had emblazoned DOUBLEDAY in either black on gray for the visiting team or black on white for the home nine. Only the handlebar mustaches were missing.

The talk buzzing through the crowd was the talk I frequently heard at similar outings across the United States. These people casually spoke of illness and death, business deals and debt; of soap opera plots and Oprah guests, store openings and foreclosures, doctors' visits and home repairs; of appliance sales and insurance costs, schoolwork and rebellious children, local politics and village bake-offs; of babies born and babies expected, the rising cost of living and the declining respect for family values; of celebrity gossip, infidelities, and divorce; of recipes and movies seen and books read and all the other everyday items that make up such a vibrant part of the vast American distraction.

Shover had set up a small concession stand, really nothing more than a well-maintained shack with a galvanized tin roof, just behind the first base dugout. He had even erected a TV platform on one side of the building for the ESPN crew that never showed up. Someone had used a penknife to notch a series of numbers into the platform planks: ⊦⊦⊦⊦ ⋯ ⊦⊦⊦⊦ ⋯ and so on up to forty-five. Either this person had recorded someone's low pitch count or the marks represented the runs for one high-scoring game.

Brad kept his grounds crew equipment and two small refrigerators stocked with soda pop and frankfurters inside that stand. He crossed the field to shake hands as soon as he saw me. Brad was a slightly balding man of average height and athletic build, as lean and corded as a sprinter. His nose was peeling, and every inch of skin that his clothing did not cover glowed red. Hard to believe he had ever spent a day indoors.

After greeting me, Brad appeared to be everywhere, a one-man grounds crew, trimming the grass, laying down chalk along the baselines, dragging the infield, setting the bases, fixing the mound, and lining up the batter's box. He even threw batting practice to both sides and umpired every game.

A PA system played music throughout the afternoon. We

heard Dan Fogarty's "Centerfield," Terry Cashman's "Willie, Mickey and the Duke," and several renditions of "Take Me Out to the Ballgame." Brad even slipped on a tape of Abbott and Costello performing their famous "Who's On First" routine. Real mainstream fare, which did not surprise me. This was Arlen Specter's turf, Republicans mostly, and these people had generally conservative tastes. You would not hear too many requests for the Goo Goo Dolls or Busta Rhymes in this part of the country.

It all seemed so ideal, Norman Rockwell could have been standing off to the side capturing the scene on canvas. Except my fears about that omen proved correct. Brad was one great guy—Tug McGraw, who had pitched for him the year before, had told me you could not find anyone with more respect for the game. A successful entrepreneur, he had started this business more out of a love for baseball than any longing for profit.

That said, he expected to fetch back a large return on that $2,500 investment. That first afternoon he had me pitch a complete game between two teams from local towns. Or rather, he had me pitch two complete games; I stayed on the mound for both sides. It would go on that way for most of the weekend.

I saw the irony in this arrangement. Throughout my professional career I had railed against the designated hitter, that symbol for baseball's age of the specialist. That was Buckminster Fuller's influence exerting itself. I had once heard Mr. Fuller declare that all forms of specialization bred extinction, a theory that struck me as one of the great universal truths.

Yet here I was the designated pitcher, doomed to stay on the mound till the final inning, never allowed to take my turn at the plate. The ultimate one-dimensional chucker. I not only pitched for both sides that day, I ended up notching sixty-four innings by the time Sunday evening rolled around. Neither Bartolo Colon nor Curt Schilling, the closest things this generation has to the workhorse pitchers of yesteryear, throws that many frames in an average month.

How did my arm survive the strain? Wasn't easy. The physical abuse was bad enough, but pitching that much in such a short time can batter your brain as well as your arm. To do it successfully, you must possess the emotional makeup of someone who likes to repeatedly hit himself in the thumb with a ping hammer. I'm not masochistic. So to meet this challenge I transformed myself from a pitcher into a master actor from the Japanese Noh theater. Every gesture I made on the mound that weekend assumed significance; any waste in my motion vanished.

Coping required me to first force my mind to go blank as slate. I had to completely reformat my hard drive. I mentally transported myself to another place. A Wal-Mart in Akron, Ohio. I rolled my shopping cart down the canned-goods aisle, somewhere near the cutlery and notions departments, searching for Cheez Whiz and Slim Jims at a discount. Those images worked on me like the hypnosis a dentist drilling a root canal might employ in lieu of anesthesia.

My only baseball thought focused on the first pitch. And after I delivered that, every next pitch became the first pitch. The thermometer read 96 degrees, humid enough to grow orchids. That sun wasn't dispensing any healing warmth, either, you know the kind that swathes a weary body through a day of heavy work. No, it was one badass coach gone frenzied with a bullwhip, lashing our backs out on the field. Had someone tossed me a bar of Irish Spring, I could have bathed in my own sweat.

Under conditions that grueling, your environment becomes as daunting an opponent as any hitter. Something I learned pitching in the hellish climes of Venezuela. Sucking in too much air too slowly and too deeply will sear your lungs. But if your breaths race too fast and shallow, you risk hyperventilating. Only a middle course will do. So my body acclimated to the surroundings. I remembered something the great sensei Suzuki wrote in *Zen Mind, Beginner's Mind*: concentrate on your exhale. My breathing turned rhythmic and measured, slowing my heartbeat and dropping my body temperature.

Once I established relative comfort, my concentration turned to minimizing all effort. When you face major-league hitters, one pitch sets up the next. For example, even in my youthful prime, the Bill Lee fastball was never torrid enough for anyone to refer to it as a heater. But I might buzz two semi-hard ones deep inside the kitchen of a slugger like Reggie Jackson—so far in there, Number 44 could never put good wood on them—just to back him off the plate a hair. Once Reggie started looking inside, setting himself to cream any pitch that traveled in that zone, I would drop a changeup over the outside corner to catch him off balance. If he tried pulling that ball, I would have a lazy pop-up or a grounder, maybe even a strikeout if Reggie came to work that day juiced and overeager.

That is the only way to attack a dangerous professional slugger. When you confront a lineup of amateur hitters, though, your approach radically changes. The whole idea in that situation is to avoid setting up anyone. Waste six or seven pitches on each batter when you are throwing to both sides and you will have nothing to pitch with come the fourth inning but a blood-dripping nub. So the strategy for this game arrived out of need: I would give the hitter the optimal opportunity to fail by seducing him into thinking he could succeed.

This required me to be a quick study. Before the game started, I stood near the batters' cage watching the players from both sides take their cuts. Want to know what a hitter looks for at the plate? Examine his stance. Watch how he sets his feet. Observe what kind of pitches he lustily offers at and which he lets pass or swings at with indifference. Combine all your data and try to intuit the type of pitch he likes to whale. Then use his strength to destroy him.

Before I could do that, I had to persuade each hitter to swing as early in the count as possible. So the first time through the lineup I allowed nothing but "show 'em" at bats. I started each batter with a sinking fastball over the plate. If he took it and tried thinking along with me, he would look in a different location on the next pitch. So he got a second fastball, same spot. Once the count reached two strikes, I became the executioner. The batter received a nasty 12 to 6 curveball. Strike three.

That pitch made a psychological impact. Once those hitters realized they could not touch my major-league-quality bender, they eagerly swung at the first straight pitch no matter where I put it. This greatly reduced my workload while allowing me the opportunity to get inside the batter's head.

For instance, that afternoon one outfielder came to the plate with the left-handed stance of Jason Giambi: coiled, aggressive, seething with testosterone. A classic low-ball hitter who obviously loved the roar he heard from the stands whenever he pulled a pitch for distance. Singles seemed an affront to him. If he slapped something to the opposite field for one base—a dandy piece of platework—he acted as though he wanted to give back the hit.

Every time this slugger faced me, I fed him that low pitch he favored. Or, at least, that's what the batter thought he was getting. In reality, I was just groundhogging the man, throwing him hard sinkers that rolled toward the plate fat and sassy. It probably looked to him as if some artisan had tattooed a HIT ME sign in neon across the horsehide. Afterward he swore to everyone that the pitch darted right through his wheelhouse. But as he swung, that sucker just kept burrowing out of his zone. He could do nothing else but top the ball to my second baseman for an easy out.

During his next at bat, he looked for that same ball down and in. He didn't realize I had already adjusted to his bat speed. The pitch did arrive in on him, but belt high at his hands, a little quicker than he expected. He could not possibly get the sweet spot of his bat on that ball. *Crack!* Nothing but a slow two-hopper back to the mound. Another quick out.

High-ball lovers saw choked-off sinkers down the middle, pitches they couldn't elevate. With the better hitters, I took a touch off the fastball to catch them swinging with their weight leaning forward. Pop-up city. If a batter wanted the ball in, he got a cutter buzzing the bat handle out of his hands.

Funny thing about that pitch. When I played in the majors,

I didn't have enough velocity to throw it with any confidence. But in 1995, Montreal Expos team doctor Larry Coughlin performed an operation that shortened the tendons in my left shoulder and increased my arm strength. So now I could break a bat in two when the ball collided with the right spot.

If someone wanted the ball outside, my pitch acted as the proverbial carrot, just barely within reach. Unless a hitter owned retractable arms, he would cue that ball off the end of the bat down to the third baseman. Should he pull it, our shortstop got a chance to show off his throwing arm.

I came at both lineups with different speeds, never full bore, putting each pitch in a place where they could hit it but seldom smack it square. And while I worked the strike zone, I also played with the hitters' egos, exploited their anxieties. No one had to explain the deal to me. I arrived on this field as the "pro from Dover," the former big-leaguer. I knew what each of these hitters wanted from this game more than any win: the chance to go home and tell everyone how they had cracked a long ball off that loony left-hander who had once played with the Red Sox. So I threw slop-drop curves they thought they could yakatow into the seats. They flailed at those pitches with back-breaking swings that produced nothing more than big can of corns to the centerfielder.

Everyone in Doubleday Field thought I was pitching. Nope. I was shelling out three-card monte on the diamond, working this flim-flam so well that at one point I recorded eight consecutive outs on two pitches. Or at least it seemed that way, the at bats flew by so fast. I threw about 320 pitches in the sixty-four innings I worked over the weekend. Sounds like a lot, huh? But when you do the math, you can see I paced myself, rarely exceeding seven pitches in any one inning. More than once it took only three tosses to retire the side.

I played God in every game, the ultimate puppet master manipulating the strings, and the feeling of power, damn near omnipotence, intoxicated me. I was never good enough to experience that on the major-league level. My one rule was not to bully any opponent, not to take advantage of their amateurish skills by burying them with breaking balls. No pleasure in that. If a team fell too far behind, I let up and allowed it to score a few runs to get back into the game. Yet I always left the winning run up for grabs. A team had to earn it. The idea was to make sure everyone had fun. Nevertheless, if I thought you acted a bit too cocky, you went down on three quick strikes. Hey, last time we checked, I do have an ego.

We played a doubleheader the Thursday I arrived. In between games, a man came out of the stands to introduce himself. Said his name was Jeremiah, and it would be. You could see he had spent his life working outdoors. He was flat-faced, as if the wind had eroded his profile. His eyes were set close together and grooved at the sides from too many days spent squinting in the sun. When Jeremiah clasped my hand in a firm grip, I noticed his fingers: bronzed, squared-tipped, and streaked with nicotine stains dark as bittersweet chocolate. They felt as if a sculptor had hewn them from granite. Farmer's hands.

Pain had drawn Jeremiah to me. At one point during the first game, someone took pity and finally allowed me to take a turn at the plate. I hit a line drive off the wall that should have been a double, but all that pitching had exhausted me. I had to stop at first after taking a wide turn. As I stepped back toward the bag, my daughter darted out from the crowd to leap into my arms. "I love you, Daddy," Anna said as she planted a kiss on my cheek.

Suddenly you had this funny picture of a middle-age man standing on first base unable to see second for all the tears in his eyes. Only five weeks before, my wife had taken Anna and the furniture and moved out of our house. Pam left behind only a letter from a lawyer I didn't know she had engaged. Can't say that I blamed her. Many professional athletes are self-centered. Our livelihoods depend on our bodies, so we obsess over every twinge, cramp, or hangnail. That sort of narcissism does not make for a well-rounded individual. No doubt it made me difficult to live with.

Yet after Pam gave birth to Anna, I immediately changed. Our daughter was cute and tiny, so very much *there*. When she looked at you, her eyes said nothing else existed but that moment. Anna was so magical, I surrendered my adolescence at forty-eight. No more late hours. The smoking and carousing stopped. I devoted myself to her. Once, after appearing at a fantasy camp in Florida, I drove twenty straight hours up to Craftsbury just to return in time to watch her wake up that morning. Nothing gave me a greater kick.

When I came home to find my wife had taken Anna without writing where they had gone or when I would see them again, my lungs stopped pumping. Something sucked the oxygen out of that empty house until there was nothing to breathe. My stomach roared into my throat. I doubled over retching and crawled off to bed.

Or at least I would have crawled off to bed, but Pam had taken that too.

I spent the next month wasting away. Drinking again, smoking again. Thirty pounds slid off me so fast, people mistook me for the victim of a flesh-eating virus. My guess is that I eventually would have evaporated, but, soon as I agreed to a divorce, Pam and her lawyer relented and allowed me to see our daughter. Coming to Landisburg was our first trip together with me as a single parent.

Jeremiah had observed my anguish as well as my joy in that moment when Anna planted her lips on my face. Turned out he had recently endured his own divorce, so he understood the anguish a father feels when he can watch his child grow up only in intervals. We talked beneath the shade of a tree overlooking a piebald hummock on the side of the field. He had a gentle, almost somber look to him as I explained how my wife had left.

But before too long, Jeremiah's eyes took on a different cast. Flame suddenly imbued them with the merry, blazing gaze of a plastic dashboard Jesus. Turned out that when he was not tending his farm, Jeremiah moonlighted as a country minister. Not a Pentecostal, mind you, but a true believer nonetheless. No one who saw him could doubt his conviction, though he did exude the air of a reformed alcoholic. All the telltale signs were present—he chain-smoked filterless Camels and consumed one diet Coke after another.

I have seen this many times before. Addicts must replace their addictions with other opiates, be it smoking, body building, cybercruising, game shows, gambling, raw sex . . . anything that can substitute for their habit. So they never truly lose their compulsions, they simply take up more benign ones . . . such as playing baseball 250 days of the year.

Jeremiah mentioned that his farm was just down the road. When I told him I had three hours off between games, he invited Anna and me to go fishing in a pond on his property. Once there, we could see that Jeremiah was no man of means. The only building on his property was a forlorn, weathered barn. He did not own a farmhouse. He lived year-round in an aging though well-tended trailer.

No sooner had Jeremiah's hook splunked through the water than that pond turned into his pulpit. "Do you read the Bible, Bill?" he asked in a matter-of-fact way, just as if he were asking what color shoes I wore.

Forget whatever catches hid near that muddy bottom. Jeremiah was fishing for my immortal soul. Touching as that was, I pitied him. He had decided to come at me with the old soft sell, apparently thinking that my pain would make my conversion a slam dunk.

A mistake. Hurting or not, I am the sort of person from whom veteran Seventh Day Adventists run uphill through fire after only a minute of conversation. Certainly all of the god squadders I had met in the major leagues considered me beyond saving. While playing with the Montreal Expos in 1981, I woke up in the trainers' room after being out all night long as well as a good part of the morning. What a view to greet the new day: I opened my eyes to seven Expos' asses on the bench directly above me, sitting through a prayer service led by our catcher, Gary Carter.

I rolled out from under the bench as quietly as possible, hoping to sneak out a side door without being noticed. Soon

as my teammates saw me, they insisted I take a seat. They had
waited for this all season—an opportunity to save the prodigal
pitcher.

But as the players stepped closer, their noses crinkled. Stay
out from dusk until past dawn, crawling through the darkest
alleys of the Montreal netherworld, there is bound to be an
unmistakable aroma about you. The moment Gary Carter
caught one whiff of my breath, smelling of Johnnie Walker
Black and last night's redhead, any thoughts of redemption
fled.

"Maybe it would be best," he said, "if you just go off to the
showers."

Gary understood his pitcher. He knew these Expos for Jesus
didn't have enough resources to deliver me to salvation. We
were playing a single a game that afternoon; there wasn't
enough time to perform any miracles. Converting me would
require a day-night doubleheader with a lengthy rain delay.

Don't misunderstand. My mind is open, and I am willing to
let you persuade me on almost any subject. Nevertheless, I rate
time as a more valuable currency than money, and if you
expect me to spend mine, you had better deliver a full return
on my entertainment dollar. Anybody who wants me born
again must come prepared. Be ready to multiply loaves and
fishes, speak in tongues, and transform water into wine. Show
me a thousand angels poised on the head of a pin. Appear
before me as a burning bush. Make my six-foot-four frame
pass through the eye of a needle. I want to see you break dancing for Christ.

Jeremiah had no idea he was dealing with one of Satan's
frontline troops. At first he was delighted to learn that I had

indeed read the good book. To jostle my memory, he quoted New Testament passages, all of them referring to sins of pride. "You tend to strut a bit out on the mound," he said, "as if you think you're better than anyone else on the field."

Sure I strutted. I *was* better than anyone else out there, and I knew it. None of those players had ever played professional ball. Why, the Grand Canyon does not stretch out as wide as the gap between a professional ballplayer and an amateur.

But, hell, I had spent my entire adult life as a pitcher. No one had to give me any lessons in being humble. I told Jeremiah, "You will not find anyone more familiar with humility than a guy who has given up three-run homers on line drives so stiff you could hang your wash on them. Spend an afternoon in front of forty thousand jeering fans getting undressed by Reggie Jackson, Mike Schmidt, Dave Winfield, Johnny Bench, or any of those other sluggers I faced in the big leagues and you'll carry enough humble with you to last until the Third Coming and beyond."

My vehemence on the subject backed off Jeremiah a half step but no more. He decided on another tack. "All right, Bill," he said, "perhaps a lesson in humility isn't what you need. But I know you feel sorry for yourself. Do you understand how we are all responsible for what happens to us, the good as well as the bad? We reap what we sow. Do you remember reading about the twelve plagues that God visited on Israel after the people turned their backs on him?"

Uh-oh. He had just allowed me my opening. I said, "Look, God didn't visit anything on anybody. All that happened was that the Nile simply overflowed, just like it usually did that time of year."

"But," Jeremiah countered, "the waters turned to blood and a great pestilence descended on the land." His voice was shaking now. "Thousands died in excruciating pain."

"No," I calmly replied, "the rising Nile merely colored crimson after the swirling currents mixed together the red sand, silt, and dead fish. And that pestilence? After the floodwaters washed through the town, they left piles of dead frogs, which attracted armies of flies and mosquitoes. That illness they spread wasn't any plague; it was just an early form of West Nile disease. Nothing divine to it, just the natural order of existence at work."

Jeremiah remained undeterred. Back and forth we debated, bashing each other toe-to-toe, substituting rhetoric for right crosses. He jabbed me with every spiritual point he could muster, quoting chapter and verse from both testaments, and I counterpunched with biological and metaphysical data. Jeremiah talked about the seven-day creation; I lectured him on the evidence paleontologists had unearthed to prove that life had evolved in a quagmire over 4.5 billion years.

To his credit, Jeremiah hung in much longer than anyone else who had ever tried to save me. But after two hours of head-butting discourse, he conceded, at least for this afternoon. Jeremiah mournfully shook his head, placed his hands on my shoulders, and whispered, "You are going to have to go through an awful reckoning before you find yourself back in the arms of God. Can't you believe that Jesus Christ is the only answer?"

"Only if you are responding to someone who just reminded you that George Bush is actually our president, and even then it must be followed by an exclamation point."

That did it. Jeremiah packed his gear, threw it in his car, and drove off. We waited awhile, but he never did come back. I do have that effect on people. My stubborn irreverence had so ruffled Jeremiah, he had forgotten we were fishing on his own property.

17

VERMONT TALES

My girlfriend, Diana, and I live in a half-way house in Crafts-bury, Vermont. It sits halfway between the bars in Montreal and the bars in Boston. Constructed the place myself—well, myself and about twenty close friends under the guidance of master builder Lyle Raymond, but it feels all mine. Like a child I helped create. I even relate to my home as if it were human. When the plumbing breaks down or the heat fails to come on, I talk to it, and what I whisper in its eaves is, "I'm going to sell you, you son of a bitch."

The house does not mind. It knows I never mean it.

I worked on nearly every inch of this building. A contractor named Billy Bolton took me on as an apprentice and taught me everything I needed to know, from working with Sheetrock to cutting wooden frames. Only the foundation escaped my touch. It takes experts to pour concrete. I hired the Bradleys, a father-son team—two tobacco-chewing, cigarette-smoking deer hunters who worked the job with the carriage of Marine grunts. Toughest people I've ever known. These men could stalk out of slippery mud holes carrying ninety pounds of plywood on each shoulder and never come close to stumbling. Shake their bare hands, you'd swear they were wearing monkey paws, the flesh felt so cracked, the bones so thick and gnarled.

A day with them and the rest of the crew on the construction site wore on me much harder than any day on the mound. I have thrown over a thousand cut fastballs and sliders throughout my career without once experiencing a sore wrist, but I developed carpal tunnel syndrome laying down the white pine floors that wind through my home. Could not get on top of my sinker for nearly a year after that. It was worth it, though. I remember sitting in my kitchen the day after we finished and thinking how great the place looked. But I knew something was missing. Was it the warmth that only an old house can exude? No, it was the basement door. I had forgotten to install one. I walked outside to go downstairs through the bulkhead and discovered we had also neglected to build one of those.

Remember what I told you before? Half cocked.

It took three days of nonstop work before I could slice a rectangle through the kitchen wall's eighteen inches of concrete. My daughter Katy wore a surgeon's mask and dripped water on my diamond-blade saw to keep it cool. I spent another two days pounding out that slab with a sledgehammer and chisel. Lost twenty pounds, but now I can walk down to the wine cellar. I have found peace here. Those wild partying days in Montreal feel well behind me. People in this region take everything in stride, and I've learned to relax more being in their company.

My friend Durwood Starr comes to mind here. He has taught Bill the Great Confronter how a touch of dry wit can defuse potentially volatile situations. Durwood lives in North Troy, where people revere him as one of the best vetenarians in our entire state. His son Greg works as a customs investigator on the border between Vermont and Canada. One afternoon, the three of us were hunting deer on the Starrs' property. After shooting a deer, you must hang it so the blood can drain from its carcass before lugging it home to be butchered. We had already slain three bucks and winched them up on tripods constructed from the trunks of freshly cut birch trees.

A fourth tripod stood in our camp, but it did not carry any prey. Only the week before, Durwood had shot at a deer from across the hood of his Ford truck. He used a new rifle that day and did not realize quite how low the gun's barrel extended under his sights. He missed the deer but scored a perfect bull's-eye through the side of his vehicle. To honor the kill, his children had hung a crumpled toy Ford truck from one of the birches.

I was checking the ropes securing the tripods, making sure

they were tight, when we heard a man yelling from the top of a nearby hill. He ran into our camp carrying a bloodied hunting dog that had just lost a wrestling match with a porcupine. The pooch whimpered from under a face full of knitting needles, each of them at least three inches long. I counted over two hundred black-tipped quills stuck in his hide.

We brought the dog to the surgery Dr. Starr maintained on his farm, only a hundred yards away. After Durwood sedated his patient, Greg and I helped him to extract the needles by hand. Twenty minutes later, the dog sat bandaged on the operating table, licking our faces, still hurting but past any danger. Durwood stepped to his desk and wrote an invoice for $115. The dog owner, a bartender from New York, went ballistic soon as he saw it. "Jesus Christ," he screamed, "this is so outrageous, it borders on usury. You only had my dog for twenty minutes. What the hell do you people do up here all winter that you have to charge such high rates?"

Now, the old me would have clamped my incisors around this ungrateful son of a bitch's throat in a heartbeat. Durwood, though, did not misplace his composure for a moment. He just looked the man in the eye, smiled, and said, "What do we do all winter? Why, raise porcupines, what else?" That bartender laughed so hard he forgot his anger. Paid his bill with a smile.

David Reed is another Vermonter who has offered me lessons in equanimity. Mr. Reed owns the farm next to mine. In fact, he sold me the land we built my house on. He recently turned seventy-eight, but like most senior citizens from these parts, he exhibits a vitality that belies his age. However, David has suffered heart trouble. Whenever he tackles a strenuous task on the portion of his property that curls around the back of our home, his wife phones and asks me to keep an eye out for him.

One wintry day David went out to work over his maple sap lines, heating with his butane burner those that had frozen and mending any that the red squirrels had gnawed. Dusk was already filming the sky when Mrs. Reed's call came. She had not heard from David in hours.

I refrain from wearing snowshoes, those oversized tennis racquets Vermonters put on to walk over the top of heavy accumulations. They just feel too awkward on this California boy's feet. So I pulled up my thick Sorrell boots and walked outside to find Mr. Reed. He had parked his olive-green tractor near the top of my driveway. I could see the prints of his snow shoes following a path into the woods.

David's heavy footsteps had packed the snow down, so traveling was initially easy. Deeper past the trees, though, the snow turned slushy in spots and I broke through its frosted crust every third step. That made for slow moving. The forest grew darker, sweat soaked my long johns, and the harsh wind iced my face. I reached the furthest end of David's property, a point maybe half a mile from my house, and saw a shovel by the side of the path.

A few feet further down I found a flashlight. I tried not to think the worst. *He's not in distress,* I told myself. *These aren't even his tools. Any minute now David's going to come walking down this path, a smug grin creasing his face, and we'll both head back to some mulled cider and his dear wife.*

Then I saw my friend's body lying prone on his stomach at the side of a sap line. He looked as though he wasn't breathing.

Seldom do I remain calm when a situation calls for panic. "Dave," I yelled, "just hang on. I'll get you out of there." I ran not three feet before my boots cracked through the top of a snowdrift. My body plummeted until the snowflakes kissed my chin. Pine branches twined around my ankles and held me fast. I could not raise my arms high enough to pull myself up from the hole. The branches afforded no leverage; the more I pushed against them with my feet, the deeper I dropped as the icy quicksand pulled me under. Dave lay dying, frostbite was setting into my limbs, and I wanted to start crying for mama when I heard a familiar voice hovering behind me.

"Nice day, ay?"

"Dave! What the hell are you doing standing there? I thought you were in trouble."

"No, Bill, from the looks of it, you're the one who's in trouble."

Turned out he had been lying on the ground splicing together a sap line, a delicate procedure that required him to keep his body perfectly still while his fingers did all the work. He never faced any danger at all. Dave placed his shovel across the hole; I leaned against the thick handle and pushed myself out. He saved my butt by reacting like the typical Vermonter, someone who approaches life with the detachment of a Zen monk and rarely gets too excited over anything. If someone had only taught me to maintain my cool that well, I'd still be pitching in the major leagues.

As laid-back as they might be, the Vermonters I know are triple tough and highly competitive. I have played hardball for Newport in the Vermont Senior League. Rollie Denton starred for our team. Years before, this North Troy butcher had become a Vermont sports legend when he led his high school basketball and baseball teams to state championships. Rollie was sixty-five years old when we played together; he could still throw a fastball in the mid-eighties with movement, and the velocity on his slider registered just a notch below major-league.

One afternoon he started for us against the Jericho Little Indians and came out of the shoot looking like a hybrid of Randy Johnson and Barry Bonds. Rollie struck out seven of the first nine batters he faced. He also rapped a two-run homer to put us ahead in the bottom of the third inning. But as he touched home plate, Rollie clutched his chest and collapsed. We carried him to the bench. He face had turned chalky, and he labored for every breath. Heart attack. We wanted to stop the game and run him to the emergency room. Rollie would not hear of it. "Just wrap me in a blanket and call the paramedics," he said. We laid him on the ground and elevated his feet against a bench. He stayed there, rooting us on, until the EMS squad carted him away.

Not long after that, I played first base in a game against a team from Chelsea. The second batter up hit a screaming one-hopper that glanced off first at a funky angle to catch me smack on the right eyebrow. Blood dyed my uniform shirt crimson. Several teammates offered to take me to the hospital. My departure would have left us with only eight players on the field, and our club would have lost the game on a forfeit. I remembered how Rollie had stayed to cheer for us after his heart attack; there was no way anyone could remove me from this field. A nurse came from the stands and butterflied my wound with duct tape. I played all nine innings and hit two home runs with blood streaming in my eyes. We won the game. Might not have made it without Rollie's example spurring me on.

I know that sounds a bit rah-rah, but, on my word, I'd run through a cheesecloth wall for that man.

Most Vermonters root for the Boston Red Sox. Many of them dream of having a son or grandson grow up to play for the home team in Fenway Park. Not too long ago one of these Sox diehards knocked on my front door. He was a tall, powerfully built elderly man with wispy white hair receding at the crown. Liver spots speckled his face. He introduced himself as Bob Sparks, a local who had worked as an athletic trainer at Dartmouth College for over forty years.

We sat in my kitchen, eating Diana's freshly baked apple pie, while he told me something of himself. His wife had died only two weeks earlier in a rest home; he still could not understand why her health had failed. A cancer operation had recently removed part of his own lung, but he assured us he felt fit as ever. His son, a heart doctor, lived in San Diego. When Bob told me how his boy made more money in one year than he himself had taken home in a lifetime, not a trace of bitterness colored his voice. Only pride.

He recalled working with Jim Beattie and several other future major leaguers while they attended Dartmouth, and asked me to show him the various grips I used to throw my different breaking balls. I had no idea where this was going until he removed a snapshot from his wallet and slid it across the table.

"That's my grandson, Bill. He's the top soccer player for his age in all of San Diego, and that's out of more than four hundred participants. But he's an even better baseball player. He can field like a pro at any position and has the same swing as Nomar Garciaparra. I came here to see if you can help us get him on the Red Sox."

The photo depicted a broad-shouldered, light-haired youth about to run from the batter's box after finishing his swing. A textbook follow-through had propelled his bat behind his back on a perfectly level plane. His right leg had already crossed over to carry him toward first. His body language indicated that his weight had shifted forward just at the point of contact, and I could see how he had kept his shoulder tucked in to generate maximum power. Garciaparra? Hell, he looked like Joe DiMaggio. Only one problem, though—this boy appeared to be no more than twelve years old.

I explained to Bob how major-league rules prohibited teams from signing anyone under eighteen. It would be at least six years before the Red Sox had an opportunity to draft this prodigy. He pondered that a moment and said, "All right, why don't we do this? I'll come back just before he graduates high school, and you can call the Red Sox and tell them to give him a look." We shook hands on that, and he rose to leave. As I walked Bob to the door, I asked if he would mind revealing his age. "Eighty-six my next birthday," he answered.

Bob was walking around on one lung and will have to make it to ninety-two to have any hope of ever seeing his grandson wear a Red Sox uniform. I have no doubt he will keep our date. After all, the man's a Vermonter.

18

BACK IN THE LAND OF BEISBOL

I visited Cuba four more times with various senior teams from 1999 to 2003. We won very few games. One does count as very few, right? I could offer any number of reasons for our poor showing, but the fact is the Cuban players were simply better than we—more talented, better conditioned, and far more competitive.

The Cuban players also played a headier brand of ball; all of them grew up in the game. Baseball may be *the national pastime* in the United States, but few people in my country embrace the sport with the passion I found throughout Cuba. For example, no U.S. city has a spot comparable to Havana's *esquina caliente,* or "hot corner," a park in the center of the city where hundreds of Cubans gather every day to discuss their favorite players and teams.

Diana and I discovered just how much knowledge those fans possessed when we attended a game with them in Latinoamericano Stadium, located in downtown Havana just off Revolutionary Square. We sat on the third base side and watched the fiesta begin before the first pitch was thrown. Cheerleaders warmed up the crowd from the dugout roofs, though the fans hardly needed any prompting. Salsa bands playing rock-your-socks-off Cuban music strutted through the stands.

I noticed the spectators around us understood baseball down to its smallest intricacies. They did not second-guess managerial decisions the way many American fans do. The Cubans prided themselves on making first guesses. During the game that afternoon, the hometown manager stepped from the dugout with two men out in the fourth inning to remove the starting pitcher, who had just walked three straight batters to load the bases. Most of the fans immediately rose from their seats to roar their disapproval. I thought they were right. The pitcher had been throwing great up to that point. He hadn't surrendered a hit, and his control was only off by a hair on the last two batters he faced. When the opposing team pounded the pitcher who came on in relief, the fans stomped their feet, filling the stadium with thunderclaps of disgust.

The Cuban players demonstrated more élan than you will see in the American major leagues. Whenever a player struck out, the team on defense flipped the ball around the diamond from catcher to third to second to first, not once as they do in the States, but twice. They performed this ritual to entertain the fans, but also to stay in the game. Cubans understand that the more a fielder touches the ball, the better he plays. An infielder can go several innings without moving a step until a batter hits a ball that requires him to suddenly range far to his left or right. That is not a time to get caught flatfooted. The throwing exhibition kept the infielders on the balls of their feet, always free, always moving, always ready to make the play.

The fans in our section went out of their way to make us comfortable as soon as they learned we were *norteamericanos*. The game was played on a Sunday, so the local laws did not allow concessionaires to sell alcohol in the stadium. Diana called to a man who sold the Cuban meat pies called *arepas*. She asked if he could get us some beer. He said, "Sure, just watch my stuff and make sure no one takes anything without paying." He returned an inning later carrying two ice cold beers he had taken from the refrigerator in his house four blocks away. No charge.

We walked through Havana after the game and were struck by the sight of the Cuban women. Not by their beauty, which was often arresting, but by their body language. Most Cuban women walked the city streets with a quiet confidence. This was not the tough, fragile arrogance too many attractive American women carry as a symptom of confusing sexual leverage with genuine power. Under Castro, Cuban women have attained economic and cultural equality with their men, and that independence has given them a powerful self-esteem that manifests itself in every gesture. And their attitudes did not appear to threaten their male companions at all.

If the Cuban people we spoke with felt oppressed under Castro, they certainly hid it well. Fidel remains a hero to members of the older generation, who remember how little they had under Batista. They reminded us that though Cuba is a poor country, it boasts a 96 percent literacy rate, the second highest in the world. Every Cuban attends school, and most graduate from college. We did meet a few young dissidents, but even they credited Castro with improving conditions for the lower classes. However, they felt Cuba had stagnated under his recent leadership and that the island would never assume a place in a modern world economy until after Castro's demise.

Speaking to any other naysayers would have required us to visit the prisons where Castro detains many political dissenters. Neither I nor any of my teammates ever met with the premier during my trips to Cuba, but we once caught a glimpse of Fidel rolling by in a town car in the middle of a two-block-long motorcade. I remember thinking, *This is one funny kind of socialism this revolutionary practices. He gets to ride in stretch limos while many of his people can barely afford to buy a decent pair of shoes.*

I had heard stories about Castro's pitching prowess, how he was good enough as a young college player to compete in the major leagues. Supposedly the Washington Senators almost signed him just before the revolution broke out. The old-timers who saw him play say the stories are apocryphal. Castro possessed enormous physical strength, and he apparently threw the ball harder than most Cuban pitchers of his day. Power, though, is apparently all he had. The word is Fidel's fastball moved little, and he could not throw a decent curve or any other breaking pitch. He did not start for any of the better Cuban teams, and no one but the most ardent Castro supporter thought he had enough talent to play in even the lowest rung of the American minor leagues.

Castro regards himself as the number one baseball fan on his island, and he encourages Cubans to participate in sports even if he cannot supply enough money to fund many organized athletic programs. Adults and children play catch on nearly every street corner. We passed one avenue and saw a group of men weaving in and around three lanes of traffic trying to retrieve a baseball. They had been fielding grounders in the center of a busy town square.

Just outside of the city, I watched a coach work in a deserted lot with a squad of talented teenage players. The second and short combination impressed me most. The coach introduced them, a pair of brothers who each could afford only one baseball shoe. The second baseman wore his cleat on his left foot; the shortstop's cleat covered his right. This allowed both of them to push off toward the middle of the diamond on the double play, which they turned as smoothly as the most accomplished major leaguers. In the United States, their skills would earn them a full ride to any college with a first-rate baseball program—provided someone first bought each of them a complete pair of shoes.

◆

Diana and I stayed at a hotel near Vinales. An American camera crew followed us around while filming a documentary on Cuban baseball. One evening the crew's sound man, a surfer dude type who resembled Brad Pitt, invited us to join him and his compadres for a party at the home of an elderly woman. She had a reputation as a *babalao,* a priestess of Santería, the Afro-Cuban religion.

Her house sat behind the main drag in Vinales. Imagine driving through a small, modern American city. You pass a post office, a bank, a few stores, and city hall. It is midnight, and no one walks the avenue. The buildings skulk just beyond the reach of the streetlights. You park at the end of the block across the street from a faded green stucco house, a Masonic temple abandoned shortly before Castro took power. The Masons' all-seeing eye, sculpted in stone, peers out from above the door. A new moon hunched behind a thin curtain of clouds threads the black sky with an eerie silver underlight.

You hear banshees in the distance, the off shore wind howling through the limestone caves overlooking Vinales. Soon as you turn the corner, the city disappears. You stand in front of a dense jungle carved into the midst of the urban landscape.

The *babalao* lived in a one-story rectangle, but I have no idea if the builders had constructed her home of wood or stone or some other material. Nature had reclaimed this structure. Thick ivy vines encased the house in a cocoon and a grove of tall trees formed a wall that semicircled the property. The branches of the trees on the side of the wide porch curved over the roof and met in the center; they resembled a pair of giant hands clasped in prayer.

Tropical flowers sprouted from the walls of the house. Their fragrance blended with the musky odor of fresh compost. Someone had scattered chunks of rotting melon on the ground near the front gate. While bending over to pick up a wedge of fruit, I saw something else on that fence, something that stared back at me: the dead eyes of a dismembered doll's head. Then I noticed the other severed plastic heads and limbs tied to the pickets.

From the forest behind the *babalao*'s yard came the low whistle of metal slashing air. Machetes glinted in the moonlight slanting between the trees. I considered leaving until one camera crew member explained that the priestess and her family had left the fruit and mangled dolls as benign offerings. The people inside this house had just celebrated the feast of Santa Barbara, a sacred night in the Santería religion when the female deity devours the male god and all the women of the earth attain their full power to rule the world for twenty-four hours.

A woman stepped from the shadows in front of the house—the *babalao*'s daughter. She appeared to be in her early thirties, with head-spinning looks: onyx hair tumbling to her shoulders, high cheekbones, panther's eyes, bare legs under a white skirt. She did not say a word, just gestured us inside with a wave of her hand.

As we walked up the path leading to the front door, I saw three bulky forms perched on the roof next to the chimney—turkey vultures with their wings black cowls drawn up around them. Those birds only eat dead flesh. Something on this place had died or was about to die. They swayed forward as we climbed the porch steps, and I could feel their eyes on us.

The sight of those figures chilled me, but as soon as we

entered the house, I heard music, a soothing refrain from my childhood, coming from the next room:

"... a three-hour tour, a three-hour tour ..."

Neighbors of the *babalao* crammed the front parlor watching a rerun of *Gilligan's Island*. Now I felt at home.

Diana and I followed the film crew into the living room. We met a party of maybe ten Cubans sitting around the room, passing a bottle of rum among them. The *babalao* must have been in her late seventies, a tiny woman with a face as wrinkled as a chestnut. Nothing frail about her, though. You could feel her powerful presence from across the room. She came over and took my hand, studied my eyes for a moment, and pinched the skin on my face. "I have something for you," she said.

She went out to the kitchen and came back with a bottle of thin white liquid. "You need this," she insisted as she poured the stuff into a tablespoon. *Whoa,* I thought, *what is this, some witch's brew that will have me crawling around the room, braying like a jackal? Or do they think I'm Chango and is she giving me a sedative to knock me out before popping my carcass in the oven as an offering to Santa Barbara?* The liquid gave off no telltale odor. *What the hell, everybody's got to die of something.* I slurped down the spoonful and immediately recognized that vile chalky taste. A witch's brew all right: milk of magnesia.

The *babalao* invited us to look around her house. She had papered over the living room walls with *Life* magazine covers dating back as far as the 1930s. In the center of each wall she had plastered three pictures of the Last Supper. Those religious depictions inspired me. With the film crew's cameras running, I launched into a monologue describing how Christ had not really died on the cross but had instead gone to France, where he worked as a real estate developer and eventually opened an office in Cannes, and how the apostles had fabricated the resurrection as a marketing ploy to win converts, and how Charlemagne and Clovis and members of the Moravian dynasty carried Christ's bloodlines into the Stuart line in Scotland and how Mary Stuart was my great-great-great-grandmother and how that made me a direct descendant of Jesus Christ.

And so on.

Diana kept trying to attract my attention, but I was on a roll and didn't notice. We left shortly after I ran out of words. Diana remained silent the entire way back to the hotel. Once we reached our room she could not contain her rage. Diana screamed at me for being so insensitive as to stand in the *babalao's* home on a sacred night and mock her religious beliefs while keeping my back turned to our hostess the entire time. If that was any indication of how I treated people, Diana did not want to know me.

She was right. I had behaved thoughtlessly, doing my Bill Lee sidewalk act without giving any regard to how my words might offend the *babalao*. The next morning I visited the woman's house to make amends. We had noticed how arthritis had restricted her movements the night before, so I brought a carton of five hundred aspirin, a rare commodity in Cuba. She smiled, clasped my hands in thanks and we said goodbye. After that Diana eventually came to see that my behavior that night was not an irreparable character flaw. My narcissism had just gotten the better of me, and that was something I could work on. Some weeks, it's a full-time job.

◆

The house where Ernest Hemingway lived from 1940 to 1960 floats on a high promontory, part of a large plantation set above San Francisco de Paulo, a town twenty miles southeast of Havana. The Hemingway hacienda is a one-story Spanish colonial-style building constructed of a ghostly white stucco so porous it seems to absorb the sun's various colors so that the building shifts its tint depending on the time of day.

A large outdoor pool stretches through the backyard. Back in the fifties, locals would often see Gary Cooper and Errol Flynn drinking cocktails with Hemingway while sitting in lounge chairs at the pool's edge. One man told me, with undisguised delight, about the night Ava Gardner and Rita Hayworth swam naked in its waters. Rita Hayworth *and* Ava Gardner! Just writing their names in the same sentence as the word *naked* arouses me.

Inside, the house appeared to be waiting for the owner to return. Someone had left a sheet of paper wedged in the Royalton typewriter on the desk where Hemingway once stood to write each morning. The author's books remain piled high on his desk and library shelves. Stuffed heads of game animals stare down on the living room. Bullfighting posters adorn the walls. Hemingway's old Victrola rests on a table next to a stack of big-band albums. There is a plate with a drawing of a bull's head propped up on a mantel. The artist's signature reads Picasso. On a tray in the center near a plump leather armchair a half-full vintage bottle of Gordon's gin wants pouring. . . .

We did not come here looking for any of these things.

During the late 1940s Hemingway founded and coached a Cuban Little League team called the Gigi Stars. His son Gregory played on the club with other boys from San Francisco de Paulo. Though baseball unquestionably ranks as the number one sport on this island, the youth leagues have suffered with the declining economy. The national sports committee directs the bulk of its funding toward the adult teams. Most Cuban boys and girls still play the game, but budget cuts have reduced them to using balls made of twine and tape wrapped around small stones. They substitute broom handles for bats. In San Francisco de Paulo, the children did not even have an organized baseball program to join.

My friend Randy White and I visited Cuba in March 2001 with a group of baseball players from our Florida senior league. Our mission: to find the surviving members of the Gigi Stars and present them with enough baseball equipment to start three new Little League teams. The cargo we brought to Cuba included six cartons of baseball caps, eight catcher's mitts, twenty-four aluminum bats, thirty batting helmets, seventy-five pairs of spikes, one hundred fielder's gloves, one hundred batting gloves, and three hundred official Little League baseballs.

The curator of the Hemingway home told Randy that only four of the Stars were still alive. Three of them owned houses in San Francisco de Paulo; one resided in the fishing village of Cojimar, just twenty miles northeast of there. We asked for the names and addresses of the men. Nothing is ever that easy in Cuba. Before the curator agreed to give us any contact information, he insisted we get permission to implement our plan from the local government representative. That official behaved as if our largesse were part of some nefarious American plot. He spent nearly two days interrogating Randy through an interpreter before finally allowing us to proceed.

We met the four Gigi Stars with their extended families in a sun-filled plaza in the middle of San Francisco de Paulo on a Saturday afternoon. The men's grandchildren and great-grandchildren chased each other in a game of hide-and-seek on the ball field next to the plaza while we chased shots of rum with tankards of Cuban beer.

The park the Gigi Stars once played on had fallen into disrepair. Cows loitered in the outfield. Rodent trails slashed through the overgrown grass. Erosion had devoured much of the infield soil, leaving the surface as grooved and rigid as concrete. Locals had removed the mound, and the winds had obliterated the base paths. Yet you could still trace the outline of a baseball diamond. Despite human neglect and the battering of the elements, the diamond had endured.

One of the old gentlemen lifted a first baseman's mitt from its package. He tossed it to me, took one for himself, and grabbed a ball. We started playing catch, and his three *compadres* soon joined us. Gregory Hemingway's former teammates had reached their seventies, slack-bellied men with rubbery biceps. Fat had narrowed their eyes to slits. But in that plaza, playing the game they loved, those men became boys again, loose-limbed and graceful. Papa Hemingway had coached them well. They caught the ball smoothly with both hands, lined up their bodies behind every throw, and more than once stung my palm with hard tosses.

When we ended our party late that evening, the Gigis thanked us and promised to use the equipment to revive Papa's legacy. They vowed to restore that old ball field so the joyful noise of bat on ball rising above the laughter of children would be heard throughout the village once more.

◆

The day after our picnic, our senior league team played in Vinales against a club from Pinar del Río. Jon Warden started for us. For three innings, Pinar could not score against him. However, Jon weighed nearly 300 pounds, and the tropical heat soon cooled his fastball. Randy White brought me in from the bullpen in the middle of the fourth with our side down 3–2.

My pitching kept us in the game. Kept Pinar in the game as well. I had thrown a lot of innings during this visit, and the workload had beaten up my arm. My pitches lacked zip. Our defense bailed me out several times, making spectacular catches on hard-hit balls.

I helped with the bat. In the seventh, my two-run homer down the right field line knotted the game 7–7. Pinar took a one-run lead in its half of the inning. I rapped another base hit with one man out in the top of the ninth and scooted to third base with the potential tying run when Randy singled.

To that point, the American teams I had accompanied to this country had lost twenty straight to the Cubans. I believed if we could just tie this game, we would finally notch a win. Our next batter hit a sharp ground ball off the pitcher's glove. I sprinted halfway down the base path, eager to score. The pitcher looked me back to third. As he threw to first base, I took off again for home, trying to steal a run.

I had forgotten that in Cuba stealing counts as a capital offense.

The Pinar first baseman stabbed the carom off his pitcher's glove and stepped on first for the second out. Without pausing, he threw a strike to his catcher that beat me by a good two feet. I started to hook-slide around the catcher's tag, but he planted his foot in my path. Sliding into his shin guard was like crashing into a concrete stump. My body halted. I lay laughing in front of home plate, too tired to feel any pain, while the umpire waved me out. Double play. Another game lost.

I kept looking out the window during the bus ride back to our hotel in Vinales. As the driver approached a familiar house, I asked him to pull over. She stood near her front door, the old woman who had given me the guava two years earlier. I did not have to introduce myself. "You came back," she said in an amazed voice, "just to see us!" Her grandson was five now, still shy, still not talking, just that same pair of large, questioning brown eyes hiding behind his grandmother's bulk.

I presented her with a rainbow-striped cotton shift and handed him a pair of ankle-high boots. "His first shoes," his grandmother told me. She shook my hand and chattered in Spanish. Her words came so quickly, I had no idea what she said, but that did not matter. I saw it all there in her eyes. After showing off her place—nothing had changed since our last visit—she kissed me on the cheek and once again insisted on sharing a handful of fruit from her meager supply, papayas this time. I ate them on the bus, and their sweetness lingered in my mouth for hours. But the smile she gave me when I handed her that dress and her grandson those shoes and the grins on the faces of those elderly Gigi Stars who discovered their youth waiting for them in a box of baseball gloves will remain with me until my memory surrenders to time.

19

HANGIN' WITH THE BIG DOG

I started hearing Ted Williams stories from the moment the Boston Red Sox signed me as a pitcher out of USC in 1968. Ted had retired eight years before, but he never relinquished his title as Mr. Red Sox, the greatest hitter ever to wear that franchise's uniform.

People who had played with Williams—Johnny Pesky and Bobby Doerr among them—would recall for us minor-leaguers how Ted's strike-zone judgment had been so precise, he could go weeks without swinging at a bad pitch, or how his eyes remained so sharp, he could still read a record label spinning at 78 rpm. A writer told me that when Ted hit .406 in 1941, he made such solid contact in every at bat he did not hit a single pop fly all season. Ted himself once claimed that his swing passed through the strike zone so quickly at times he could smell burning leather when he grazed a pitch.

I had no idea how much embellishment colored these tales, but we enjoyed hearing them. Yet when a coach described how Ted once hit a ball so hard, it cleaved in two, well, that carried the legend-making too far. "You guys," I told him, "make Williams sound as if he's God."

"Oh, that's silly," the coach replied. "God could never hit like Ted."

It was not until 1971 that I finally had the opportunity to watch Ted swing a bat against live pitching. I had just established myself as a member of the Red Sox starting rotation. He was managing the Washington Senators and had come to a sold-out Fenway Park to join other Boston heroes such as Frank Malzone and Walt Dropo in a home run–hitting contest. For every ball the participants smacked over the fence that day, the Red Sox donated $500 to the Jimmy Fund, a New England–based charity that raises money for juvenile cancer research. Williams had supported the organization throughout his career.

From the moment Ted left the dugout for his turn at bat, you could tell he was someone special even if you had never heard his name. You just needed to watch his walk. There was no swagger in his stride. He approached home plate with the nonchalant assurance of a man who knew everyone in the place awaited his arrival.

Red Sox pitching coach Lee "Stinger" Stange faced Ted that day. Stinger had retired from the major leagues only the year before. He had just turned thirty-five and could still throw his fastball in the high eighties. He started Ted off with a blooping batting-practice pitch that arrived waist-high in the middle of the plate. It had nothing on it, a meatball your great-aunt Sadie could have bashed over an outfielder's head. Ted had expected something carrying a little more bite. He swung too hard, pulling the ball on a line into the Red Sox dugout, scattering several players sitting on the bench. He shook his head in disgust. "God damn it," he screamed at Stange, "give me your real stuff. Put some muscle on the ball."

Stinger nodded. He delivered a hard, cross-seamed fastball that looked like a strike. Except it never passed home plate. Ted hit that pitch more than 380 feet into the bullpen for a home run. After that he put on a show. The faster Stinger threw, the harder Ted whacked the ball. Nearly every shot off Williams's bat either soared over the fence or rattled against it. Boston manager Eddie Kasko had placed me in right field to shag fly balls for the contest, and I can tell you that not one of Ted's home runs was a cheapie. He cost the Red Sox a lot of money that afternoon.

Watching him effortlessly stroke one long ball after another convinced me that he could have ended his retirement to play in the major leagues that very afternoon. He would not have hit .350 like the Williams of old. He no longer possessed reflexes sharp enough to cope with professional breaking pitches. But Ted's hands still retained so much quickness, he could time any pitcher's fastball. Had he made a comeback, I imagine he might have hit .270 while finishing among the league's home run leaders. He was fifty-three years old.

So I'm thinking, those stories those coaches told me? They were not bullshitting. From that point on, I believed anything anyone ever said about Ted Williams.

Ted and I occasionally met after that in spring training. We didn't get to know each other until 1986, when he worked as a special hitting instructor at the Red Sox fantasy camp in Winter Haven, Florida. I came down to manage a team of fans who had paid hefty fees to play baseball with former major leaguers. Ted spent hours with these weekend athletes, patiently honing their swings and discussing the nuances of hitting such as weight shift and strike zone judgment.

One afternoon he lumbered onto the practice field hours before any of his pupils and found me sitting alone in our dugout. Ted seldom said much to the pitchers; he still considered us the enemy. Nevertheless, he plopped down on the bench and draped a beefy arm around my shoulder.

"Christ," Ted growled at the empty field, "they got me stuck in here with a fucking pitcher. And he's a damned Communist too!" He gave me that charming who-gives-a-shit grin of his and said, "You're a California kid like me, Lee, so you must be all right. For a pitcher, that is. But you are dumb. All pitchers are dumb. The only thing dumber than you pitchers are the hitters you get out."

"You don't really think pitchers are dumb. . . ."

"Oh, no? Just look at you! You throw that curveball, right? But I bet you don't even know what makes the damned thing curve."

"Sure I do. The same thing that lifted those jet fighters you used to pilot off the ground only in reverse. Bernoulli's principle."

His eyes widened in feigned astonishment. "You know about that?" he squealed.

"It's basic physics. The seams on a curveball rotate over the top, creating a high-pressure area above the ball and a low-pressure area below it. The high pressure pushes down, and the pitch drops as it crosses the plate because the low pressure on the bottom cannot withstand the thrust."

My explanation impressed Ted. Sure, he constantly challenged people with his jibes, but that was his way of thumping their brains, forcing them to think about their craft. He got in your face like some Marine drill instructor who knows his way *is* the highway, but Ted loved it whenever a player stood his ground and fired back. So I said to him, "Now it's my turn. Bet I can tell you something about why you were such a great hitter that even you don't know."

You might have described his response as laughter, but no, it was something much deeper, a gut rumbling that quaked his whole body until the bench shook under us. A groundskeeper walked through the dugout on his way to the diamond to trim the grass along the infield. "Look," Ted's voice boomed after him, "at who's going to tell me about hitting." But then his mirth-filled eyes turned serious. Hitting was never a laughing matter to Ted for very long. "All right, hot shot. Tell me. Why did I hit so well?"

Pointing to his right eye, I said, "This is your dominant eye, even though you're left-handed. For most left-handers the left eye dominates. When you stand at the plate facing the pitcher, you look at him through your dominant eye. That gives you a perfect view of every pitch."

"And what exactly does that bullshit mean?" He sounded gruff and scoffing, but I heard the little boy's excitement coloring his words. He was genuinely interested in hearing more. Ted never passed himself off as a learned man. He did not impress me as particularly bright or worldly. I never heard him discuss a book or a play or a work of art. His cinematic tastes ran to cowboy movies, the oaters more than the classics. Ted's politics, such as they were, came across as predictably hard-hat conservative and revealed little self-reflection. But when it came to hitting, Ted fit the role of scholar. The decades spent obsessively studying his craft had left him with a mind as inquisitive and flexible as Einstein's. He appeared eager to learn something new about a subject he understood better than anyone in the world.

On that bright, cloudless Florida morning, we could clearly see a water tower half a mile in the distance. I asked Ted to stare at the tower with both eyes for several seconds.

"Okay, now keep looking but cover your right eye so that you can see the tower only with your left."

"The damn thing skipped over," he shouted. "It moved about three inches."

"Now do it again, only this time cover your left eye."

"Son of a bitch. It didn't move at all that time."

"That's what right-eye dominance means," I explained. "Your right eye gives you a true, smooth perspective of an object. If you were left-eye–dominant and looking at a pitcher with your right eye, the ball would appear to jump slightly when you first caught sight of it. Most people need a split second to adjust to that movement. You didn't have to waste time making that adjustment, so you picked up the ball's spin and location faster than most hitters."

"Isn't that something."

Some of Williams's students started running past us toward the outfield. A grounds crew member motored his golf cart over to our dugout to taxi Ted out to them. As they drove off, I watched him cover one eye, then the other, while looking at various points around the ballpark. "You believe it?" he said between laughs. "A goddamned crazy pitcher had to tell me this. Son of a bitch."

We were friends from that day on. Ted would see me in the morning and cover his left eye in a salute. Whenever we had a free moment, he joined me at my locker to talk fishing. Professional anglers rated Ted an expert fly caster, and he loved to tease me for preferring to hook my lines with bait. "Takes no skill to fish with bait," I can still hear him growl, "it's like cheating. Old ladies can do it." That was his guy's way of showing affection.

I marveled at how he performed his duties. Ted was sixty-eight, but his energy seemed inexhaustible; none of us could keep up with him. Most coaches in our camp contented themselves to merely pass on a generic tip or two to each player. Ted took more of a hands-on approach when he imparted his lessons. He would wrap his powerful arms around some hitter at home plate and wrestle him into a perfectly balanced stance while roaring instruction and encouragement: "Keep your eye on the ball. . . . Your weight stays back until you identify the pitch. . . . Don't just use your arms, get that big ass of yours into the swing. . . . Make that son of a bitch throw strikes. . . .

Swing up and swing hard. . . . Screw grounders, drive that ball into the air. . . . Put some gin-a-ger in it. . . . There ya go, that feels good, am I right, am I right, am I right?"

At night, Ted occasionally joined a group of the campers for a dinner that would soon turn into a marathon discussion about hitting. He would sit at the head of the table sipping his branch water—Ted's name for a whiskey straight up with water on the side—and pepper the campers with questions about whatever they had practiced that day. He treated them as professionals.

In their eyes, Ted could do no wrong, even when he flirted with their wives. One camper, though, did take exception. When he complained to me, I said, "You have to understand Ted doesn't mean anything by it. He's the Big Dog, and it's just his way of being playful." That mollified the husband somewhat. "Yeah," he said, "I guess it's all right if he just wants to sniff around. Just so long as that Big Dog doesn't wag his tail in my bedroom."

The thing you noticed about Ted once you spent time with him was his dedication to achieving excellence. He had no patience for halfhearted efforts in anything. One night my team dined with him in a Chinese restaurant where the service responded sluggishly. When the pu-pu platter arrived at a pace much too slow for his liking, Ted yanked the circular aluminum dish from the waiter's hands and sailed it across the room like a Frisbee. The glassine noodles, pastel-colored won tons, and seared red ribs stuck to the wall in a paste of dark sauce, an abstract of textures and hues that Jackson Pollock could have painted.

That was pure Williams. Even when he behaved inappropriately, he responded as an artist. Ted paid for the order, even left a generous tip. But he never apologized. He did not censor his actions, words, or feelings, and he did not give a good goddamn what anyone thought about him. He was a man who had the courage to live an imperfect but honest life. I loved him for that.

So when the news reported Ted's death from a stroke on July 5, 2002, well, it knocked me over. I called the Red Sox to ask where the William family planned to hold the funeral. Found out there would be no service. Ted's son had already arranged to have his father's body flown from their Florida home to the Alcor Life Extension Foundation, a cryogenics company in Scottsdale, Arizona.

We all learned what happened later. I read stories that described how Alcor's engineers had removed Ted's skull from his torso, froze the separated parts in a pool of liquid nitrogen, and stored them at subzero temperatures in two metal cylinders (Alcor has never confirmed this). This procedure supposedly preserved the remains until some future date when science discovered a way to revive the body.

I attended a dinner for the Jimmy Fund fourteen months after Ted died. Many of his closest friends sat at my table. Rage. That's what they felt. They wanted to kill the people who had put this great man on ice.

The idea of Ted hanging in a freezer did not appeal to me either. I don't hold with many traditions. Few things strike me as undignified, but this certainly qualified. Someone had to put the situation right. "I visit Scottsdale with my sons, Andy and Mike, every year," I announced, "to compete in the father-son baseball tournament. We pass the Alcor factory whenever we drive to the ballpark. Why don't I visit the place and find out where they keep Ted's remains?"

"What good will that do?" one of Ted's friends asked.

"I'm a bonded locksmith. Once we know where they've stored the body, my sons and I will return to Alcor after closing hours. That's when we'll steal the cylinders. You know how Ted loved to fish the waters off Key West? We'll drive the remains down there and give him a proper send-off."

Bet you can hear that table hush even from where you're sitting. Every eye turned my way. They looked at me as though Alice's Mad Hatter had just joined the party, but you know what? No one objected to the plan.

"What sort of ceremony do you have in mind?" someone asked.

"Viking funeral. We get a boat, build a pyre, and put Ted on it with two virgins. Light the whole thing up and push it out to sea."

Some of Ted's friends later privately told me they would lend whatever assistance they could—cash, transportation, men, ordnance, anything—if I carried out my scheme. I should have gone for it that evening, when anger put my judgment on hold. As the Scottsdale trip drew closer, doubts intruded. This recurring nightmare haunted me:

My sons back out of the trip, leaving me alone with Ted in the Pathfinder, the only car driving down the Lost Highway. It is midnight. Heavy clouds cover the moon, and workmen have removed all the street lamps. The landscape appears desolate. No billboards, houses, rest stops, or gas stations.

I quit smoking months ago, but the ride makes me so nervous I chew on a wad of Nicoderm patches. No help there. I reach for

the stale pack of Camels jammed in the rear of the glove com-
partment. Suddenly Ted's parade-ground voice booms from that
chrome container on the seat next to mine: "Put those butts down
and show some goddamned willpower . . . Let up on the clutch,
you cannot drive scared . . . Change the radio station, no one
wants to hear that rock and roll shit . . . And get off this highway,
there's a quicker way through the mountains . . . Don't pussy
around with that pedal, floor the son of a bitch . . . Now we're
making time, am I right, am I right, am I right!"

You know it would go on that way for the rest of the trip.
Think Ted was the kind of guy who would let a little thing like
death alter the habits of a lifetime? After pondering it, I
decided against attempting the Alcor caper. Hated to disappoint Ted's friends, but let's face it: if heaven exists our bodies
are merely temporary shells. We cast them off at death before
traveling on to a higher plane. I may be rationalizing here, but
we can comfort ourselves knowing that Ted is off fly casting
with Babe Ruth and Richard Nixon on some river in the Great
Beyond. And that the Big Dog spends his nights—if they have
nights up there—chasing Marilyn Monroe and Jayne Mans-
field around a baseball-shaped waterbed. He is probably enjoying himself too much to care whether the body and head
that used to be him are stuck in a deep freeze.

Okay, let's turn this around to play devil's advocate. Suppose nothing exists after death but the void. Which means
even the void doesn't exist. Bonus. Now Ted isn't worried about
anything. Alcor could sell his remains as Fudgsicles for all he's
concerned.

Of course, the company would make many of us happy by
simply ending this silly exercise. Call me a skeptic, but it

seems absurd that anyone could believe cryogenics will ever revive Ted. The science just does not add up. Once you deprive the brain of blood and oxygen for only a few minutes, the cells permanently die. To reanimate a coherent, functioning Teddy Ballgame, the doctors would have to undo the stroke that killed him, clean out the blocked arteries, reverse years of organ degeneration, stimulate new cell growth, reintroduce emotional memory, and implant new mitochondria to turn back the aging process.

I ain't holding my breath.

Come to think of it, neither is Ted.

Let's go wacky for a moment and imagine that Alcor can revive my friend's corpse. Now the cryogenicists are treading in unknown territory. Not one of them can guarantee that Ted's essence—his soul, if you will, that wonderfully profane and exuberant personality that made him him—would return to it. Stay with me here. Let's suppose he has already reincarnated. Why would he wait? Ted returns to this existence as some baby born in New Delhi who is destined to grow up to become the world's top cricket player. Know what that means? Ted's old body would be up for grabs. Any spirit could enter it. Those cryogenecists might unknowingly conjure Jefferey Dahmer with a great batting eye. Then where would we be?

I doubt any insurance company would protect Alcor for the potential liability. So if the company has the remains and its president is reading this, he should call. I know where we can get a Viking burial ship at a good price and constructing a proper funeral pyre is a snap. Finding two virgins in Key West . . . that will be the difficult part.

20

OF FATHERS AND
THEIR CHILDREN

I had just turned nine years old when my father first handed me that ancient baseball glove. It did not resemble any glove I had ever seen before. For one thing, the manufacturer had not attached the five fingers to each other as with modern gloves; a fielder could not count on snaring a ball in the top of the webbing. No ice-cream cone catches. And it felt dinky on my hand, more a mitten than the baskets fielders wear today.

My own glove had emerged from its package colored a dull yellow brown and gave off the same smell as my book bag on the first day of school. Time had buffed and stained the leather of this older glove into a burnished oxblood. It did not give off any one scent, but a blend of rich, gamy odors. In my boy's imaginings, that glove carried the smell of sweat and liniment and cigar smoke and the dirt from one hundred different infields. The aroma of something that had traveled many miles in the company of men.

My grandfather William F. Lee Sr. wore that glove when he played second base for the Hollywood Stars of the Pacific Coast League in 1918. Many players in that era regarded the PCL as a third major league. Its star performers routinely refused to sign with teams like the New York Yankees or St. Louis Cardinals, since joining those clubs would have required these players to accept pay cuts. William Lee stood on a rung just below star, an excellent contact hitter, dangerous in the clutch, and one of the best fielders in the entire circuit.

Dad slipped the glove on his own hand and explained how his father would slice the leather from the center of it, exposing his palm. My grandfather believed it was easier to control a catch when you could feel the ball against your skin. This practice also gave him a decided edge over rival second basemen. During Grandfather's playing days, the home team fielders left their gloves at their positions so the visiting players could wear them when they took their turn to play defense.

Other second basemen hated using Grandfather's glove. They lacked the thick pad of callus that had formed on his palm and acted as a cushion against hard-hit balls. Many of them yelped in pain whenever they fielded a searing grounder or line drive while wearing my grandfather's doctored mitt, and some even shied away from plays rather than risk damaging their hands.

My grandfather's webless glove would not let you stab at balls the way infielders do today; a hot smash could rip away your finger. He had to move his body behind every grounder and quickly transfer the ball to his throwing hand. This left no time to double-clutch. He either made the play right or he didn't make it at all. And from what I've heard, Grandfather rarely botched a grounder.

He studied the rudiments of defense and practiced his art for hours every day, taking ground balls of various speeds from every conceivable angle until his legs melted. Grandfather schooled my dad in baseball fundamentals and taught him the proper way to play every infield position. During the 1940s, my father started at shortstop for Jackson Paint, a semipro team that played its home games in Griffith Park, just to the side of the Los Angeles River.

Scotty Drysdale managed that club and his son Don, the future Hall of Fame pitcher, served as bat boy. Don was fourteen when we first met, a long-muscled string bean and already a schoolboy pitching legend renowned for throwing shutouts in almost every start. We did not say very much to each other, though we met at the park many times. I was only five years old at the time, and the caste system all children recognized prohibited me from mingling with teenage boys.

I saw my father play enough games with Jackson Paint to know he could have excelled in the major leagues. He fielded his position expertly, with quick feet and even quicker reactions. Dad could dive to his right to catch a hot grounder on his belly and scamper up to throw from his knees to nip even the fastest runner at first base. Smart hitter too. He kept his hands above the ball and smacked line drives to all fields. I never saw him strike out or look bad on a swing. But he entered the Army Signal Corps during World War II, and by the time Dad left the service professional teams considered him too old to tab as a prospect. My mother was pregnant with me, so he went to work for the telephone company and played semipro baseball at night and on weekends.

Dad excelled at every sport he tried. He averaged 200 the first year he joined a bowling league, top man on his team. He all but gave up the game after that. Needed something more challenging. My father just turned eighty-three as we write this and has shot his age or better at golf for the last ten years. In fact, he probably ranks as the best over-seventy-five golfer in all of California. And he remains fiercely competitive. I bested him on the links not too long ago. He refused to talk to me during the entire ride home.

Soon as I grew big enough, he passed on everything his father had taught him about baseball. He sized me up as a pitcher right away. Dad showed me how to properly throw a curve by snapping it off with my thumb and index finger rather than using my elbow to provide torque. I pitched nearly fourteen years in the big leagues without suffering an elbow injury, largely due to his advice. He also helped me develop a big-league attitude. "Don't get down when someone gets a hit off you," he would say. "Give him credit. But remember what pitch he hit, and don't throw it in that situation to that hitter again. Learn from your mistakes instead of brooding and you'll get him out next time."

That lesson stayed with me. I can't tell you what I ate for breakfast yesterday, but I do remember the sequence of pitches I threw to Del Unser of the Washington Senators before he homered against me in 1969. When I signed to play professional baseball, Dad gave me a glove bearing an inscription that continued his tutelage and formed the credo for my entire career: "Throw strikes. Keep the ball down. Be smooth. Don't alibi." Across the front of each finger on the glove he wrote six letters wide in black marker: HUSTLE.

When dad could not catch me in the backyard, my aunt Annabelle Lee put on a mitt. During the 1940s she had starred as the ace left-hander for several women's baseball teams, including the Minneapolis Millerettes and the Fort Wayne Daisies. Annabelle earned her living, and a good one at that, as a professional ballplayer for nine seasons. She pitched a perfect game and two no-hitters while posting a lifetime ERA of 2.19. Her uniform hangs at the entrance of the Baseball Hall of Fame, right next to Jackie Robinson's.

My aunt worked on my control and mechanics and taught me how to change speeds. She also smoothed my delivery and insisted I throw every pitch from the same release point and with the same motion. "That way," she would remind me, "the batter can't read your motion and figure out what you're going to throw." Annabelle and my father were the best pitching coaches I ever had, though Dad could be a difficult man to satisfy. He praised me when I played exceptionally well and acted proud of my accomplishments.

But he also used sarcasm to prod me to do better even after a win, and I grew up thinking I could never completely please him. In the winter of 1975, I brought some Red Sox teammates to his house in San Rafael for a barbecue and some beers. Before long he was sitting in the middle of them, smoking a cigar and holding court. "My son could be a pretty good pitcher," he announced, "if he just had the balls to knock someone down once in a while." He analyzed all the things I needed to improve—a long list. I had won seventeen games that season for the American League champions, yet, according to Dad, I was just getting by.

I have forgotten much of what he said that day, but I recall how his words hurt. They also toughened my hide, which was his purpose all along. Dad shared a trait with that father in the Johnny Cash song who named his son Sue so he would grow up a fighter. And he still knows how to wield the needle. The other day, I phoned to tell him how I had hurt my wrist and he said, "Gee, son, I figured you hurt that thing a long time ago, what with all the shit you've been slinging from the mound."

I have no doubt he loves me deeply. All those hours he spent teaching me the game, showing me how to hunt and make my own way in the world represented his way of expressing how much he cared. When Dick Williams invited me to try out for the Padres in 1984, my father got so excited, he grabbed a mitt and called me outside for a catch. He wanted to help get my arm in shape. I stood at one end of the yard while Dad squatted on his haunches and raised his mitt.

My first pitch got on him a little too high. A little too quick. His 64-year-old hands could not raise his glove in time. The ball hit him a glancing blow off the top of his cap and rolled away. Left a small bump on his forehead. He stood up, told me to retrieve the ball, and went inside. I could see that muffing the catch embarrassed him. He spent the rest of the afternoon unusually quiet. Dad did get over it by dinner—that's his way—and when we discussed the incident recently, he even laughed. "That," he said, "was a pretty dumb thing for me to do."

I didn't think so. You grow up wanting your father to be your hero, to be the best at everything. Dad seldom failed at anything he attempted, and I have looked up to him my whole life. Yet I cannot remember admiring my father more than that day when he tried to catch me even though his hands could no longer keep up with my speed. My career meant that much to him. He is a man of high integrity and character, and I am proud to call him my father. I understand that he comes from a generation of males who never learned how to articulate affection, who thought fathers were always right and that saying "I'm sorry" to anyone but particularly to a slighted son was a sign of weakness.

The John Wayne code.

That is something he and his father passed on to me as well. My son Michael constructed his first hunting bow from scratch shortly after turning fourteen. One day, his brother Andy and sister Katy ran into the house to tell me Mike was shooting at chipmunks with it. "Don't worry," I said, "those things are so small, he'll never hit one." Fifteen minutes later Mike came cartwheeling into the kitchen carrying his kill.

"Goddamnit," I screamed, "don't you ever shoot anything you can't eat!" Mike blanched. He could not understand what he had done to make me so angry. I ripped into him for a good ten minutes. We didn't speak the rest of the night. All through the silence, I knew I had behaved badly. Part of me wanted to go to him and say, *This is my fault. I should have said something to you in advance, told you not to shoot at the chipmunks, but I made the mistake of thinking you couldn't hit anything with that bow.*

But that's not what I know.

It's not what I learned.

You see, my father had yelled the very same thing at me when I was fourteen and shot a blue jay out of a tree with a .22 at a hundred yards. He didn't think I could hit that target either.

Twenty years have passed since Mike killed that chipmunk. I still haven't said I'm sorry. Let me do that now. No. Let me do more than that. I want to say, *Mike, there is so much of me in you. You try to please me just as I tried to please my own father. It is not necessary. You have a wonderful wife and family. You work a job you love, and live your life on your own terms, and you and Andy and Katy and Anna are the best damned kids anyone could want. I love you all and could not be prouder to be your father. Nothing any of you do could ever disappoint me.*

Funny. I can write those words easily enough. Perhaps one day I will find the courage to say them.

❖

I have heard people describe baseball as a family game. The first pitch most children catch is thrown by their fathers, and boys and men can talk baseball when they have nothing else in common to speak of. However, the sport does not bring together families when the father pursues it professionally. The teams I played on trained in Florida for six weeks every spring while my children attended school in Massachusetts. I traveled another 90 days or so during the season. Add in the charity events and the promotional dinners and the golf outings and the television appearances, and I ended up spending less than half the year at home.

My children resented those encroachments on my time. I make up for that now by traveling to see them every chance I get. Katy is a veterinary technician in Memphis, Tennessee. We think of her as the patron saint of flawed dogs. She inherited her love of animals from me. Katy loves to save them; I love to eat them. But my daughter doesn't hold that against me. Mike works as a graphic artist in Seattle, Washington. Andy, a former pitcher just out of the Boston Red Sox minor league organization, coaches baseball at Hines Junior College in Mississippi.

Since 2000, we have kept a date every November to gather—with my parents and Annabelle—in Scottsdale, Arizona, for the father-son baseball tournament. The event organizers invite thirty-two teams composed of fathers and sons from all over the country to compete against each other in a round-robin tournament.

The first year my sons and I participated, we played against a team from San Diego in the second playoff round. I came to the plate in the bottom of the ninth with two men out, our team behind 6–4, and runners on second and third. The San Diego manager brought in his left-handed closer, a large, slope-shouldered twenty-year-old who featured an intimidating running fastball clocked in the mid-eighties. His first two pitches missed the strike zone. He came back with two ferocious sliders that I barely fouled off for strikes. My weak swings made that pitcher cocky. He threw one more slider to finish me off, but this one hung in my eyes. I hit a line drive into centerfield to score the tying runs.

Earlier in the tournament, I had pulled a hamstring tripping over my birth certificate while running out a slow ground ball. Now my right leg dragged, but our team had no pinch runners left. I prayed for a long ball and took a healthy lead off first base. Mike came to the plate and hit the first pitch deep over the right fielder's head. Home run, or so I thought when it first left his bat. But topspin curled the ball back into the park, and it landed at the foot of the outfield fence 345 feet from home plate.

I rounded second in good time and decided to score despite my barking hammy. Adrenaline rocked through my veins. I ran as fast as I could while taking slow, deep yoga breaths to prevent my leg from seizing. The hammy spoke to me rounding third: *This feels good, Bill, time to pour it on!* I opened the throttle and hit home plate with hands held high. The winning run.

I waited for the team to mob me at home plate. No one moved from our bench. They looked stunned. I turned around to see what they were gaping at and discovered that a relay throw had caught Mike at third base right before my foot touched home. The umpire ruled my run did not count.

Limping back to our bench, I noticed my father sitting behind the backstop. He wore a nautical cap pulled low over his eyes to protect him against catching skin cancer in the hot Arizona sun. I also saw that chaw of tobacco wedged in his cheek. A true Lee. That double-edged sword never stops dangling over our heads.

Suddenly my uniform grew too big. My shoes flopped around my feet. My shirt cuffs hid my hands and dangled to my knees. The waist of my baseball pants fell down my legs and snagged my ankles. I became a little boy again, shuffling forward in droopy drawers, eager to gain that man's approval. I grabbed the chain link fence and blurted, "Dad, Dad. I ran as fast as I could." He spit a glob of tobacco on the dirt next to my cleats and said, "Yes, son, I could see that. But you were running in place."

So what if he can't catch my fastball anymore? He can still buzz one under my chin whenever he's of a mind to.

The right-handed batter swaggered to home plate and crouched into a stance that mimicked the Seattle Mariners' designated hitter supreme, Edgar Martinez. Feet set far back in the batter's box, hands cocked at the waist, head down with his eyes riveted on the pitcher. Scouts had yet to give me a rundown on this masher, but I assumed he liked the ball low, as he only measured four feet tall. Six-year-old Hunter Lee. My grandson.

We faced each other during an impromptu batting practice on a deserted Scottsdale field in between games of the father-son tourney. Aunt Annabelle, all seventy-two years of her, squatted behind the plate as our catcher while my father stood over her calling balls and strikes. Except Dad did not have to open his mouth. Hunter wore me out, going with each pitch with the patience of a pro and smacking line drives to every field.

"Hey, you're a pretty good hitter," I told him.

"Yeah, well, I can hit you."

Oooh, cocky! I admired that—up to a point. And Hunter had just passed it. Time for a tough-love pitch. I jammed the

Wiffle ball deep between my fingers and threw a wicked-ass splitter that flashed up in his eyes as it reached home plate. The ball plunged straight down before skipping in the dirt. Hunter wildly swung over it.

"Grandpa," he said in a voice full of pout, "you didn't throw me a strike!"

"That's right, my boy. Next time you'll remember not to swing at everything."

I know. I should have played Wilfred Brimley, the doting grandfather, and just let Hunter keep raking me. But baseball is a hard game. Best he learn that now.

◆

My son Andy pitches for our team in the Scottsdale tournament, but he also occasionally catches. In a game against Los Angeles in 2001, he impressed all of us with his athleticism. The score was tied 4–4 in the seventh inning when our opponents put a runner on third with only one man out. Andy came out to the mound and reminded me to keep my pitches down. We did not want the batter hitting any deep fly balls to score the go-ahead run.

I threw three straight sinkers to run the count to 2–1. My next pitch got away from me. It passed through the strike zone, but much higher than I intended. Good thing the batter was looking for another sinker. He swung under the ball for strike three. Too bad Andy had been looking for that sinker as well. The ball soared past his glove, past the umpire, past everything until it hit the wrought-iron railing at the bottom of the backstop screen and bounded eight feet into the air.

With the runner bearing down on home plate, the common impulse for an inexperienced catcher is to quickly retrieve a ricocheting ball by jumping for it. That's a good way to muff the catch. Andy maintained a professional's cool and waited for the rebound to plop into his mitt. He somehow shoveled the ball from under his armpit to me waiting at home plate.

Andy's toss reached my glove just as the runner dipped into his slide. He plowed into me with such force, the collision flipped us into the air. I landed on top of him. We rolled around near home plate, a gaggle of thrashing limbs. When the umpire at last saw I had retained possession of the ball, he ruled the runner out.

Great piece of teamwork between my boy and me. Makes a father proud.

◆

The competition in the father-son tournament is lively and entertaining, so rambunctious at times, the unexpected passes for routine. Last November, a team the Lees played went all the way to the championship final against Sacramento. We entered the bottom of the third inning losing 1 0 with no one out. I led off with a weak single to centerfield. Mike followed with a base hit to put runners at first and second. The next batter tried bunting us over; Sacramento retired me at third on a force play.

Our pitcher hit a short fly over second base. The Sacramento centerfielder was playing so deep, he could not cover enough ground in time to make the catch. My son lit out for third. He read the play correctly. Our third base coach did not. He thought the centerfielder would glove the ball on the fly for an out. Instead of sending the runner halfway down the baseline, the coach made him tag up before trying to score.

When the centerfielder picked up the base hit on one hop, Mike had to slow down until the runner in front of him reversed course and headed home. That delay gave the centerfielder all the time he needed to unloose a perfect throw. The ball rushed toward home plate. Mike sprinted down the third base line, moving so fast he could have jumped on the runner in front of him for a piggyback ride. His teammate tried to score standing up. Mike slid under his legs and flipped him into the air before either could touch home. The catcher touched the plate for a force-out on the first runner and tagged Mike for a rally-ending double play.

You will not see that happen at your local ballpark anytime soon.

We eventually lost that game 2–0. Soon as the Sacramento pitcher recorded the final out to win the tournament, his manager dropped to his knees, flung up his arms in triumph, and burst into tears as the entire team crowded around him for a group hug. It was such a passionate, heartwarming reaction, we did not mind losing. Besides, the father-son tournament has never been about the final score. It is about fathers and sons breaking the barriers of familial constraints to roll around in the same dirt, to become best pals in a common cause. We play hard, we play to win, but we do *play*, and that's the important thing.

◆

The Blue Adobe Mexican restaurant stands on the corner of Country Club and Main Streets in Mesa, Arizona. My family often drives over from Scottsdale to dine there after a full day of baseball. We stuff ourselves with poblano chiles, *puerco adobado,* and enchiladas while swilling margaritas late into the night. During a recent outing, my father stood next to his great-grandson Hunter, instructing him to lower his body close to the ground while perching on his tiptoes, the classic stance for an infielder waiting for a hot smash to come his way. It was what his father had taught him and he had taught me and I had taught my sons. Now Hunter joined us, a recipient of the legacy.

My aunt Annabelle sipped a cocktail with Katy and reminded me to slow down my motion the next time I pitched, to make sure my body did not lunge too far out in front of my arm. Mike and Andy walked over from the bar, where they had just watched a baseball game. Andy wrapped his arm around me and said, "We have to keep doing this. Being here with you guys, it's the greatest time of my life."

"Yeah, Dad," Mike added, "you better promise to stay in shape so we can come back and play next year."

My father sat at our table and told the bartender, José, to sprinkle the infield, a secret phrase that let him know it was time for another round. Andy and Mike talked baseball with Dad. The excitement in their voices made me realize something I had only suspected before: that my sons and I have long shared the same passion for a sport the Lees have played for nearly a century. And I realized something else: in baseball, you cannot go home without first circling the bases. Looking around the room, I saw that the game that had once separated me from my family had finally come full circle to bind us. We had reached home together.

EPILOGUE

Have Glove, Still Travel

It is a November afternoon in 2002. I am playing for the New England Sox in the Roy Hobbs Senior League in Florida. The left-hander on the mound throws in the high eighties and he just broke the bat of the last hitter he faced. I walk to home plate determined to wait him out, to discover how many weapons his arsenal holds.

His first four pitches crackle in the catcher's mitt. Electric stuff, but I can see he delivers everything at the same speed. He has not thrown a breaking pitch since entering the game. With the count 2–2, I look for a fastball, down the middle, knee high. The pitch leaves his hand, and I hear my father's voice: *Keep your head down and your front shoulder in.* I follow his instructions and swing from my ass. The ball climbs high over the outfield. It carries past the fence. Home run.

I am fifty-seven years old and still playing a game I first picked up as a child. And as we reach the end of this book, after all the miles and all the stories, I finally know why.

I play because the game's mystery still entrances. A pitcher can throw the ball to the same spot with the same velocity in game after game, and hitters cannot touch him. Next game, the same batters smack those same pitches all over the lot. No idea why that happens, but I might just continue throwing to batters until I find out.

I respect the justice of the baseball diamond. The dimensions of some ballparks favor hitters and others grant an edge to pitchers, but the arrangement of the four bases around the mound remains constant in every park and does not favor one player over another. I appreciate how the law of averages evens out for everyone if you play the game long enough. Make perfect pitches, surrender three bloop singles that someone should have caught, and just before you can bitch, someone swats a vicious line drive your first baseman snags to start an inning-ending double play.

I enjoy pulling on the uniform. It means I'm going to match my skills against an opponent and only one of us can emerge the winner. When I slip on spikes I am dressing for battle, and the confrontation between hitter and pitcher holds all the drama and allure of two gunslingers facing off at high noon.

I still love breaking in a new glove, kneading the leather with oil until it feels tacky and wrapping it around an old ball to form a deep pocket. That glove will remain stiff and foreign the first few games I play wearing it, but over time the cowhide will turn floppy and mold itself into the best part of my hand.

I love the ritual of preparing a new bat, scraping the soft wood from its surface, laying resin in the cracks, rubbing the barrel with a femur to flatten the fibers, and roasting the lumber until it hardens. Just like honing a saber.

I love pitching at dusk, when I can lurk in those shadows stretching out over the mound and jump on my prey at home plate. Standing on the rubber puts me at the center of attention and I don't have to say a word. The game cannot start, nothing can happen, until I let go of the ball.

I love stretching before a game. I stand on the side of the field, my spikes flat on the ground, palms flat out in front of me. Take a deep breath, hold, contract the back of my calves, and exhale as I lengthen. I push forward, the earth moves. I become Atlas shrugging.

I keep lacing up my spikes because I hate wearing suits and I never learned to play cornet like Miles Davis.

Or dance like Fred Astaire

Or sing like Billie Holiday.

I love to hear vendors hawking their peanuts, popcorn, beer, candy, and soda in the ballpark. The sound of people having a good time.

I love the pop the ball makes when a fielder catches it

cleanly. Or that rifle crack you hear when a pitch crashes against the sweet spot on the bat. Even if the sound comes to you with your eyes closed, you know that line drive will send the outfielders scampering and no matter how fast they move, the ball will bound past them and slam against the wall on one hop, and the runner will switch gears into overdrive to grab that extra base, and the ball and the runner will converge on the bag simultaneously, and we will all stand on our feet holding our breaths until the umpire makes his call.

And I love another sound that is not a sound at all, but the quiet that enfolds a ballpark when the game is on the line in the late innings and you can hear the heartbeats of the fans as they inch up to the edge of their seats, just waiting to scream in joy or anguish.

I play because whether you win or lose, the cold beer tastes better after a game.

I love rolling in the newly mowed outfield grass, where the oxygen hides on late summer afternoons. You run wind sprints till sweat drenches your uniform and your lungs emit the sound of gasping bellows. Your body drops to the cooler ground, where the grass respires, and you dig your face deep into the green and take in the breath of life and you know you can play another game. In the spring the ground feels soft, same as your muscles, still not quite in top shape, and it cushions you when you dive or stumble chasing after the ball. As your body hardens, the field hardens with it, and it pounds you all summer until your bones and joints ache and you feel your age and mortality and all the distance you've run over a thousand base paths and your body comes close to breaking until that first cool fall rain gentles the ground, so when you slide tough into second base to bust up the double play, the earth gives and catches you in its arms like a teammate.

I continue to take the field because I fear growing old, not the wrinkles or the gray hair—I can live with those—but the muscles turning slack and my mind growing numb. You don't work baseball, you play it, and the little boy in me never wants recess to end. I love the dance on the mound, my body flowing through my pitching motion. I love the feel of the ball sliding from my left hand, sweet as a lover's caress. The years have notched my fingers with calluses that fit perfectly around the seams on that horsehide. The world resting in my palm.

After a hard afternoon on the mound the resin has stained my nails black; they remind me of an artist's fingers dipped in paint. I cup my hands around my nose and breathe in deeply. The smell of freshly cut pines transports me to that Christmas morning when I found my first baseball glove wrapped in ribbons and colored paper.

I love running out ground balls. My spikes bite deep into the ground to produce perfect traction. My ankles and calves shove against the earth, and I explode out of the batter's box. Running down the baseline, the wind blows off my cap and scurries on its tiptoes to catch me, but I am fast and I am elusive and I am free and I am beyond the reach of the wind and pain and time and I am eighteen again forever.

I still play because I have no choice.

I am a ballplayer.

INDEX

ABOUT THE AUTHORS

BILL LEE is a pitcher. From 1969 to 1982 he compiled a laudable .569 winning percentage while starring in the major leagues for the Boston Red Sox and the Montreal Expos. In 1984 he collaborated with Richard Lally to write the best-selling autobiography *The Wrong Stuff,* and he wrote *The Little Red (Sox) Book* with Jim Prime in 2002. Today, Bill continues to play baseball in countries all over the world while appearing regularly as a commentator on television and radio in the United States and Canada. He lives in Craftsbury, Vermont.

RICHARD LALLY has written nineteen books. He has collaborated with celebrity authors to produce three international bestsellers, including *The Wrong Stuff.* In 2002, Princeton University Library added Mr. Lally's critically acclaimed *Bombers* to its prestigious Dixon Collection, a collection of books "illustrative of contemporary life and thought." He lives in New York City.